North Carolina's Confederate Hospitals

1861-1863

Volume I

Also by Wade Sokolosky:

"To Prepare for Sherman's Coming": The Battle of Wise's Forks, March 1865

"No Such Army Since the Days of Julius Caesar":
Sherman's Carolinas Campaign from Fayetteville to Averasboro, March 1865

North Carolina's Confederate Hospitals

1861-1863

Volume I

Wade Sokolosky

FOX RUN
PUBLISHING
QUALITY PUBLISHING ONE BOOK AT A TIME

Publisher's Cataloging-in-Publication Data
provided by Five Rainbows Cataloging Services

Names: Sokolosky, Wade, author.
Title: North Carolina's confederate hospitals : 1861-1863, volume I / Wade Sokolosky.
Description: Edition. | Burlington, NC : Fox Run Publishing, 2022. | Series: North Carolina's Confederate hospitals, vol. 1. | Includes bibliographical references and index.
Identifiers: LCCN 2022940272 (print) | ISBN 978-1-945602-23-8 (hardcover) | ISBN 978-1-945602-24-5 (paperback)
Subjects: LCSH: North Carolina—History. | Hospitals--Confederate States of America. | Military hospitals--Confederate States of America. | United States--History--Civil War, 1861-1865--Hospitals. | Confederate States of America. Army. Medical Department. | United States--History--Civil War, 1861-1865--Medical care. | BISAC: HISTORY / United States / Civil War Period (1850-1877) | HISTORY / United States / State & Local / South (AL, AR, FL, GA, KY, LA, MS, NC, SC, TN, VA, WV) | HISTORY / Military / United States. | MEDICAL / History.
Classification: LCC E625 .S65 2022 (print) | LCC E625 (ebook) | DDC 973.7/76--dc23.

Cover design by Sandra Miller

Cover images:

Emeline Jamison Pigott, Courtesy: North Carolina Office of Archives and History

Stephens' Brick Block, Craven Street, New Bern, ca. 1864–1865. Courtesy: #P0001, North Carolina Collection Photographic Archives, Louis Round Wilson Special Collections Library, University of North Carolina at Chapel Hill.

Surgeon Ashton Miles, Courtesy: From the Collection of Jonathan O'Neal, MD

Library of Congress Control Number (LCCN): 2022940272

Published by
Fox Run Publishing LLC
2779 South Church Street, #305
Burlington, NC 27215
http://www.foxrunpub.com/

This Book is Dedicated to
the Men and Women that it Entails

Table of Contents

List of Images

List of Maps

List of Tables

Preface

In recent decades, historians have advanced the scholarship regarding the history of North Carolina's Confederate hospitals. David A. Norris' "For the Benefit of Our Gallant Volunteers": North Carolina's State Medical Department and Civilian Volunteer Efforts, 1861-1862," published in the *North Carolina Historical Review*, provides the first detailed, albeit short, analysis of North Carolina's hospitals during the war's first two years. Nursing historian Dr. Phoebe Ann Pollitt has contributed immensely to telling the often-neglected story of Tar Heel women, both Black and White, and the important role they played as hospital staff during the war. Others have also helped blaze a path to further our knowledge. Robert J. Cooke's research on Wilmington and the Lower Cape Fear River hospitals, as well as Hugh B. Johnston's work on the hospital in Wilson, have greatly expanded our understanding.

North Carolina's Confederate Hospitals builds upon the excellent work previously done by those listed above. Until the publication of this volume, no book-length study existed on the state's Civil War hospitals, which is odd considering that at one point, North Carolina had the fourth-largest number of military hospitals in the Confederacy. This study originated as only a history of North Carolina's Confederate hospitals during the Civil War's final months, which was an obvious choice considering my previous writings on the 1865 Carolinas Campaign. However, despite the good work done in recent decades, I discovered the subject still lacked a full analysis, and because many of the 1865 hospitals had operated since 1862, I needed to encompass the entire war. By utilizing existing hospital records and reports, individual service records, period newspaper accounts, as well as diaries, letters, and journals, I have pieced together a more definitive study of North Carolina's Confederate hospitals.

This book is much less a medical history of the state's Confederate hospitals than it is an organizational examination of why those hospitals existed. The book's first two chapters provide the reader with a general understanding of the Confederate Medical Department and the military and civilians that were essential in the day-to-day operations of a hospital. The remaining chapters are arranged chronologically and discuss the key military operations and events that occurred in the state or in Virginia that drove hospital requirements. Two key factors within the scope of military operations influenced the need for hospitals: the density of troop populations in certain regions of the state or the sheer volume of sick and wounded, the latter influenced by the use of the railroads. But in dealing with these, I have, as far as possible, avoided entering into the minute technical details of the fighting and have instead tried to portray the effect of those military events—such as Union General's Ambrose Burnside's 1862 expedition—which significantly impacted North Carolina's early coastal hospitals.

This study also addresses the human story: the men and women, both Black and White, who staffed the hospitals. These individuals provided an interesting perspective, both good and bad. Without these personal experiences, the story of North Carolina's Confederate hospitals is incomplete, so they help me to tell the complete story. This proved challenging at times due to the nature of the research, specifically, the lack of letters, diaries, and such regarding hospital service by the state's lower-class and enslaved individuals.

I discuss all these topics, and others as well, throughout this volume, which covers the period from the beginning of the war and the establishment of the state's first hospitals in April 1861, through the expansion of state-operated wayside hospitals in December 1863. I do not discuss in this volume of *North Carolina's Confederate Hospitals* the Confederate naval hospitals that operated in the state, as research is still ongoing. A second volume will cover the war's final two years, 1864-1865, which includes the major expansion of government-operated hospitals in the Piedmont region of North Carolina, and two titanic events: the fall of Wilmington and Maj. Gen. William T. Sherman's 1865 Carolinas campaign, both of which stressed the state's hospital system to the brink of failure.

In describing this near-decade-long labor of love, I think it is appropriate to borrow a quote from Wake Forest College historian George W. Paschal. Early in the process of writing the school's history, Paschal was advised to, "Put in everything; no one will ever work over again the documents from which you draw your account, and what you omit will be permanently lost to the history of the College and the State." I have followed the advice given Paschal to ensure this aspect of North Carolina Civil History is not lost, with the hope that it may provide the source for further scholarship. Despite the many years of work and effort, I know that likely, I have made errors for which I alone am responsible.

Acknowledgments

This study has benefited from the help and advice of many people. Throughout this journey, nearly everyone I know has helped me in some way or another. Others, whom I have never met, have graciously responded to my requests for assistance and have provided source material or aided me in the quest to get copies of such. For this, I am forever grateful. This project began with historian Robert J. Cooke handing over his extensive research files on the Wilmington and Lower Cape Fear hospitals. Bob's mountain of folders quickly became my jumping-off point. Thank you, my friend.

An army of archivists, librarians, and historians quickly followed to aide and assist me, which has not been easy during the coronavirus pandemic. But these lovers of history refused to let research stop. I am forever grateful for your willingness to provide services to individuals such as myself. I cannot list them all, but I feel I must highlight a few, especially those who went the extra mile. Taylor de Klerk and Matthew Turi, Wilson Special Collections Library, University of North Carolina at Chapel Hill; Elise Allison, archivist, Greensboro History Museum; Marian Inabinett, curator, High Point Museum; Shelia Bumgarner, Sydney Carroll, and Jane Johnson, Charlotte Mecklenburg Library, Robinson-Spangler Carolina Room; Vann Evans, archivist, State Archives of North Carolina; staff and volunteers at the History Museum of Carteret County; distinguished Civil War historian, Libra R. Hilde, who provided me copies from her research files relative to North Carolina's hospitals; Peter J. D'Onofrio of the Society of Civil War Surgeons for providing information from Dr. F. Terry Hambrecht's unpublished register on surgeons who served in the Confederacy; Michael P. Zatarga, for assisting me in identifying the locations of the Confederate hospitals on Roanoke Island; Steve Shaffer, New Bern battlefield historian; Civil War historian Randy Sauls of Goldsboro; Frank Hall for sharing his Civil War hospital postal collection; and Skip Riddle, who kept a steady flow of research finds coming my way. To Pattie Smith, president of the Friends of Bentonville Battlefield Association, for her unwavering support to see this project to completion. Lastly, to Sarah Powell and Margaret Anne of the North Carolina Division of the United Daughters of the Confederacy, for always answering my calls for assistance.

To fellow New Bern Historical Society members, Nathaniel Glasgow, Jim Hodges, and Claudia Houston, who can ever forget the day when we discovered a forgotten past of New Bern's Civil War history—the former Confederate hospital located in the Stephens' Brick Block. It was truly a collaborative effort on the part of everyone. To honor the hospital and its discovery, I selected its wartime image for the front cover of this book.

Throughout my research, I received a wealth of assistance from several of North Carolina's state historic sites. I especially want to recognize Amanda Brantley, Jim McKee, and Becky Sawyer, who never once failed to answer my calls for help. To Charlie Knight, North Carolina Museum of History, and Chris Meekins at the state archives, gentlemen, you never hesitated to assist or to share discoveries. I am forever grateful to these fine individuals for their willingness to help. Thanks for all that you do every day to preserve North Carolina's rich history.

This project would not have been possible without the help of special individuals. I want to thank the following historians for taking the time to read and provide excellent recommendations that improved the overall quality of this study: Derrick Brown; Michael Hardy; Chris Hartley; Hampton Newsome; Rick Walton; and James W. White III. Heather Ammel, once again, provided excellent editorial assistance. The maps that grace this study attest to George Skoch's extraordinary skill and professionalism. His contribution has resulted in a far better book. Thanks to Sandra Miller, whose wonderful graphic skills grace the book's cover. None of this would have been possible without Keith Jones of Fox Run Publishing, who enabled this dream to ultimately come true.

Finally, I could not have written this book without the love and support of my family. I remain grateful to my much-loved wife, Traci, without whose infinite patience for my need to tell this Civil War story, none of this would be possible.

Wade Sokolosky
Beaufort, North Carolina

Guide to Abbreviations Used in Footnotes

AIGO	Adjutant and Inspector General's Office
CV	*Confederate Veteran Magazine*
CSR	Compiled Military Service Records, National Archives, Washington, D.C.
DU	Perkins Library, Duke University, Durham, NC
ECU	Joyner Library, East Carolina University, Greenville, NC
GO	General Orders
LCHS	Lower Cape Fear Historical Society
LCFHSB	*Lower Cape Fear Historical Society Bulletin*
NA	National Archives and Records Administration, Washington, D.C.
NCHR	*North Carolina Historical Review*
NCOAH	North Carolina Office of Archives and History, Raleigh, NC
OR	*The War of Rebellion: A Compilation of the Official Records of the Union and Confederate Armies.* 128 vols., Washington, D.C.
RG109	Records Group 109, War Department Collection of Confederate Records, National Archives, Washington, D.C.
SHC/UNC	Southern Historical Collection, Wilson Library, University of North Carolina at Chapel Hill
SHSP	Southern Historical Society Papers, Richmond, VA
SO	Special Orders
UNCW	Randall Library, University of North Carolina at Wilmington
VMCH	Virginia Museum of History and Culture, Richmond

Additional Notes

I have written the names of North Carolina towns, cities, and counties without the comma, then NC. All out-of-state locations are marked as such when first referenced. The town of Washington is the one from North Carolina, unless otherwise identified with D.C. North Carolinians used to spell city names differently, such as Goldsborough / Goldsboro, New Bern / Newberne, Tarboro / Tarborough, etc.; I have chosen to use the contemporary spelling, only retaining the former spelling when part of a directly quoted source. I have attempted to keep the writings from letters, diaries, and journals as unaltered as possible. When necessary, I added words in brackets for clarity.

CHAPTER 1
Organization of Confederate Hospitals

"[I]t should do the sick no harm."

"Never, never, never believe any war will be smooth and easy." These words, written by Winston Churchill 70 years after the Southern states seceded from the Union, aptly illuminate a commonly held misconception that existed at the start of the American Civil War. Many Americans predicted a short-lived conflict, not the bloody, drawn-out struggle that ultimately transpired. As high losses from sickness and casualties began to accumulate, the war quickly exposed just how unprepared both sides were to treat wounded and sick produced by the war. Because of these deficiencies in providing proper care, particularly in its military hospitals, many soldiers held an unfavorable opinion of inexperienced or incompetent army surgeons and poorly-staffed and ill-equipped hospitals. Describing the hospital surgeon at Fort Macon, North Carolina, one Tar Heel soldier wrote, "Anything that he goes at he don't half do it, he has set several bones here and they either growed crooked or they had to be set even again."[1]

In mid-nineteenth-century North Carolina, and throughout the country for that matter, hospitals, as we know them today, did not exist. Quite naturally, a volunteer from rural North Carolina would have felt apprehensive if admitted to a hospital. Before the war, female family members were the primary caregivers to the sick and requested a local physician to visit if necessary. In Southern society, caring for ill family members was a "fundamental aspect of female duty and self-sacrifice," which is why soldiers welcomed the care of women at their hospital bedsides.[2]

The hospitals in North Carolina were for sick travelers or the mentally ill, and in 1861, there were only three. At Portsmouth Island and Wilmington, along the coast were two U.S. Marine Hospitals, tending to sick and injured sailors. The third hospital at Raleigh, called

1. Winston Churchill, *My Early Life: A Roving Commission* (London, 1930), 246; Phoebe Pollitt and Camille N. Reese, "War Between the States, Nursing in North Carolina," *Confederate Veteran* (*CV*) (2002), 2:24; North Carolina soldier, quoted in H. H. Cunningham, *Doctors in Gray: The Confederate Medical Service*, 2nd ed. (Baton Rouge, LA, 1958), 255-56.
2. Libra R. Hilde, *Worth a Dozen Men: Women and Nursing in the Civil War South* (Charlottesville, VA, 2012), 135.

Dix Hill, later known as Dorothea Dix Hospital, served as the state asylum. Additionally, the state's larger plantations, like Somerset Place in Washington County, had facilities on the property for local physicians to treat and care for enslaved people. The facility offering the closest example to organized health care in North Carolina was located at a Moravian settlement, known today as "Old Salem," where a physician provided community care, along with male and female nurses who administered aid when required.[3]

The establishment and operation of Confederate hospitals in North Carolina occurred in the context of a broader development, namely the creation and administration of the Confederate Medical Department throughout the South in the war's first years. During this challenging period, the department struggled to provide adequate care for the sick and wounded while simultaneously trying to build a medical corps from the ground up. Critical to bridging the gap between chaos and stability were the invaluable services of individual state medical departments, charitable organizations, and the efforts of Southern women and African Americans, both enslaved and free. The role of women, especially those whose work in the hospitals provided them opportunities to "carve out positions of independence and authority and to gain valuable experience with medical care." The valuable lessons from this period resulted in action from the Confederate government that ultimately helped to develop an effective hospital system in North Carolina for the remainder of the war.[4]

Because the Confederacy had no medical system at the war's outset, Confederate officials established their Medical Department with the U.S. Army model in mind. In some aspects, the absence of an existing organization proved beneficial to the developing medical department. First, with no medical officers on the rolls, the department avoided selecting personnel based on seniority, relying on merit instead. Second, unlike its Union counterpart, bureaucracy and red tape were nonexistent in the new organization. This allowed for creativity, which was beneficial as resources became more and more strained while the war dragged on. Finally, as within the U.S. Army, where the regular army and the volunteer corps did not always have a

3. Phoebe Pollitt, "Information about North Carolina Women in the Civil War," *North Carolina Nursing History*, accessed on October 17, 2020, http://nursinghistory.appstate.edu. According to Pollitt, as early as the 1770s, both male and female nurses provided care to their respective sexes when needed at Old Salem; The earliest documentation of physician care in eastern North Carolina occurred at Edenton in 1703. Randy D. Kearns, M.D., *Sanatoriums and Asylums of Eastern North Carolina* (Charleston, SC, 2018), 7; Somerset Place is now a State Historic Site that belongs to the NC Department of Natural and Cultural Resources.
4. Hilde, *Worth a Dozen Men*, 17.

cooperative relationship, no such distinction existed in the Confederate army, thus allowing for "the sense of single-minded purpose within the Medical Department."[5]

The Confederate Medical Department, created on February 26, 1861, in Montgomery, Alabama, initially consisted of a surgeon general, four surgeons, and six assistant surgeons, all of whom were responsible for establishing the army's medical corps. The limited staffing reflected expectations for a short war and the notion that the department would merely assist in coordinating the efforts of individual state medical staffs. This decentralized system required the governors from each Southern state to appoint a surgeon general.

On May 4, President Davis named Dr. David C. DeLeon, a South Carolinian and former U.S. Army surgeon, the acting surgeon general for the newly created medical department.[6] Following the attack on Fort Sumter, South Carolina, in April 1861, the Southern states that had remained in the Union seceded. The Confederate government absorbed the individual state forces, which had operated independently, into the provisional army. Also, during this timeframe, the government selected Richmond, Virginia, as the site for the new capital of the Confederacy.[7]

In late July 1861, President Davis appointed 47-year-old Dr. Samuel Preston Moore as the acting surgeon general. Moore, a native of Charleston, South Carolina, was a 25-year U.S. Army Medical Department veteran. Recently resigned from the U.S. Army, he had settled in Arkansas to practice as a private physician before accepting the position. Earlier in March, Moore had declined a surgeon's appointment in the C.S. Army. But, for an old soldier like Moore, who had spent almost half of his adult life in the army, declining to answer the call to duty may have proved onerous, coupled with the constant appeals from his closest friends.[8]

5. Carol C. Green, *Chimborazo: The Confederacy's Largest Hospital* (Knoxville, TN, 2004), 2-3.
6. Guy R. Hasegawa, *Matchless Organization: The Confederate Army Medical Department* (Carbondale, IL, 2021), 4. *Matchless Organization* is the most detailed examination of the Confederate Medical Department. For additional treatment, see also Cunningham, *Doctors in Gray*. In May 1861, the Confederate Congress authorized an additional twenty staff positions in the department. DeLeon served as the acting surgeon general from May 6 to July 12, 1861. After DeLeon's dismissal, Surgeon Charles H. Smith served in the interim until Samuel P. Moore arrived in Richmond; Green, *Chimborazo*, 3.
7. Green, *Chimborazo*, 4; In May 1861, the provisional Confederate government relocated to Richmond. In November 1861, the Confederate Senate confirmed Moore's rank as surgeon general.
8. Cunningham, *Doctors in Gray*, 27-28; Green, *Chimborazo*, 3-4; Hasegawa, *Matchless Organization*, 12. President Davis appointed Moore surgeon general on November 7, and confirmed by Congress on December 13.

Samuel Preston Moore served as the surgeon general of the Confederacy throughout most of the war.

(Courtesy of National Library of Medicine)

On July 30, 1861, Surgeon General Moore arrived at Richmond to begin his official duties. At Richmond, Moore walked into a hornet's nest. The rapidly growing Confederate army suffered from rampant diseases and illnesses, conditions exacerbated by poor diet, hygiene, and exposure, leaving thousands incapacitated. Childhood diseases, such as measles, reached epidemic levels in the army camps. In addition to confronting the issues with caring for the sick, Moore arrived at his Richmond post shortly after the battle of First Manassas (First Bull Run), where he witnessed the wounded cared for in hastily established hospitals.[9]

As surgeon general, Moore's broad responsibilities covered "the administrative details of the medical department, the government of hospitals, the regulation of the duties of surgeons and assistant surgeons, and the appointment of acting medical officers, when needed, for local or detached service." Although Moore ultimately performed well in his roles as surgeon general, he initially experienced a rocky transition into his new role, as "the still coalescing Confederate government responded slowly to the medical crisis at hand." This was especially true regarding the establishment of hospitals. The organizing and staffing of hospitals "vexed the Medical Department from the start," along with the authorities' inability to "predict the length and severity of the war," which further exacerbated

---

9. Samuel P. Day, an English observer, noted 12 Richmond hospitals provided care for approximately 1,500 Confederate soldiers following the battle. According to Day, the figure was only "a fractional part of the sick and wounded," while Richmond private residences housed the remaining men. See Cunningham, *Doctors in Gray*, 45.

the problem. Consistent with short-sightedness, the Confederate Congress appropriated only $50,000 for hospitals.[10]

Throughout the conflict, the Confederate Medical Department operated several types of hospitals, each varying in size and purpose. General hospitals were the largest of these organizations, "intended for more permanent occupation" and "more complex in organization." Medical officials used the term "general hospitals" throughout the war to describe those facilities in which admitted patients regardless of their state or unit affiliation. Various employees staffed general hospitals, such as matrons, nurses, cooks, laundresses, and others who provided long-term care for sick and wounded soldiers. Unlike field hospitals, which were temporary and moved with the armies, medical authorities located general hospitals in rear areas with access to rail or waterway transportation to receive the wounded evacuated from battle. Typically, general hospitals were more permanent, often clustered in major transportation hubs like Atlanta, Raleigh, and Richmond. Although in some instances, notably during the Atlanta and Carolinas campaigns of 1864 and 1865, the deteriorating military situation required general hospitals to relocate.[11]

At the beginning of the war, general hospitals were nonexistent in the army, so Confederate authorities converted existing structures for military use. Ideally, officials preferred multistory structures, like hotels, warehouses, and schools, as the facilities provided larger patient capacity. When demand exceeded hospital capacities, authorities pressed into service churches, personal homes, and tents. One North Carolinian, Surgeon Edward Warren, witnessed the tragic overflow of patients in the aftermath of the battle of First Manassas (First Bull Run). He recalled that "the whole country, from Manassas Junction to Richmond in one direction, and to Lynchburg in another, was one vast hospital, filled to repletion with the sick and wounded." Indeed, there is no doubting historian H. H. Cunningham's conclusion that the "early hospital picture was confused and depressing." During this

---

10. Quoted in Cunningham, *Doctors in Gray*, 27; Hilde, *Worth A Dozen Men*, 19; Hasegawa, *Matchless Organization*, 107, 110.
11. W. A. Carrington to S. P. Moore, April 14, 1863, quoted in Hasegawa, *Matchless Organization*, 107. Cunningham, *Doctors in Gray*, 45; Hasegawa contends "that many general hospitals were intended for the treatment of patients from particular states," for example, the two general hospitals established in Petersburg, Virginia, by the North Carolina Medical Department. However, the general hospitals established within North Carolina admitted soldiers from various states. Hasegawa, *Matchless Organization*, 107, 216-17n1; Hilde, *Worth A Dozen Men*, 17-18; Glenna R. Schroeder-Lein, "The Wounded," Essential Civil War Curriculum, accessed on November 9, 2020, https://www.essentialcivilwarcurriculum.com/the-wounded.html.

chaotic period, North Carolina and other states established hospitals in Virginia to care for their soldiers. In addition to state-operated hospitals, private citizens established hospitals, often founded and operated solely by women.[12]

Much of the initial heavy fighting of the war occurred in Virginia between Richmond and Washington, D.C. Consequently, both capitals became destinations for the sick and wounded. Large numbers of soldiers requiring medical care transformed Richmond into a *de facto* hospital center. Many of these facilities scattered about Richmond were either state or privately owned, and the Confederate Medical Department operated them with limited purview. With Richmond's patchwork of hospitals overflowing, Surgeon General Moore was eager to find a solution. Upon the advice of a local Richmond physician, Moore selected a sprawling 40-acre site east of the city, known to the locals as Chimborazo Hill, for the site of a new hospital. Moore's vision for a new, larger facility yielded Chimborazo Hospital, which became "the best-known hospital in the Confederacy and the largest hospital anywhere in the world at that time."[13]

Confederate officials constructed Chimborazo Hospital utilizing the pavilion design, which consisted of separate single-story buildings with multiple windows on each side, allowing for excellent lighting and cross ventilation. Hospital administrators designated each building as a different ward. The pavilion design had originated in France at the end of the eighteenth century. Still, it was not until the 1850s, when Florence Nightingale printed her *Notes on Hospitals*, that support for this design gained momentum in British government circles. Nightingale, a veteran nurse from the Crimean War and crusader for hospital reform, preferred the pavilion design for its low mortality rate. In *Notes on Hospitals*, Nightingale begins with the following

---

12. The medical department rented from the city of Richmond the newly constructed four-story Almshouse (poor house), which the government later designated as General Hospital No. 1. See Rebecca B. Calcutt, *Richmond's Wartime Hospitals* (Gretna, LA, 2005), 41, 74, 110; Edward Warren, M.D., *A Doctor's Experiences in Three Continents* (Baltimore, MD, 1885), 270. At the time Warren observed the disastrous situation with the Confederate wounded, he had just completed a brief four-month duty as the first surgeon of the North Carolina navy, and was in Virginia seeking a position in the Confederate army; Cunningham, *Doctors in Gray*, 45; Hilde, *Worth a Dozen Men*, 18-19. In addition to North Carolina, Alabama and Georgia provided excellent support to their sick and wounded.
13. Doctor James B. McCaw suggested the Chimborazo Hill site to Moore. McCaw later served as commandant, or "surgeon-in-chief," for Chimborazo Hospital. Green, *Chimborazo*, 8. A lengthy discussion of Chimborazo Hospital strays far beyond the scope of this book. Green's superb study provides the most detailed examination of the hospital.

Chimborazo Hospital, Richmond, Va., April 1865. The pavilion-style hospital consisted of 150 buildings.

(Library of Congress)

statement: "It may seem a strange principle to enunciate as the very first requirement in a hospital that it should do the sick no harm."[14]

American physicians preferred the pavilion design of hospital architecture. Surgeon Charles S. Tripler, Medical Director of the Army of the Potomac, was an advocate for the design's use in the U.S. Army. Tripler's explanation as to why he and so many of his fellow medical officers favored the pavilion design provides an excellent summary of its benefits: "They admit of more perfect ventilation, can be kept in better police, are more convenient for the sick and wounded and their attendants, admit of a ready distribution of patients into the proper classes, and are cheaper." First opened in October 1861, Chimborazo Hospital eventually consisted of 150 individual pavilions, with a total capacity of 8,000 beds. Because of Chimborazo's success, the medical department adopted it as the standard for all new hospital construction. In North Carolina, the government later constructed three significantly smaller pavilion-designed hospitals at Charlotte, Raleigh, and Salisbury.[15]

Throughout the war, shortages of hospital attendants impacted hospital efficiency. Early on, the Confederate Medical Department adopted the U.S. Army's antebellum practice of using able-bodied or convalescent male soldiers as hospital attendants. However, as the number of sick and wounded increased, so did the requirement for nurses and other supporting staff. To help alleviate the problem, on August 21, 1861, the Confederate Congress authorized surgeons to hire civilians, White or Black, as hospital attendants. When civilian hires failed to lessen the critical shortages in the hospitals, the government turned to the South's primary workforce: its large African American population. The Confederate Congress passed laws allowing the impressment of Blacks, free or enslaved, into hospital service. For the remainder of the war, the labor of African Americans, mainly enslaved people, hired or impressed from their owners, would prove vital to keeping Southern hospitals functioning.[16]

By the summer of 1862, the Confederate government began instituting "a more centralized administration" regarding military

---

14. Hasegawa, *Matchless Organization*, 147; Florence Nightingale, *Notes on Hospitals* (London, 1859), iii.
15. According to Green, it is unclear who suggested implementing the pavilion plan at Richmond. Green, *Chimborazo*, 12; Charles S. Tripler, quoted in Cunningham, *Doctors in Gray*, 50; In April 1862, the Confederate Medical Department opened a second pavilion-style hospital, Winder Hospital, on the western outskirts of Richmond, followed by a third, Howard's Grove Hospital. In June 1863, authorities constructed Jackson Hospital, a smaller pavilion-style, not far from Winder. Green, *Chimborazo*, 14-16.
16. Hilde, *Worth a Dozen Men*, 134; Cunningham, *Doctors in Gray*, 72; Green, *Chimborazo*, 47-48.

hospitals. Since the beginning of the war, the Confederacy contained a patchwork system of various government, state, and privately operated hospitals, with limited oversight by the Confederate Medical Department. Surgeon General Moore believed it an imperfect system that affected efficiency and military discipline.[17]

In September 1862, the Confederate Congress passed "An Act to Better Provide for the Sick and Wounded of the Army in Hospitals." The law required that hospitals "be named and numbered as hospitals of a particular state" and, when feasible, that hospitals admit soldiers representing their state. One early lesson learned was that soldiers typically fared better when grouped with fellow patients from their home state. Moving forward, general hospitals were either primarily associated with an individual state or contained geographically segregated wards. The act's wording was a compromise that appeased "states' rights proclivities" while "maintaining a national medical bureaucracy."[18]

The September 1862 act's most significant impact was in the area of hospital staffing. The law authorized surgeons in charge of hospitals to employ matrons, assistant matrons, ward masters, and additional nurses and cooks as needed, "giving preference in all cases to females where their services may best subserve the purpose." It was "generally recognized . . . that women made better nurses than men and acted also as morale boosters of hospitalized troops." The low mortality rate in hospitals where women had cared for the soldiers reinforced this belief.[19] In *Mothers of Invention*, Drew Gilpin Faust describes how the legislation "not only changed the status of women in the South but made a political statement about the policy of the government regarding women in society." This proved significant because Southern society considered hospital work a calling for poor people, inappropriate for and beneath a respectable, upper-class woman in the mid-nineteenth century. Additionally, the act "revolutionized

17. Pollitt and Reese, "War Between the States, Nursing in North Carolina," *CV*, 27; Cunningham, *Doctors in Gray*, 70-71.
18. *The War of Rebellion: A Compilation of the Official Records of the Union and Confederate Armies*, 128 vols. (Washington, D.C., 1888–1901), Series 4, vol. 2, 199-200. Hereafter cited as *OR*, 2:199-200. All references are to Series 1 unless otherwise noted; Hilde, *Worth a Dozen Men*, 22, 24; In one instance at Richmond, the surgeon in charge at the Florida hospital denied a North Carolinian's transfer request to the North Carolina hospital in the city. Outraged, Surgeon Otis F. Manson, surgeon-in-charge at Gen. Hosp. No. 24, wrote Governor Zebulon B. Vance that the surgeon's refusal ". . . afforded positive proof of the injustices that which our men are treated but is a direct violation of the Act." O. F. Manson to Vance, August 3, 1863, Zebulon B. Vance Papers, North Carolina Office of Archives and History (NCOAH), Raleigh.
19. *OR*, series 4, 2:199-200; Cunningham, *Doctors in Gray*, 71.

Confederate medical care because henceforth, each hospital was a microcosm of southern society." The day-to-day operations of a Confederate hospital now depended on a very diverse workforce made up of both men and women, "whites and blacks, slaves and free people, soldiers and civilians, and medical professionals and amateurs," which sometimes proved troublesome to the surgeon in charge.[20]

Despite the September 1862 act's noted benefits, two issues still existed that hindered the Confederate Medical Department's effort to assume control of all hospitals. First, many private hospitals operated autonomously from the Medical Department while receiving government support with food, supplies, and medical officers. Officials in the Department believed that private hospitals failed to measure up to military hospital standards from centralized control and economies of scale. To improve efficiency, and because he disfavored such private hospitals, Moore sought to either shut down or consolidate all facilities with a capacity of fewer than 100 beds. Although Moore's plan applied to hospitals throughout the Confederacy, the Medical Department focused its initial efforts on Richmond's large concentration of hospitals. Understandably, these actions met immediate pushback, especially in hospitals supervised by women. In *Worth a Dozen Men*, Libra R. Hilde wrote, "Because the Confederate government stepped into the medical business relatively late, officials faced women armed with confidence derived from practical experience." Surgeon General Moore was acutely aware of the sensitivity of the subject, going as far as to recommend to the then acting medical director for the Department of North Carolina and Southern Virginia, Dr. William A. Carrington, that "the better plan appears to let these private hospitals alone for the present. As the ladies are very desirous of attending to sick soldiers, they should be gratified."[21]

The second issue impeding the Department's consolidation of facilities was uncertainty regarding its authority over general hospitals. Until 1863, a surgeon overseeing a general hospital received orders

---

20. Drew Filpin Faust, *Mothers of Invention: Women of the Slaveholding South in the American Civil War* (Chapel Hill, NC, 1996), 98; Nancy Schurr, "Inside the Confederate Hospital: Community and Conflict during the Civil War," PhD diss., (University of Tennessee, 2004), 1.

21. Hilde, *Worth A Dozen Men*, 31; Hasegawa, *Matchless Organization*, 118-19; S. P. Moore to Wm. A. Carrington, February 2, 1863, Letters, Orders, and Circulars Sent, Surgeon General's Office, 1861–65, vol. 741, pt. 1, ch. 6, Records Group 109 (RG109), National Archives and Records Administration (NA), Washington, D.C. Carrington was a strong proponent of closing hospitals; W. A. Carrington to S. P. Moore, April 14, 1863, William A. Carrington, Compiled Service Records of Confederate General and Staff Officers, and Nonregimental Enlisted Men, M331, roll 49, RG109, NA. Hereafter, cited as CSR, M331, followed by the roll number.

from the medical directors of corps, armies, or departments, the commanders of such organizations, and, indirectly, from the surgeon general in Richmond. This situation created difficulties for the unfortunate surgeon in charge, who served at the beck and call of multiple superiors. The medical director served as the principal medical adviser to the commander and, additionally, was an essential link between the "surgeon general's office and the surgeons serving in regiments, or hospitals." However, the development and refinement of the director's roles and responsibilities proved challenging during the war's first two years, especially regarding general hospitals. Who controlled the general hospitals—the military commander or the medical director?[22]

In October 1862, the Confederate War Department attempted to clarify who had ownership of general hospitals by publishing General Orders No. 58, which stated local commanders had authority over the hospitals. Still, general management was the responsibility of the senior surgeon or medical director. "[O]nly in special cases" could commanding officers interfere, but even still, such incidents were to be "referred to the Commander of the Department." Although this arrangement clarified roles, it burdened the medical director, especially during active military operations when his focus was on the immediate wounded, not necessarily on general hospitals located miles to the rear. Surgeon General Moore recognized this shortcoming, writing, "[T]wo years of experience have fully shown, how utterly impossible it is, for the ablest Medical Directors, serving with Troops in the Field, to bestow upon hospitals in the rear, that care, and attention so essential to their efficiency and usefulness."[23]

In March 1863, the Confederate War Department issued General Orders No. 28, placing general hospitals "under the supervision and control of medical directors specially selected for the purpose," thus relieving all responsibility and control of general hospitals from the various medical directors in the field. Whether an individual state or a designated geographical area, each had an assigned medical director of hospitals who was responsible for the supervision and control of general hospitals. In the case of North Carolina, the Confederate Medical Department considered the state a separate hospital district

---

22. Cunningham, *Doctors in Gray*, 71. Hasegawa, *Matchless Organizations*, 33.
23. General Orders (GO) No. 78, Adjutant and Inspector General's Office (AIGO), October 28, 1862, General Orders and Circulars of the Confederate War Department, 1861–1865, M901, roll 01, RG109, NA, Washington, D.C. Hereafter cited as Orders and Circulars, AIGO, M901, to include relevant order and roll numbers; S. P. Moore to Samuel Cooper, November 6, 1863, Letters Received by the Confederate Adjutant and Inspector General, 1861–65, M474, roll 84, RG109, NA. Hereafter cited as Letters Received, AIGO, M474, to include relevant roll numbers.

within the Confederacy. The order further directed: "Medical directors of armies, army corps, and departments will not interfere with this arrangement in respect to general hospitals." Although the order did not specify so, the chain of authority now ran directly from Surgeon General Moore to each medical director of hospitals and then to the surgeons overseeing general hospitals.[24]

Although the decision to establish the director position was "a departure from the Union army system on which the Confederate Medical Department had based their organization," General Orders No. 28 effectively removed the awkward command structure under which general hospitals had previously operated. It improved efficiency by eliminating the field medical directors' burden of managing both field and rear area hospitals. Additionally, the order strengthened Moore's position as surgeon general regarding the day-to-day management of general hospitals, thereby facilitating his goal of more centralized control in Confederate military hospitals. How well Moore carried out this task is questionable. Due to the geography of the Confederacy and delays in communication, the extent to which Moore could rapidly handle situations is suspect. Extant records indicate Richmond's proximity to North Carolina facilitated effectively centralized control.[25]

In May 1863, the Confederate Congress took another key step in further improving the care of its soldiers by amending the September 1862 act to require the establishment of wayside hospitals. Wayside hospitals, or "Way Hospital" as the Medical Department officially identified them, provided limited medical attention for transient Confederate soldiers, who might require limited medical attention, meals, or places to stay overnight. Until this point in the war, the Confederate Medical Department had relied primarily on general hospitals to treat its sick and wounded, even though state and private organizations had successfully operated wayside hospitals since March 1862. In addition to existing general hospitals, the amendment directed the surgeon general to establish wayside hospitals. For the remainder

---

24. GO No. 28, Orders and Circulars, AIGO, March 12, 1863, M901, roll 01, RG109, NA. Although Surgeon General Moore benefited greatly from the publication of General Orders No. 28, neither the Confederate secretary of war nor adjutant general consulted Moore before its release, and it took him by complete surprise. Hasegawa, *Matchless Organization*, 39; Not all senior commanders in North Carolina welcomed the general order, as it essentially removed their command authority over hospitals operating within their area of responsibility. Chapter 7 explores those issues further pertaining to the Old North State; Cunningham, *Doctors in Gray*, 70-71.
25. Glenna R. Schroeder-Lein, *Confederate Hospitals on the Move: Samuel H. Stout and the Army of Tennessee* (Columbia, SC, 1994), 21, 64; Cunningham, *Doctors in Gray*, 70-71; Hasegawa, *Matchless Organization*, 112.

of the war, wayside hospitals were essential in the medical department's hospital system.[26]

By the summer of 1863, under Surgeon General Moore's leadership, the Confederate Medical Department had largely overcome its initial challenges and advanced significantly as an organization in its ability to provide essential medical services to the Confederate military. From North Carolina, Doctor Edward Warren observed that the Department consisted of "competent, devoted and patriotic men ... who were ... small in number, deficient in organization and unsupplied with such materials as the exigencies of the situation demanded." However, problems would remain, mainly as the war dragged on. Despite establishing a functioning hospital system, surgeons and hospital staff faced increasing shortages of food, medical supplies, and other essential items necessary for a hospital to function correctly.[27]

---

26. Cunningham, *Doctors in Gray*, 38-39.
27. Warren, *Doctor's Experience*, 271.

Dr. John F. Shaffner

Graduate of Jefferson Medical College, was Assistant Surgeon of the 7th, 21st, and 23rd North Carolina Regiments.

(Brethren with Stethoscopes)

CHAPTER 2
Confederate Hospital Personnel

"[G]lides among the suffering like an angel of mercy."

Prior to the Civil War, the U.S. Army did not have an extensive medical department. The staff of a typical hospital consisted of a surgeon, a hospital steward, and detailed convalescent or able-bodied soldiers serving as nurses or in other capacities. The facilities were small. The 40-bed hospital at Fort Leavenworth, Kansas, for example, was the U.S. Army's largest hospital before the war. Nevertheless, this simple personnel structure and modest facilities proved effective for a small, 16,000-soldier peacetime army. Anticipating a short conflict, the Confederate Medical Department adopted the U.S. Army's model. However, it soon became clear that this approach was not well suited for a large army or a protracted war. The Confederate government's response resulted in a diverse group of personnel employed in its hospitals, which relied on civilian workers, including women and Blacks. For the remainder of the war, a typical hospital contained medical officers, detailed soldiers, and civilian employees, each of whom performed an essential function in the hospital's day-to-day operation.[1]

Medical Officers

The Confederacy faced an immediate challenge trying to organize a corps of physicians at the start of the war. Only 24 medical officers had resigned from the U.S. Army and entered Confederate service, which posed a serious problem as newly raised regiments experienced shortages in authorized medical positions. In 1861, John W. Ellis, North Carolina's governor, and a board of three Raleigh physicians appointed surgeons to the state's newly raised regiments. Other Confederate states implemented similar practices for assigning medical officers, and in some instances, a military unit simply elected its surgeon.[2]

1. Silas W. Mitchell, "On the Medical Department in the Civil War," *Journal of the American Medical Association* (1914), 62:1,445-50; Robert F. Reilly, M.D., "Medical and Surgical Care during the American Civil War, 1861–1865," accessed on December 23, 2021, https://www.ncbi.nlm.nih.gov/pmc/articles/PMC4790547/.
2. Cunningham, *Doctors in Gray*, 31; About 834 surgeons and 1,668 assistant surgeons served in the Confederate army. Bonnie B. Dorwart, Dr., "Civil War

Such expedient measures resulted in individuals of questionable abilities obtaining surgeon positions within the rapidly expanding army. Although prior to the war individual states did not require licenses to practice medicine, most physicians received a level of training commensurate with the times. The education of American physicians before the Civil War ranged from medical courses at universities in Europe and in the United States to informal apprenticeships with practicing physicians. However, deficiencies in the competence of some of the early state-appointed medical officers soon drew sharp criticism, even from members of the medical profession. For example, a physician practicing in Petersburg, Virginia, expressed such sentiment to Dr. John G. Brodnax, of Rockingham County, who had been unsuccessful in obtaining a surgeon's position. "I wish you could get a Surgeon's place," Dr. Thomas Withers wrote. "I am sure I know some who have received the appointment of surgeon to a regiment, who never saw a gunshot wound except in a squirrel." Brodnax eventually received his commission. He served in South Carolina and Virginia hospitals before returning to North Carolina as surgeon-in-charge of General Hospital No. 14 in Wake Forest.[3]

To establish a standard for medical officers and to weed out the incompetent, the Confederate Congress granted President Jefferson Davis authority to appoint army surgeons and assistant surgeons after candidates had satisfactorily passed a Medical Examination Board. The War Department tasked the surgeon general of the Confederacy with establishing the board, which required candidates to pass both a written and oral examination. One of the first boards to convene in North Carolina occurred at Goldsboro on February 8, 1862, for 13 previously appointed state medical officers. Only one failed—Assistant Surgeon Joseph L. McConnaughey, a medical officer assigned to Fort Macon. For McConnaughey, as well as those deemed unqualified from other board locations, Surgeon General Samuel P. Moore acted swiftly to seek their immediate resignations.[4]

Hospitals," accessed on December 23, 2021, https://www.essentialcivilwarcurriculum.com/civil-war-hospitals.html; David A. Norris, "For the Benefit of Our Gallant Volunteers: North Carolina's State Medical Department and Civilian Volunteer Efforts, 1861–1862," *North Carolina Historical Review* (*NCHR*) (July 1980), 75:299; Hasegawa, *Matchless Organization*, 139.

3. Cunningham, *Doctors in Gray*, 9-10; Dr. Thomas Withers to John Brodnax, dated August 28, 1861, John Grammar Brodnax Papers, Southern Historical Collection, Louis Round Wilson Library, the University of North Carolina at Chapel Hill (SHC/UNC); Brian C. Miller, *Empty Sleeves: Amputation in the Civil War* (Athens, GA, 2015), 18; John G. Brodnax, CSR, M331, roll 34.

4. Hasegawa, *Matchless Organization*, 139; S. P. Moore to AIGO, March 3, 1862, Letters Received by AIGO, M474, roll 46, RG109, NA; S. P. Moore to Samuel Cooper, March 6, 1862, ibid; McConnaughey received a state

Not all medical officers agreed to appear before the examination board. Assistant Surgeon Windal T. Robinson, 1st North Carolina Cavalry, informed his father back home in Wayne County that there was "a majority of assistant Surgeons who will not stand." Although Robinson felt confident in both his "competency and ability" to practice medicine, to include the "theory of Surgery," he admitted to his father, "I had much rather resign . . . then present myself before the board for a permanent commission." Despite his lack of credentials, Robinson believed his knowledge of practicing medicine was "not inferior to those who have their diplomas." True to his word, Robinson resigned from the Confederate army on January 2, 1862.[5]

The Confederate Medical Department adopted from the U.S. Army three grades of rank for its medical officers: surgeons, with the rank of major; assistant surgeons, with the rank of captain; and, when necessary, acting assistant surgeons (contract civilian physicians), with the pay of a second lieutenant of infantry. Surgeons possessed the best qualifications in experience and education, whereas assistant surgeons were generally younger and less experienced. All three medical officer ranks served in hospitals and military units.[6]

Hospital Surgeons

The surgeon-in-charge of a Confederate hospital was "responsible for the efficient administration of his institution," which encompassed a wide range of administrative duties, allowing little time for actual hands-on care. Regulations required he maintain a patient registry, individual record books related to diet, prescriptions, and hospital requisitions, and an order and letter book. In addition, the Confederate Medical Department required various daily, weekly, and monthly

appointment as assistant surgeon on September 9, 1861. Joseph L. McConnaughey, CSR, M331, roll 170. See also, Joseph L. McCannaughy. See CSR, M331, roll 168.
5. Windal T. R. to My Dear Pa, December 4, 186[?], quoted in Brenda C. McKean, *Blood and War at My Door Step: North Carolina Civilians in the War Between the State*, 2 vols. (n.p., 2011), vol. 1, 123-124; W. T. Robinson, CSR, M331, roll 215.
6. By 1863, Confederate regulations changed the pay scale for acting assistant surgeons to $30-50 per month depending on the number of patients treated. War Department, *Regulations for the Army of the Confederate States, 1863* (Richmond, VA, 1863), 239; Hasegawa notes, "Used generically, 'surgeon' was a catchall term that encompasses all army medical officers, whether they performed surgical operations or not." Hasegawa, *Matchless Organization*, 4; Glenna R. Schroeder-Lein categorized medical officers as "those who cared for soldiers in the field and those who attended them in hospitals." See, Stout, *Confederate Hospitals on the Move*, 69-70. Because this study deals specifically with the rear area hospitals, the author does not discuss the organization and functioning of the field service.

reports entailing patient information, such as number admitted, deaths and discharges, and surgical cases, as well as hospital returns, which listed by name the medical officers, hospital stewards, and detailed men assigned to the hospital. To assist him in this mountain of regulatory paperwork, the surgeon-in-charge oftentimes employed a clerk, either civilian or detailed military, who provided relief so that his boss might make daily visits through the hospital wards to ensure compliance with rules and regulations. Depending on the number of patients treated, the Confederate Medical Department authorized an additional assistant surgeon or contract physician to every 70 or 80 patients.[7]

The individual rank of the surgeon-in-charge and the number of assigned medical officers varied within North Carolina's hospitals and often fluctuated throughout the war depending on patient workload. The larger hospitals typically consisted of a surgeon and two to three assistants. Alternatively, a locally contracted physician often solely directed a smaller hospital; for example, Dr. Richard K. Gregory was in charge at Charlotte's first general hospital, and Dr. Benjamin W. Robinson oversaw the Fayetteville Arsenal and Armory Post Hospital.[8]

Hospital Stewards

On May 16, 1861, the Confederate Congress authorized the position of hospital steward. Hospital stewards held the rank of sergeant and received their appointments from the secretary of war upon recommendation of the Confederate surgeon general. If necessary from the absence of military personnel, the surgeon-in-charge could employ a civilian as a steward. In contemporary terms, the hospital steward was the pharmacist for the hospital. Additionally, medical regulations made the steward "responsible for the cleanliness of the wards and kitchens, patients and attendants, and all articles of use." He was also the custodian of the hospital property and stores, and as such, prepared the provision returns and received and distributed the rations. In reality, because of these diverse responsibilities, the steward was "an all-purpose errand boy," and one who often bore "the brunt of patient complaints," especially regarding hospital meals, frequently keeping him in an unfavorable spotlight. Surgeon General Moore considered stewards key managers and of great value to the hospital, spurring him to publish a circular on July 8, 1864, proclaiming "stewards were the only able-bodied white men

---

7. Cunningham, *Doctors in Gray*, 74.
8. Cunningham, *Doctors in Gray*, 74-75; See files of Robert Gregory and Benjamin W. Robinson, CSR, M331, RG109, NA.

between the ages of seventeen and forty-five employed in hospitals who were exempted from field duty."[9]

When the Confederates established the general hospital at Wilson in April 1862, Pomeroy P. Clark, a local civilian merchant, served as the hospital steward. The hospital's muster rolls note Clark's civilian status during this period with the annotation: "employed as a non-enlisted man." Along with Clark, the rolls included his wife, Susan, and their 12-year-old son, George P., both identified as nurses. Not only was hospital service a family affair for Clark, but records also show he profited by acting as an agent for 11 hired enslaved.[10]

Because the various responsibilities were "too great for one person to handle" in the state's larger hospitals, records list an additional steward who was on permanent assignment or a detailed soldier in a temporary or "acting" capacity. When two stewards were present in a hospital, the surgeon-in-charge divided the duties into druggist and mess steward. Hospital returns for the month of September 1864 note the presence of two stewards at the larger hospitals in Goldsboro, Raleigh, Wilmington, and Wilson. At Raleigh's General Hospital No. 13, Henry M. Pettit, who was an apothecary, served as the druggist, and William C. Barker, who was previously detailed as a nurse at the hospital, performed the duties of mess steward.[11]

Like the congressionally mandated surgeon boards, the Confederate surgeon general, by his own initiative, instituted an examination board for all hospital stewards after an increasing number of reports suggested "a general distrust that had begun to develop about mess stewards." Because mess stewards frequently purchased commissary items from the general public, there was concern about potential unscrupulous dealings. The guidance provided to a board conducted in Virginia specified the requirement to investigate the "the moral fitness of the Steward for his office. He should be temperate, honest, and every way reliable and known to be such."[12]

9. Green, *Chimborazo*, 59; Cunningham, *Doctors in Gray*, 75; Calcutt, *Richmond's Wartime Hospitals*, 34-35; S. P. Moore, *Circular No. 11*, July 8, 1864, quoted in Green, *Chimborazo*, 60.
10. Clark served as the hospital steward for approximately 21 months. P. P. Clark, CSR, M331, roll 56; U.S. Federal Census (1860), Schedule 1, Wilson District, Wilson County, NC, 61; "Wilson Confederate Hospital Muster Rolls: Records of the Wilson Confederate Hospital, 1862–1865," Hugh Buckner Johnston, comp., unpublished file obtained by the author.
11. Green, *Chimborazo*, 58-59, "Return of Hospital Stewards for the Month of September 1864," Statistical Reports of Patients and Attendants, Office of the Medical Director of Hospitals in NC, 1863–65, ch. 6, vol. 280, RG109, NA. Hereafter cited as NC Medical Director Reports, ch. 6, vol. 280.
12. Green, *Chimborazo*, 60.

*Dr. Henry M. Pettit, hospital steward at various Virginia and
North Carolina hospitals, served in the Raleigh area hospitals
during the war's final two years.*

(Courtesy of Jeff Giambrone)

Records pertaining to these boards indicate the examiners categorized the results into three categories: favorable for all the duties of a steward; favorable for either mess steward or druggist; or unfavorable, not sufficient in either. A February 1863 Examining Board of Hospital Stewards in Raleigh tested the competencies of 14 currently serving stewards from various North Carolina hospitals, three of whom were determined "not sufficiently skilled in pharmacy or the other duties of a steward." The individuals who failed the examination were "acting" hospital stewards at the Charlotte, Tarboro, and Weldon wayside hospitals. The results from another board determined Acting Mess Steward William C. Barker "Favorable as Mess Steward," with the additional comment, "He is honest, capable, industrious and moral."[13]

Ward Masters

Ward masters were responsible for cleanliness, as well as supervising nurses assigned to an individual hospital ward. They also "assigned new patients to their beds, collected and listed, and stored all effects," and maintained accountability for hospital property issued to the ward by the hospital steward. Additional duties varied by hospital. The ward master, according to one surgeon's orders at a Raleigh hospital, was to "carry the Diet Rolls as soon as made out by Asst. Surgeons of Wards to the Matron in charge of the culinary department." Confederate law authorized a ward master a monthly salary of no more than $25.[14]

War Department General Orders No. 93 provided "for the permanent detail of soldiers as nurses and ward masters in case a sufficient number of these attendants could not be attained outside the military service." Records indicate most North Carolina hospitals throughout the war employed at least one ward master on staff. Raleigh's larger pavilion-style hospital used 14 ward masters to supervise the 10 individual one-story structures that constituted the hospital, whereas General Hospital No. 8 in Raleigh employed four ward masters to supervise the multistory Peace Institute building.[15]

---

13. "Report of Examining Board of Hospital Stewards held at Raleigh," February 17, 1864, Ernest Haywood Collection of Haywood Family Papers, SHC/UNC. Hereafter cited as Haywood Papers.
14. Stout, *Confederate Hospitals on the Move*, 75; GO No. [blank], July 24, 1863, Pettigrew General Hospital No. 13, Haywood Papers, SHC/UNC; Cunningham, *Doctors in Gray*, 76; See also, GO, No. 93, November 22, 1862, AIGO, General Orders and Circulars, Nos. 1-22 (1861) and Nos. 1-112 (1862), M901, roll 01, RG109, NA. Hereafter cited as AIGO, General Orders and Circulars, M901, and the relevant roll number.
15. GO, No. 93, November 22, 1862, AIGO, General Orders and Circulars, M901, roll 01, RG109, NA.

Soldiers as Nurses

At the beginning of the Civil War, the Confederacy adopted the U.S. Army's prewar practice of using convalescing or able-bodied detailed men as nurses. Confederate hospital regulations specified one nurse for every 10 patients. Although acceptable for a small peacetime army, the staggering losses early in the war from combat and sickness quickly exposed the policy's shortcomings. Field commanders frowned upon the practice of taking able-bodied infantrymen and detailing them to rear area hospitals on a permanent basis—a situation that only worsened as the Confederacy could no longer replace its combat losses. Hospital surgeons preferred healthy detailed soldiers as nurses; however, because these men were subject to recall, hospitals experienced a constant turnover in nurses, which "made it difficult to establish consistent routines and affected standards of care." The frustration these surgeons held is understandable, especially after training an individual to proper efficiency.[16]

On the other hand, commanders approved the detailing of a convalescent soldier as a nurse until the individual sufficiently recovered to return to the unit. Oftentimes these individuals had physical limitations from injuries, thus limiting their effectiveness. For example, Private William C. Bruce, 4th North Carolina, suffered a severe gunshot wound in the right shoulder at the battle of Chancellorsville. After recovering sufficiently enough in a Richmond hospital, authorities transferred Bruce to Raleigh's General Hospital No. 7, where he served as a nurse. The surgeon-in-charge at the hospital, Dr. Edmund B. Haywood, disagreed with the policy of using convalescent soldiers as nurses, a point he expressed to the Surgeon General Moore, writing, "It will be impossible to keep a hospital in fine order and the patients well cared for with broken down disabled men."[17]

A detailed soldier at Wilson's General Hospital No. 2, Peyton A. Cox of the 52nd North Carolina, initially served as an assistant clerk, but within a few short weeks, the hospital's surgeon-in-charge, Dr. Samuel S. Satchwell, had reassigned Cox as both a nurse and ward master. Cox informed his brother that the ward consisted of "the worst cases in the hospital—and have but one assistant and fear I shall not keep him long as changes go on every day." On one occasion, Cox's dentistry background from back home in Forsyth County proved

16. Hilde, *Worth a Dozen Men*, 44. For additional reading on the role of male soldiers as nurses, see Green, *Chimborazo*, 41–46; Schroeder-Lein, *Confederate Hospitals on the Move*, 76; Cunningham, *Doctors in Gray*, 72.
17. Wm. W. Bruce, CSR, M270, roll 136; Haywood to Moore, October 8, 1863. Order and Letter Book, Fair Grounds Hospital, Haywood Papers, SHC/UNC.

useful when he "extracted one old tooth today for a soldier & did it before the old Dr. . . . it seemed to please him. I am fearful all that sort of work will fall on me & will I ever get thanks or pay for it?"[18]

A different group of military men called "Galvanized Rebels" served as attendants in the Confederate Military Prison Hospital (General Hospital No. 9) in Salisbury. Galvanized Rebels were imprisoned Union soldiers who Confederate authorities recruited with offers of parole in exchange for military service to escape the privations and sickness plaguing the prison during the war's final months. As late as December 1864, the surgeon-in-charge of the hospital utilized the deserters as nurses, ward masters, and cooks, as well as for other administrative duties.[19]

Pvt. William Henry of the 31st North Carolina served as a nurse in the general hospital at Washington, NC.

(Library of Congress)

Because "competent nurses were hard to find," the need for detailed nurses at North Carolina hospitals continued throughout the remainder of the war. In March 1864, detailed soldiers represented 58 percent (69 of 119) of the total nurses employed in North Carolina hospitals, as compared to hired nurses, which included Blacks, free or hired from their enslavers, and White civilians, as shown in table 2.1. When analyzed on a weekly basis, later records reveal the state's

18. Peyton A. Cox to Dear Brother [Romulus L. Cox], September 17, 1863, "1862–64: Peyton Alexander Cox to his Siblings," Spared & Shared, accessed on November 1, 2021, https://sparedshared22.wordpress.com/2021/10/22/1862-64-peyton-alexander-cox-to-john-henderson-cox/.
19. Heather Clancy, "Galvanized Rebels," accessed on December 25, 2021, https://www.nps.gov/ande/learn/historyculture/galvanized.htm; "List of Federal Deserters on Parole from C.S. Military Prison of Salisbury, N.C," December 24, 1864, List of Miscellaneous Rolls, Returns, and Reports, #9023 Louis Brown Collection, Rowan County Library, Salisbury, NC.

hospitals continued to rely on detailed men for the duration of the war. For example, when Raleigh's General Hospital No. 13 opened in the summer of 1864, it employed a total of 23 detailed nurses.[20]

Table 2.1: Comparison of Detailed and Hired Nurses, week ending March 21, 1864[21]

Location	Designation	Detailed Nurses	Hired Nurses	Total Nurses
Wilson	General Hospital No. 2	15	3	18
Goldsboro	General Hospital No. 3	8	10	18
Wilmington	General Hospital No. 4	12	12	24
Wilmington	General Hospital No. 5	4	1	5
Fayetteville	General Hospital No. 6	2	4	6
Raleigh	General Hospital No. 7	8	5	13
Raleigh	General Hospital No. 8	10	13	23
Salisbury	General Hospital No. 9	5	0	5
Charlotte	General Hospital No. 10	4	2	6
Fayetteville	Arsenal & Armory	1	0	1
Total		69	50	119

Alternative to Detailed Nurses

On August 21, 1861, the Confederate Congress transformed the makeup of Confederate hospitals for the remainder of the war when it authorized the hiring of civilians "when necessary" to alleviate the suffering of the sick and wounded. During the initial transition from detailed nurses, North Carolina newspapers indicate the surgeons superintending the larger hospitals preferred White civilian male nurses. Wilmington's *Daily Journal* advertised the requirement for "15 or 20 good nurses" who would earn liberal wages at Goldsboro's General Hospital No. 3, stipulating, "civilians preferred not subject to

20. Cunningham, *Doctors in Gray*, 72; Consolidated Weekly Report, March 21, 1864, North Carolina Medical Director Reports, ch. 6, vol. 280, 19, RG109, NA; "Roll of Non-Commissioned Officers and Privates employed on Extra Duty as Stewards and Nurses," December 1, 1864, Haywood Papers, SHC/UNC. Historian Drew Gilpin Faust argues that hospital records indicate that Blacks served in greater numbers as nurses, cooks, and laundresses than detailed soldiers or Confederate women. Faust, *Mothers of Invention*, 112.
21. Data from Consolidated Weekly Report, March 21, 1864, North Carolina Medical Director Reports, ch. 6, vol. 280, 19, RG109, NA.

conscription," which implied White males only. In preparation for opening the Peace Institute Hospital in Raleigh, Surgeon Thomas A. Hill actively sought "White men over 35 years old."[22]

Despite the preference for White male civilian nurses, the passage of the Conscription Act by the Confederate Congress in April 1862 made it increasingly difficult for hospital surgeons to continue the hiring practice. The act restricted the number of eligible White males allowed to work at a hospital, as it made all able-bodied White men between the ages of 18 and 35 (later amended to 45) liable for service in the Confederate army. The specific wording of "middle-aged men preferred" used in one hiring announcement for nurses highlights the impact the 1862 Conscription Act had on the hiring of White male nurses.[23]

The inability of the Medical Department to thoroughly staff detailed soldiers as nurses without negatively affecting its field armies was problematic for the Confederacy. Additionally, the prewar model of staffing male soldiers as hospital nurses had a significant downside for providing quality care to the sick and wounded. By spring 1862, it had become apparent to patients and surgeons, as well as elected officials, "that women made better nurses than men." Women had voluntarily risen to the occasion early on when the government was incapable of providing quality health care. A congressional committee report cited "the superiority of female nurses as compared with males ... When males have charge, the mortality averages ten percent; when females manage, it is only five percent."[24]

According to historian Robert W. Waitt Jr., "The hospital system of the Confederacy was an evolving one thru out [sic] the War—one which was still changing as the War ended." From summer 1862 onward, authorized staff serving at a Confederate hospital consisted of a diverse group of individuals, relying heavily upon Confederate women and, to a greater extent, hired or impressed Blacks.[25]

---

22. Cunningham, *Doctors in Gray*, 71-72; *Daily Journal* (Wilmington, NC), June 30, 1862; "Nurses Cooks and Waiters Wanted," *The State Journal* (Raleigh, NC), May 21, 1862.

23. Mathews, James M. "Public Laws of the Confederate States of America, passed at the First Session of the First Congress; 1862," The statutes at large of the Confederate States of America (Richmond, VA, 1862), 29-32; ibid., "Public Laws of the Confederate States of America, passed at the Second Session of the First Congress; 1862," *The statutes at large of the Confederate States of America* (Richmond, VA, 1862), 62; "Wanted to Hire," *The State Journal* (Raleigh, NC), August 13, 1862.

24. Hilde, *Worth a Dozen Men*, 24-25.

25. Robert W. Waitt Jr., *Confederate Military Hospitals in Richmond* (Richmond, VA, 2002), 4; Hilde, *Worth a Dozen Men*, 134; Cunningham, *Doctors in Gray*, 72; Green, *Chimborazo*, 47-48.

Confederate Women in Hospitals

Prior to the war, the Roman Catholic sisterhoods, often referred to as "Sisters of Charity" or "Sisters of Mercy," were the only women in the United States with any formal training as nurses. Because of their superior reputation for hospital work, the sisters' services were highly sought after at the start of the war. Throughout the conflict "at least 617 sisters from twenty-one different communities, representing twelves separate orders, nursed both Union and Confederate soldiers." The United States had no formal training for nurses, so Florence Nightingale's "Notes on Nursing" became a widely popular reading. As one Confederate woman noted in 1861, "The young ladies are exceedingly anxious to imitate Florence Nightingale . . . To be sure, not every southern woman was a would-be Nightingale."[26]

These "would-be Nightingales" sparked debates inside well-to-do families, as well as the public at large, about whether hospital work was a suitable vocation for upper-class Confederate women. To some, the mere presence of women from the elite class of Southern society threatened their "delicacy, modesty, and refinement." An essayist in the *Southern Monthly* of May 1862 believed women should confine their charitable work to providing hospital "comforts and delicacies" and sewing items for the soldiers. "Such services can be performed without a doubt of their propriety."[27]

But such reservations did not deter everyone. Indeed, the Confederate Government's initial inability to properly care for its sick and wounded motivated many young Confederate women to serve as nurses. They were driven by several reasons, including "patriotic fervor, a sense of duty, and a belief they could be of use." Various North Carolina newspapers trumpeted the call for women to serve in the hospitals. The October 3, 1861, edition of the *Daily Journal* printed, "[W]e now have in active service another generation of Spartan women, whose ranks are filled with whole legions of Florence Nightingales." Hospital service also provided a source of income for women struggling financially as the Southern economy deteriorated. For example, Mrs. M. E. Roberts, a widow from North Carolina, served as a ward matron at the 2nd North Carolina Hospital in Petersburg. The hospital's steward, E. D. Smith, described her as "a

26. Mary Denis Maher, *To Bind Up the Wounds: Catholic Sister Nurse in the U.S. Civil War* (Baton Rouge, LA: 1999), 69-71; Stout, 75-77; Quoted in Miller, *Empty Sleeves*, 93; For a more detailed study of Confederate women's service in hospitals see, Hilde, *Worth a Dozen Men*, and Faust, *Mothers of Invention*; see also, Calcutt, *Richmond's Civil War Hospitals*.
27. Faust, *Mothers of Invention*, 92-93; "Florence Nightingale and Southern Ladies," *Southern Monthly* (May 1862), 2:7.

widow without any means of support except what her hands can earn."[28]

Other women in need also answered the call. Alice G. Beale, a refugee from New Bern who had relocated to Goldsboro along with her parents, personally wrote Confederate President Jefferson Davis seeking employment. "I am anxious to serve my country," Alice wrote, but she also confided with President Davis the financial difficulties her parents faced because of their refugee status. "I am rather young for a Hospital Matron; can you not give me writing to do . . . I am sure I can relieve some young man that can take the field." The plight of Alice and her parents was a common one in eastern North Carolina during the war, as those families with Confederate sympathies fled to other regions of the state to escape Union occupation. A nurse at a High Point hospital noted in her diary the presence of 30 refugee families, "all are from New Berne, nearly." Whatever motivated these women to step out from the confines and safety of their homes and into the army's hospitals where misery and suffering abounded, their contributions were essential.[29]

Deadly Side of Nursing

Civil War nursing was not without its dangers. During Wilmington's yellow fever epidemic, Julia E. Capps contracted the deadly disease while working as a nurse in General Hospital No. 4, and later died, leaving a small child in her mother's care. Laura Wesson, a 20-year-old refugee from Virginia, fell victim to smallpox while volunteering as a nurse at High Point. The widow of one North Carolina soldier, Eliza J. Gore from Sampson County, died while serving as a nurse in a Richmond hospital.[30]

28. Hilde, *Worth a Dozen Men*, 58; *Daily Journal* (Wilmington, NC), October 3, 1861; E. D. Smith to H. M. Pettis, November 17, 1864, Ernest Haywood Papers, Series 4, SHC/UNC.
29. Pollitt and Reese, "War Between the States, Nursing in North Carolina," 24; "Strange Phenomenon," *Weekly Progress* (New Bern, NC), September 10, 1861; Hilde in *Worth a Dozen Men* contends financial concerns drove more women to work in hospitals than the records suggest; Alice Beale to Mr. Davis, November 6, 1863, Alice G. Beale, Confederate Papers Relating to Citizens or Business Firms, 1861–65, M346, roll 50, RG109, NA; Kate S. Sperry, diary, March 27, 1865, Virginia Museum of History & Culture (VMHC), Richmond.
30. B. L. Capps, Citizens or Business Papers, M346, roll 140; Michael Briggs, *Guilford Under the Stars and Bars* (published by the author, 2015), 230-31; The Laura Wesson Chapter of the Order of the Confederate Rose in High Point was named in honor of her hospital service; According to family tradition, Eliza Gore served in one of the Richmond hospitals, until, she died of unknown causes on an unspecified date. Greg Mast, *State Troops and Volunteers: A Photographic Record of North Carolina's Civil War Soldiers*

Pvt. Morris Gore, and his wife, Susan M. Gore. Pvt. Gore was mortally wounded at the battle of Malvern Hill in June 1862. Following his death, Susan Gore served as a nurse in a Richmond hospital until, on an unknown date, she died of unknown causes.

(North Carolina Office of Archives and History)

Early Hospital Service

In summer 1861, the grim news of disease outbreaks and terrible sickness within the Tar Heel encampments located in Virginia reached the North Carolina home front. The situation provided the impetus for groups of North Carolina Confederate women to volunteer their services in hopes of alleviating the suffering of fellow Tar Heels. In

(Raleigh, NC, 1995), 196, 214n4.2.16; Eliza's husband, Pvt. Morris Gore of the 20th North Carolina, was mortally wounded at the battle of Malvern Hill on June 29, 1862. Morris Gore, CSR, M270, roll 270, RG109, NA; Morris Gore, and his wife, 27-year-old Eliza Gore, are listed on the U.S. Federal Census (1860), Schedule 1, Taylors Bridge District, Sampson County, NC, 15.

July, the Ladies Hospital Association of Mecklenburg County sent "four experienced nurses," which included Miss Catherine Gibbon, Mrs. Charles C. Lee, Mrs. Bolton, and an enslaved woman named Nancy, with necessary supplies to Yorktown to nurse the sick and wounded, as a reported 200 North Carolinians were "suffering for the want of proper attention."[31] Surgeon General Charles E. Johnson, who personally inspected the situation in Yorktown, notified Governor Henry T. Clark that the men "suffered very much from measles, diarrhea, dysentery, some pneumonia and typhoid fever." The Nelson House, a two-story brick home that once served as the Revolutionary War headquarters for the British, was one of several Confederate hospitals established in the Yorktown area for ill soldiers from the state's regiments. Surgeon Peter E. Hines of the 1st North Carolina Volunteers superintended the hospital's operation.[32]

Later that September, 14 civilian volunteers from Forsyth County departed Salem en route to Fauquier County, Virginia, where the 11th North Carolina Volunteers (later redesignated the 21st North Carolina) encamped. Since July, scores of the regiment's soldiers had suffered from measles, typhoid fever, and other non-battle illnesses. One of the nurses was a 21-year-old Salem school teacher, Miss Margaret (Maggie) E. Clewell. The group left Salem for the railroad depot at High Point in one "fully loaded four-horse stagecoach," with Miss Clewell and another traveling up top with the driver. "We had carried many things with us, knowing we could get nothing in the way of supplies when we reached the camp," Clewell remembered.[33]

31. Michael C. Hardy, *Civil War Charlotte: Last Capital of the Confederacy* (Charleston, SC, 2012), 24-26; "The Hospital Association," *Daily Bulletin* (Charlotte, NC), July 17, 1861; "The War Hospitals and the Memorial Association," *Charlotte Observer*, May 20, 1896; N. H. Whitaker to Gov. John Ellis, July 1, 1861, quoted McKean, *Blood and War at My Door Step*, 1:114; Mrs. Anna P. Lee's husband, Col. Charles C. Lee, was mortally wounded during the Seven Days' Battles on June 30, 1862.
32. Hilde, *Worth a Dozen Men*, 57; *The State Journal* (Raleigh, NC), August 14, 1861; *Hillsborough Recorder* (NC) July 31, 1861; Chas. E. Johnson to His Excellency, August 28, 1861, Henry T. Clark Papers, NCOAH; Norris, "For the Benefit of Our Gallant Volunteers," *NCHR*, 306.
33. Lee W. Sherrill Jr. *The 21st North Carolina Infantry: A Civil War History, with a Roster of Officers* (Jefferson, NC, 2015), 56. The Forsyth County group included: Elizabeth V. Kremer; Laura Vogler; Leana Shoub; Lizetta Stewart; Ann Burt; Mr. and Mrs. Tandy; Malena White; Mr. and Mrs. Byhan; Mr. Keller; and Henry Holder and his wife. See Sherrill, *The 21st North Carolina Infantry*, 464n27; Louis H. Manarin, Weymouth T. Jordan Jr., Matthew M. Brown, and Michael E. Coffey, comps. *North Carolina Troops 1861–1865 A Roster*, 20 vols. to date (Raleigh, NC, 1966–), 6:530. Hereafter cited, Manarin, et al., *North Carolina Troops*; Margaret Clewell Jenkins to Mrs. Wilson [NC, United Daughters of the Confederacy], September 28, 1906, Military Collection, NCOAH.

The volunteers first encountered approximately 30 or more gravely ill soldiers "all on the floor, on straw [and] old blankets, [and] no comforts at all" in an old stone mill building at Thoroughfare Station. "We could not do anything here," Clewell wrote, "except fixing them something to eat, [and] our hearts grew heavy, as it was our first real experience of what we could expect." Nearby, Assistant Surgeon John F. Shaffner, the unit's only medical officer—two were severely ill and one recalled to North Carolina—obtained as a temporary hospital the use of the Blantyre Plantation manor house, capable of accommodating approximately 50 patients. Shaffner put 50-year-old Elizabeth V. Kremer, president of the Relief Association of the Ladies of Forsyth County, in charge of the hospital, as well as the "nurses . . . the entire cooking [and], etc." Shaffner welcomed Kremer's presence, as it relieved him of ancillary duties. In describing the amount of trust he placed in her, Shaffner wrote, "I have given all into her hands."[34]

Local women from the area assisted Mrs. Kremer at the hospital by providing various food items, four milk cows, which nurse Anna Burt "assumed as her personal responsibility," and an unidentified enslaved woman, "strictly to help with the wash."[35] A nurse from Salem, 32-year-old Laura Vogler, wrote letters providing a glimpse into the women's daily routine at Blantyre. On October 7, Vogler wrote her sister, "We . . . have to cook for about forty men, well and sick, well men come to nurse the sick. We go and feed them three times a day, talk to them and try to [make] them believe they are getting better."[36]

The services of Kremer and her nurses allowed Shaffner to "devote himself to patient care." In a letter home to his future wife, Carrie L. Fries, Shaffner praised Kremer and the "Forsyth Samaritan' nurses," as he called them, but also noted his decision to send several of the women home "whom he deemed to be too nice . . . along with another who refused to accept Mrs. Kremer's supervisory authority." By

34. Ibid.; Sherrill, *The 21st North Carolina Infantry*, 56-57; J. E. Shaffner to Miss Carrie L. Fries, October 6, 1861, Shaffner Diary and Papers, NCOAH.
35. Laura to Dear Sister, October 7, 1861, Vogler Letters, Moravian Archives, Winston-Salem, NC; J. E. Shaffner to Miss Carrie L. Fries, October 7, 1861, Shaffner Diary and Papers, NCOAH; Sherrill, *The 21st North Carolina Infantry*, 56-57.
36. Laura to Dear Sister, October 7, 1861, Vogler Letters, Moravian Archives, Winston-Salem, NC; Sherrill, *The 21st North Carolina Infantry*, 56. The reference to "cooking" as part of the nursing duties at Blantyre contrasts with the contemporary view of nursing. Drew Gilpin Faust in *Mothers of Invention* contends, "What southern women called 'nursing,' we might better designate as 'hospital work,' for it encompasses a wide variation in activities and levels of commitment."; The Relief Association of the Ladies of Forsyth County was formed on August 24, 1861, "to minister to the comforts and necessities of the brave Soldiers who have left this county." See Sherrill, *The 21st North Carolina Infantry*, 464n23.

November the regiment had relocated, and the Forsyth County volunteers returned to North Carolina. During their brief service in Virginia, death surrounded the women at Blantyre Plantation. At the temporary hospital, an estimated 122 soldiers died, with typhoid claiming 82 percent of the deaths. The work Kremer's nurses performed in 1861 was merely an opening act in the drawn-out, bloody war that would transpire.[37]

Not all Confederate women who answered the call that summer served in Virginia. A measles out-

Elizabeth Vierling Kremer, ca. 1855.

(Collection of Old Salem Museums
& Gardens, Acc. 3134.5.)

break on Portsmouth Island, along the North Carolina Outer Banks, ran rampant through the army garrison located there. In the absence of a military hospital on the island—authorities chose to use the former U.S. Marine Hospital on Portsmouth as barracks—local families nursed many of the ill soldiers from their private residences. Following the death of one soldier, Captain Thomas Sparrow, the garrison's senior officer, remarked, "I believe that he received far better attention in the family of Mrs. Gaskill when there were three females to provide for his wants than he would have received in a hospital."[38]

---

37. Sherrill, *The 21st North Carolina Infantry,* 57; J. E. Shaffner to Miss Carrie L. Fries, October 7, 1861, NCOAH; Sherrill, *The 21st North Carolina Infantry,* 57.
38. Sparrow to Gentlemen, July 15, 1861, Thomas Sparrow Papers, East Carolina Manuscript Collection, J. Y. Joyner Library, East Carolina University, Greenville. Hereafter cited as Sparrow Papers, ECU; According to the U.S. Federal Census (1860), Schedule 1, Carteret District, Carteret County, NC, Post Office Portsmouth, 57, there were three separate Gaskill households living on the island at the time of the measles outbreak. It is unclear which specific one Captain Sparrow refers to in his letter.

Jane Renwick Smedberg Wilkes, ca. 1845, volunteered as a nurse in the Charlotte area hospitals throughout the war. In the years following the war, she was a major civic leader in Charlotte helping to raise money for two hospitals, one for Whites at St. Peter's and a second for Blacks at Good Samaritan. In 2014, a statue of Jane Wilkes was unveiled at the Little Sugar Creek Greenway in honor of her untiring work.

(Original owned by family member, digital image courtesy of Robinson-Spangler Carolina Room, Charlotte-Mecklenburg Library, Charlotte, N.C.)

In Charlotte, Jane Renwick Smedberg Wilkes volunteered throughout the war in the city's various hospitals. As the mother of five children, Wilkes was unable to serve full-time, but when able, she found time to comfort the ill soldiers. These early North Carolina Confederate women, whether traveling to Virginia to care for the sick and wounded or by remaining right at home in North Carolina, gained valuable experience, lessons they passed on to the next group of Confederate women.[39]

Matrons

In September 1862, President Jefferson Davis signed into law "An Act to Better Provide for the Sick and Wounded of the Army in Hospital," which officially established a structure of female matrons within a military hospital. Two months later the War Department issued General Orders No. 95, effectively incorporating the act into regulations. Matrons were strictly responsible for administrative tasks—at least on paper—in daily hospital operations. In setting the hierarchy of the matron structure, General Orders No. 95 authorized the hiring of two chief matrons, with a monthly salary not to exceed $40 per month, whose responsibilities were to help "exercise superintendence over the entire domestic economy of the hospital."[40]

One of the benefits of the act was that it "eased potential hostility between physicians and female employees by codifying a clear hierarchy and defining realms of male and female labor." Chief matrons were subordinate to the hospital's surgeon-in-charge, and subordinate to the chief matrons were assistant matrons and ward matrons. The order allowed for up to two assistant matrons who superintended the laundry and mending of hospital linens and patients' clothing and the preparation of meals in accordance with dietary and scheduling requirements. Assistant matrons could make up to $35 a month. Ward matrons, whose salary could not exceed $30 per month, were responsible for all matters related to their respective wards. Her duties included: "[T]o prepare the beds and bedding; to see that they are kept clean and in order; that the food or diet for the sick is carefully prepared and furnished to them; the medicine administered,

39. J. Wilkes, Unpublished autobiography (1903), Wilkes-Smedberg Family Papers, Charlotte-Mecklenburg Public Library, Carolina Room, Charlotte, NC.
40. The genesis for the September 1862 Act originated from a special committee of the Confederate Congress that recommended the establishment of a corps of nurses. The committee maintained "Good nursing, is of equal value to medical attention." Quoted in Cunningham, *Doctors in Gray*, 72-73; Hilde, *Worth a Dozen Men*, 39; GO No. 95, AIGO, November 25, 1862, General Orders and Circulars, M901, roll 01, RG109, NA.

and that all patients requiring careful nursing are attended to." In addition to their salaries, General Orders No. 95 authorized hospital matrons to receive rations and lodging.[41]

Prior to the official authorization of matron positions in September 1862, women had already been serving in administrative capacities for more than a year. In April 1861, Dr. James F. McRee, acting medical director of the Southern Coastal Defense Department in Wilmington, allowed the hiring of Mary E. Stuart as a matron at the newly established military hospital in Smithville (present-day Southport). The hospital was later identified as General Hospital No. 6. Documents suggest Stuart was one of the first women to serve as a matron in a North Carolina Confederate hospital. Remembered years later as "an uncompromising rebel," Stuart operated a boarding house, known locally as the "Stuart House." Stuart received $50 per month as the matron for overseeing the preparation of food for the patients. In addition to her paid services, Stuart donated bed sheets, pillows, quilts, and blankets for use in the hospital. Weeks later in Wilmington, McRee announced in the *Daily Journal* that he was seeking a "respectable and experienced white woman to act as a matron" at the recently established Marine General Hospital.[42]

As early as October 1861, North Carolina Confederate women served as matrons in Petersburg, Virginia. Sixty-year-old Catherine G. DeRosset Kennedy of Wilmington served as head matron for the 1st North Carolina Hospital before returning home in March 1863. Alongside Kennedy serving as assistant matrons were fellow North Carolinians Mary Beasley of Plymouth, who later served as an assistant matron in the hospital at Wilson, Nancy (Nannie) C. Beckwith, and Tyrrell County native Mary B. Pettigrew, sister to Confederate Brig. Gen. James J. Pettigrew. Mary Pettigrew later served as chief matron for the Virginia division of Chimborazo Hospital in Richmond, where she met her future husband, Surgeon Peter F. Brown.[43]

---

41. Calcutt, *Richmond's Confederate Hospitals*, 36; GO No. 95, AIGO, November 25, 1862, General Orders and Circulars, M901, roll 01, RG109, NA.

42. Jane E. Schultz, *Women at the Front: Hospital Workers in the Civil War* (Chapel Hill, NC, 2004), 111; Bill Reaves, "Inside Old Wilmington," *Brunswick County Historical Society Newsletter* (February 1999), 39:4; File of Mrs. Mary E. Stewart, Citizens or Business Papers, M346, roll 984. The correct spelling of the surname is Stuart; "Wanted," *Daily Journal* (Wilmington, NC), July 15, 1861.

43. "North Carolina Hospital in Virginia," *The State Journal* (Raleigh, NC), November 27, 1861; *Daily Journal* (Wilmington, NC), October 2, 1861, March 20, 1863; Johnston, Wilson Confederate Hospital Muster Rolls, Bi-monthly Report No. 13, August 1 to September 30, 1863; John R. Gildersleeve, "History of Chimborazo Hospital, Richmond, Va., and Its

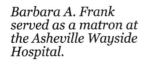

Barbara A. Frank served as a matron at the Asheville Wayside Hospital.

(Courtesy of
Mary Kay Frank Armstrong)

Often women of lesser economic or social standing served as matrons in North Carolina's hospitals. Barbara A. Frank of Asheville was 48 years old when authorities established the wayside hospital there in late 1862. At the time, Frank was a divorced single mother who made a living as a seamstress. Unfortunately, life had not always been easy for Frank. When her only child, Cornelius, turned 13, she indentured him to the editor of the *Asheville News*. According to her obituary, which is the only known record of her hospital service, Frank served as the "manager of the Wayside Hospital at this place . . . and her ministrations to the sick and wounded can never be forgotten." The obituary's reference to management implies Frank likely served as the chief matron, although it is unclear whether she volunteered or worked as an employee. As a single woman, a matron's salary would have provided her additional income.[44]

Lydia Prichard answered the call to nursing following the death of her brother Rev. John L. Prichard of the First Baptist Church in Wilmington. The reverend contracted yellow fever during the city's outbreak, and Lydia "tenderly watched over and nursed" her brother for almost a month until his passing in November. While her brother

Medical Officers During 1861–1865," *Virginia Medical Semi-Monthly* (July 1904), 148-54.

44. Calcutt, *Richmond's Wartime Hospitals*, 38; U.S. Federal Census (1860), Schedule 1, Asheville, Buncombe County, NC, 37; "Died," *Asheville Democrat*, September 17, 1890. Cornelius Frank enlisted in the 1st North Carolina Volunteers.

was bedridden, several Sisters of Charity from Charleston, South Carolina, visited the ailing reverend. Although nursing one's family member was an accepted practice in the Antebellum South, the sisters' visit may have inspired Lydia Prichard. Two months after her brother's death, Prichard became the chief matron at Wilson's General Hospital No. 2 in January 1863, a position she maintained through December 1864.[45]

Matron Janet McCallum served as a matron at the C.S. Military Prison Hospital in Salisbury. Little could have prepared her for the humanitarian crisis that would occur at the prison late in the war. To help alleviate prisoner suffering, McCallum on her own initiative planted a garden right outside the prison wall. With the assistance of detailed prisoners, McCallum grew fresh vegetables. Her simple act of planting a garden demonstrated how Confederate women implemented their talents from home to the benefit of their patients.[46]

The Civil War created a divide within some families regarding whether one's personal loyalty lay with the Union or Confederacy. Often family members served on opposing sides. Such was the case for 33-year-old Catherine (Kate) Gibbon of Charlotte. Kate had three brothers enlist in the Confederate Army, including Surgeon Robert Gibbon, who later returned home to superintend Charlotte's General Hospital No. 11. Her oldest brother, John Gibbon, was a graduate of the U.S. Military Academy. He chose to remain in the U.S. Army, and achieved the rank of brigadier general of volunteers by May 1862.[47]

Following her volunteer work at Yorktown, Gibbon relocated to Richmond where she served as a matron in Moore Hospital (General Hospital No. 24). Unfortunately, she never escaped the suspicion some fervent Confederates felt regarding John. A convalescing soldier at the Moore Hospital, then Private Thomas F. Wood of the 7th North Carolina, who later became an assistant surgeon in the Confederate army, recalled Gibbon's service at the hospital. "There was a matron in the hospital, a sister of Dr. Robert Gibbon of Charlotte, who had left her home to minister to the sick. She had a good deal of zeal but little knowledge of her duties." During his time in the army, Wood personally witnessed the challenges many women faced while serving

45. J. D. Hufham, Rev., Memoir of Rev. John L. Prichard: Late Pastor of the First Baptist Church, Wilmington, N. C. (Raleigh, NC, 1867), 167; Hugh B. Johnston, comp., Wilson Confederate Hospital Muster Rolls, Bi-monthly Report No. 17, August 1 to December 31, 1864, Wilson Public Library, Wilson, NC. Hereafter cited as Wilson Confederate Muster Rolls, followed by the relevant report number and date.
46. *Weekly Sentinel* (Raleigh, NC), May 15, 1866.
47. Edward J. Warner, *Generals in Blue: Lives of Union Commanders* (Baton Rouge, LA, 1999), 171.

in the hospitals. "In fact, many ladies wanted to imitate Florence Nightingale, but who had not prepared themselves by study or practice in the art of nursing, and who having some success at home nursing ... were greatly at sea when they undertook to look after numbers of rough soldiers with few of the appliances at home," Wood observed.[48]

Despite Kate Gibbon's shortcomings, Wood described her as "very kind to me in many little ways . . . and was the friend to whom I was indebted." Her eventual departure from the hospital "pained" Woods, noting "that she left the city under a cloud" because of her brother's service in the Union army. By 1864, Gibbon had returned to Pennsylvania, where she had been born.[49]

Wood's description of Gibbon highlights the importance of the emotional support Confederate women provided to men while patients in a hospital. Whether reading or writing a letter to a family member back home, holding their hand, or just the sound of a soft voice, such seemingly trivial actions contributed greatly to a soldier's healing. Because these women were usually the "first and most constant face injured men saw," oftentimes they developed an attachment with their patients. And in so doing, a matron performed perhaps her "most valuable and important responsibility," that of "comforting her sick and wounded and sometimes dying patients." Kate Sperry, who served at the Confederate hospitals in Goldsboro and High Point, developed a close bond with one severely wounded officer. Sperry recorded in her diary: "I've a special pet upstairs, Lt. Lenham, 1st Fla. Regiment—nice man—wounded through the elbow of the left arm and right shoulder and neck—suffers a great deal—he says I talk just like his wife and it does him good to know I'm here even when he doesn't see me—I go upstairs and sing for him and do what I can for his comfort."[50]

48. Fanning Wood, *Doctor to the Front: The Recollections of Confederate Surgeon Thomas Fanning Wood*, Donald B. Koonce, ed., (Knoxville, TN, 2000), 36.
49. Prior to the No. 24 designation, medical officers referred to the hospital as "Moore Hospital," in honor of Surgeon General Moore. When Dr. Otis F. Manson, the surgeon-in-charge of General Hospital No. 24, learned that Wood had been a medical student of a former colleague in Wilmington, he immediately put Wood to work in the hospital. Koonce, Doctor to the Front, 36; Catherine Gibbon never married nor did she continue hospital work. Instead she chose to follow in her father's former footsteps as an employee at the U.S. Mint in Philadelphia. She died at the age of 68 in Atlantic City, New Jersey, but her surviving family members laid her to rest in Charlotte's Oakdale Cemetery alongside her parents. Despite Gibbon's service to the Confederate cause as a North Carolinian, she is noticeably absent from Lucy L. Anderson's *North Carolina Women of the Confederacy* (1926).
50. Miller, *Empty Sleeves*, 95; Calcutt, *Richmond's Confederate Hospitals*, 36; Sperry Diary, April 27, 1865, VMHC. The officer was Lt. Andrew Denham Jr. of Company C, First Florida Infantry. Denham suffered his wounds on

Kate Sperry, a refugee from Winchester, Va., volunteered as a nurse at General Hospital No. 3 in Goldsboro, where she worked with her husband, Dr. Enoch Hunt, who served as the hospital steward.

(Fred Barr Collection, Stewart Bell Jr. Archives Room, Handley Regional Library, Winchester, Va.)

March 19, 1865, at the battle of Bentonville. Andrew Denham, Compiled Service Records of Confederate Soldiers Who Served in Organizations from the State of Florida, M251, roll 26, RG109, NA.

The number of matrons employed at North Carolina hospitals varied between institutions. As table 2.2 shows, an end-of-week report from May 1863 indicates that those institutions with bed capacities greater than 200 employed at least four or more matrons, whereas the small hospitals employed no matrons. Surprisingly, only two of the 11 general hospitals, Wilson's General Hospital No. 2 and Wilmington's General Hospital No. 4, employed all three types of matrons—chief, assistant, and ward—as General Orders No. 93 authorized. When analyzed on a weekly basis, later records reveal most of the state's hospitals never hired the total amount of ward matrons the War Department had authorized.

Table 2.2: Matrons Employed in North Carolina General Hospitals, week ending May 7, 1863[51]

Location	Designation	Chief Matrons	Asst. Matrons	Ward Matrons	Total Matrons	Number of Beds
Weldon	Gen. Hosp. No. 1	1		1	2	54
Wilson	Gen. Hosp. No. 2	1	2	1	4	225
Goldsboro	Gen. Hosp. No. 3	2	2		4	220
Wilmington	Gen. Hosp. No. 4	1	2	3	6	229
Wilmington	Gen. Hosp. No. 5	1			1	51
Smithville	Gen. Hosp. No. 6				0	42
Raleigh	Gen. Hosp. No. 7	1			1	150
Raleigh	Gen. Hosp. No. 8	1	2	1	4	300
Salisbury	Gen. Hosp. No. 9				0	19
Charlotte	Gen. Hosp. No. 10	1			1	37
Tarboro	Gen. Hosp. No. 11				0	56

Private Relief Organizations

Throughout the Confederacy, various women's benevolent societies supported the sick and wounded by providing food, clothing items, and other sundry goods, that were otherwise unavailable to the hospitalized soldiers. Society work provided an alternative for those middle- and upper-class Confederate women who "faced turmoil over the etiquette" of physically serving in a hospital but held a strong desire to contribute. The majority of these groups in the Confederacy functioned locally and never organized on a national scale like the U.S. Sanitary Commission or U.S. Christian Commission, which carried out relief work for Union soldiers.[52]

51. Date from Consolidated Weekly Report, May 7, 1863, North Carolina Medical Director Reports, ch. 6, vol. 280, 3, RG109, NA.
52. Stout, *Confederate Hospitals on the Move*, 112n47.

At the beginning of the war, relief societies emerged throughout North Carolina in Charlotte, Fayetteville and Raleigh, and even smaller rural towns such as Tarboro. Two relief associations operated in Wilmington during the war: the Wilmington Relief Association and the Soldier's Aid Society. In July 1861, Charlotte's Hospital Association "morphed into the Soldiers Aid Society." In addition to raising money, during the society's first year of existence, its 65 members "made 301 garments of which 207 were sent to a Virginia hospital for use by North Carolina soldiers."[53]

The following month at New Bern, local women formed the Soldiers' Relief Society of New Bern. These women primarily focused their efforts on providing "proper nourishment" for sick soldiers in local hospitals. Shortly after the society's establishment, the women found it necessary to define "the boundaries of charitable work" with the hospital surgeons, who expected large quantities of food to be prepared. The women declared their mission was to feed the sick, "not to feed the army." Although postwar reminiscences typically recognize women more often than men for their relief work, the Young Men's Christian Association of Raleigh helped raise funds and collect food and clothing items for the state-operated hospital in Petersburg. Locally, the young men helped those soldiers arriving at the railroad depot who required assistance in finding the hospital.[54]

Wartime residents of Wilmington remembered Mary Ann Buie of Augusta, Georgia, who took up residence in the port city during the war, for her "untiring devotion to the soldier." Because of her distinguished work in providing necessary relief for Confederate soldiers, she earned the title "The Soldier's Friend." Others, went as far as to call her the "Florence Nightingale of the South," although the preponderance of her work had nothing to do with physically caring for the sick and wounded. She began her work early in the war by raising funds for North Carolina soldiers stationed in Charleston, South Carolina. But by 1863, Buie had focused her efforts primarily on "the hospitals in North Carolina and Virginia, particularly those in the Wilmington area."[55]

Buie targeted the captains of the various blockade runners who frequented the port of Wilmington for cash donations—she raised $600

53. Leora H. McEachern and Isabel M. Williams, "Miss Buie, The Soldier's Friend," *Lower Cape Fear Historical Society Bulletin* (*LCFHSB*) (October 1974), 18:3; Michael C. Hardy, *Civil War Charlotte: Last Capital of the Confederacy* (Charleston, SC, 2012), 26.
54. Record Book of Secretary Nannie Daves, 1861–1862, New Bern Soldiers' Relief Society, VMHC; "A Kindly Work," *The Spirit of the Age* (Raleigh, NC), September 25, 1861.
55. McEachern and Williams, "Miss Buie," *LCFHSB*, 1–4.

Mary Ann Buie was known as "The Soldiers Friend" for her untiring efforts in collecting money and other necessary items for North Carolina's Confederate hospitals.

(#01526, James Ryder Randall Papers, Southern Historical Collection, Louis Round Wilson Special Collections Library, University of North Carolina at Chapel Hill.)

in just two hours one day—along with material goods. One appeal she had published in a Fayetteville newspaper raised $5,000 in just a few days. Buie possessed a keen business savvy and used it to raise money. One of her fundraising techniques consisted of selling donated items, such as barrels of turpentine and bales of cotton, and purchasing necessary hospital supplies from the proceeds.[56]

General Pierre G. T. Beauregard valued Buie's benevolent service and had taken such a "kindly interest" in her work that he detailed a soldier to assist her. "I am still doing all in my power to aid the Southern cause," she informed the general. "I have supplied many hospitals with tea, coffee, [and] brandy, besides sending many articles of clothing to hospitals." But despite all her work, she told General Beauregard that "the Sec. of War, Pres. Davis [and] others do not appreciate my services to the country." However, the attention the general showed Buie inspired her "not to give up [and] I know I have saved many valuable lives."[57]

James R. Randall, a poet and newspaper editor from Augusta, Georgia, who served in Wilmington at the Confederate naval

---

56. M. A. Buie to Gen. G. T. Beauregard, October 10, 1863, Citizens or Business Papers, M346, roll 117.
57. M. A. Buie to Gen. G. T. Beauregard, January 29, 1864, ibid.

headquarters, recalled meeting Ms. Buie for the first time while she was having a photograph done for the *London Illustrated*. According to Randall, Buie's notoriety had reached across the Atlantic Ocean to England and the newspaper was doing a story on her benevolent work. In a letter to Miss Katherine Hammonds, Randall informed his future bride, "I regard her as the very Empress of Benevolent Scavengers."[58]

The state's various charitable societies performed a vital service to Confederate hospitals by collecting money, clothing, food items, and other necessary goods that the government could not provide. North Carolina hospitals benefited greatly from the port of Wilmington and the steady flow of goods from blockade runners. This enabled women, such as Buie, to gain access to items that otherwise were unavailable in other parts of the Confederacy. Although few received Buie's notoriety, the untiring effort on the part of North Carolina's Confederate citizens, particularly women, deserve a place in the state's Confederate hospitals' history.

Black Hospital Attendants

The noticeable absence in contemporary writings regarding the contributions of Blacks in North Carolina's hospitals is in part resulting from the trying nature of research. Unfortunately, first-person accounts are almost nonexistent. And postwar writings by Confederate women who served in the hospitals rarely note the contributions of Blacks in hospitals. Given these realities, and in the absence of traditional source materials, the best, if not the only way, to assess the service of Blacks in North Carolina's Confederate hospitals is to look at an individual's presence on extant hospital records, albeit, oftentimes only a name is evident.

Several of the state's larger hospitals' records shed some light on the numbers of Blacks employed at those institutions and the jobs they performed. Although not all-inclusive of the North Carolina hospital system, these records provide sufficient evidence to indicate enslaved Blacks constituted a sizable portion of an individual hospital's total workforce. An analysis of employee records for a 19-month period at General Hospital No. 7 in Raleigh highlights the increasing importance of hired slaves for daily operations. The August 1862 record lists a total of nine Black attendants, four "free persons of color" and five enslaved. However, by March 1864, the number of enslaved had increased to 80 percent (16 of 20) of the total Black attendants at the hospitals. In comparison, the hospital muster rolls for Wilson's

---

58. Jimmie to My Dear Katie, May 20, 1864, James Ryder Randall Papers, 1855-1864, SHC/UNC.

General Hospital No. 2 note the presence of seven enslaved attendants in August 1862, and by March 1864, the number had increased to 13 hired slaves.[59]

The Union occupation of much of coastal North Carolina in the spring of 1862 forced enslavers in the region to relocate their slaves to safer regions within the state. This relocation benefited the Confederate hospitals located in those areas, as it provided a source of cheap labor from enslavers who eagerly sought opportunities to hire out their slaves. One of North Carolina's wealthiest enslavers, Josiah Collins of Somerset Place Plantation in Washington County, relocated many of his slaves to several locations in the Piedmont. During the war's final two years, the widowed Collins hired out more than 30 slaves as nurses, cooks, and laundresses. Clarrissa, a laundress at General Hospital No. 13, earned Collins $26 a month. Another slaveholder from Edenton, Mrs. Judge Moore, hired out Maria Moore as a laundress to the hospital.[60]

Although North Carolina hospitals employed large numbers of slaves, the payroll documents for General Hospital No. 7 (August 1864–March 1864) include four "free persons of color," two of which, Nils Richardson and Henry Dunston, each received $40 a month as nurses. Both Richardson and Dunston had the longest tenure of all the nurses employed at the hospital because of the high turnover of detailed military nurses. Two other free Blacks worked at the hospital; 52-year-old Jeff Richardson worked in the kitchen for $40 a month, and Alice Dunston received $30 a month as a laundress.[61]

Not all free Blacks employed in the hospitals served of their own volition. As early as February 1862, the Confederate Congress had passed legislation allowing the impressment of free Black men for up to six months. Later in January 1864, the Confederate Congress passed "An Act to increase the efficiency of the army by the employment of free negroes and slaves in certain capacities." The act specified that all free Black men residing in the Confederate States, between 18 and 50 years old, "shall be held liable to perform such duties" as required, at a

---

59. Haywood Papers, SHC/UNC; "Wilson Confederate Hospital Muster Rolls," Hugh B. Johnston, comp., Wilson Public Library, Wilson, NC; Enslaved Blacks frequently served as nurses on the larger plantations. See, Bennett H. Wall, "Medical Care of Ebenezer Pettigrew's Slaves," *The Mississippi Valley Historical Review* (December 1950), 37:451-70.
60. David Silkenat, *Driven from Home: North Carolina's Civil War Refugee Crisis* (Athens, GA, 2016), 141-42; Haywood Papers, SHC/UNC.
61. Haywood Papers, SHC/UNC; U.S. Federal Census (1860), Schedule 1, Free Inhabitants, Wake County, NC, 84.

cost to the government of $11 per month. In describing the various duties, the act included the wording "in military hospitals."[62]

Although the act specified free men, in one instance at General Hospital No. 1 at Kittrell, a free Black woman, Mrs. Stellin Parker Smith of Vance County, allegedly served against her will. According to Smith's 1932 Confederate Pension application, she notes authorities forced her to serve as a laundress, despite her status as a free woman. The state government denied her pension application.[63]

Harriet Frost, whose status as either free or enslaved is unclear, served as a nurse at Wilmington's General Hospital No. 5. In September 1863, Frost contracted smallpox, and later recovered while a patient at the Confederate army's "Camp Hill Small Pox Hospital," located several miles south of Wilmington. The circumstances which led to Frost being present in an exclusive hospital for Confederate soldiers are unclear. One probable explanation is that authorities had detailed Frost to the hospital as a nurse, and while performing her duties she contracted the disease. Because of the short-term nature of such hospitals, it was standard practice to temporarily assign attending surgeons, stewards, and others from local units or hospitals.[64]

In recognizing the service of Blacks in Confederate hospitals, historian Drew Gilpin Faust wrote, "For all their undeniable and important contributions, it was not the Confederacy's ladies but its African Americans who cared for the South's fallen heroes." Despite the paucity of information, by mid-1862, it is abundantly clear Blacks constituted a majority of the attendants serving in the state's hospitals. This trend would continue throughout the remainder of the war. Although the service of Blacks in North Carolina's hospitals seems forgotten, they served side by side with Whites, contributing significantly to the day-to-day operations of North Carolina's Confederate hospitals.[65]

62. Louis Round Wilson Special Collections Library, "The Civil War: Day by Day," accessed on November 27, 2020,
   https://web.lib.unc.edu/civilwar/index.php/2014/01/05/5-january-1864/.
63. Stellin Parker Smith (Vance County), 1932, Record ID: 5.22.399.26, State Auditor Record Group, NCOAH.
64. Stephen D. Doar, *CSR*, M331, roll 77.
65. Faust contends that in the "domain of nursing" Confederate women proved themselves "less able and less effective than their supposed inferiors." Faust, *Mothers of Invention*, 112.

List of Black hospital attendants
at General Hospital No. 13, Raleigh.

*(#01290 Earnest Haywood Collection of Haywood Family Papers,
Southern Historical Collection, Louis Round Wilson Special Collection Library,
University of North Carolina at Chapel Hill)*

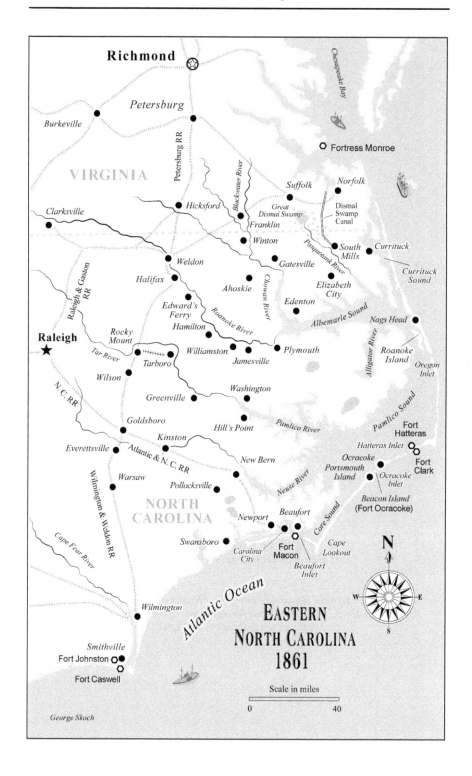

George Skoch

CHAPTER THREE

1861: North Carolina Goes to War

"I never had a harder job."

The presidential election of 1860 proved to be the final act that thrust the United States into chaos and, ultimately, a path to war. Abraham Lincoln's election as president was the end of national unity, as a bloc of Southern states, primarily from the Deep South, chose secession. In North Carolina, despite the efforts of Governor John W. Ellis's call for a secession convention, a watch-and-wait policy of conservative Unionists remained hopeful that President Lincoln might find a peaceful solution to the country's divide, without embarking on such a significant course. However, the attack that South Carolina troops carried out on Fort Sumter on April 12, 1861, and Lincoln's subsequent call for volunteers to "put down the rebellion," ended North Carolina's opportunity to come up with a nonviolent resolution. At approximately 6:00 p.m. on May 20, "a handkerchief dropped from the west balcony of the State Capitol signifying an affirmative secession vote." Shortly thereafter the boom of cannons and the ringing of church bells reverberated across Raleigh. North Carolina was now at war, even though many of the state's citizens favored remaining in the Union. The Tar Heel State joined the Confederacy the next day.[1]

Despite the watch-and-wait strategy that many North Carolinians had adopted prior to seceding, on the same day that Lincoln called for troops, Governor Ellis ordered local militia to seize Forts Caswell, Johnston, and Macon. With the coastal fortifications secured, Ellis issued additional orders five days later for the takeover of the U.S. arsenal at Fayetteville and the Branch Mint at Charlotte. On April 21, 1861, former U.S. Army officer Major William H. C. Whiting accepted the position of inspector general of the state militia headquartered at Wilmington. Ellis had selected Whiting for his reputation as a military engineer. Authorities directed Whiting to plan and initiate the

---

1. North Carolina did not formally adopt the Confederate Constitution until June 6, 1861. NC Historic State Sites, "The Road to Secession," accessed on November 24, 2020, https://historicsites.nc.gov/resources/north-carolina-civil-war/road-secession; Semi-Weekly State Journal (Raleigh, NC), May 22, 1861; K. Todd Johnson, *Historic Wake County: The Story of Raleigh & Wake County* (San Antonio, TX, 2009), 33. John W. Ellis was the first of three wartime North Carolina governors.

strengthening or construction of coastal defenses, with instructions to pay close attention to Forts Caswell and Johnston in the Lower Cape Fear, Beaufort Harbor, and Ocracoke, on the Outer Banks.[2]

At Wilmington, Whiting immediately issued General Orders No. 6, published on April 22, which established rules and procedures for the supervision and reporting of all things medical within the provisional command. It also announced Dr. James F. McRee as the "Chief of the Medical Staff attached to these Head Quarters." Whiting further specified that the medical reports submitted by the surgeons in the post hospitals at Forts Johnston and Caswell were to route through McRee at his Fort Johnston post at Smithville (present-day Southport). McRee's announcement as the medical chief with staff responsibilities for hospitals, albeit small camp and post hospitals, was a precursor to the later chief surgeon or medical director's position. Whiting, who was known for his engineering prowess, demonstrated his organizational acumen by assigning a staff officer to provide oversight of all medical affairs, a decision no doubt informed by his years of prior experience in the U.S. Army. Unfortunately, in the coming months, other less-experienced officers at posts elsewhere in North Carolina would fail to address such crucial issues of management and oversight, leading to disastrous results.[3]

North Carolina Medical Department

While Whiting was busy with the provisional forces in Wilmington, the Secession Convention members established the Military Board of North Carolina, and appointed U.S. Congressman Warren Winslow of Fayetteville as its chairman to administer military affairs within the state. Because defending the state's vast coastal region presented a host of challenges, the board divided the state's coastal expanse into two separate military departments. The Northern Coastal Defense Department, headquartered in New Bern, included the area from the Virginia border heading south to the New River in Onslow County. The Southern Coastal Defense Department encompassed the

2. John G. Barrett, *The Civil War in North Carolina* (Chapel Hill, NC, 1963), 10-15.

3. GO No. 6, Hdqrs. Provisional Forces, W. H. C. Whiting, April 21, 1861, found in the file of James F. McRae, CSR, M331, roll 174. The correct spelling of the surname is McRee. According to historian Chris Fonvielle, Battery McRee, named after James F. McRee, was part of Wilmington's outer defenses. Whiting obviously held McRee in high esteem. Chris E. Fonvielle email to author, December 12, 2020; Confederate authorities renamed Fort Johnston to Fort Branch on July 2, 1863, and later to Fort Pender. Chris E. Fonvielle Jr., *The Wilmington Campaign: Last Rays of Departing Hope* (Campbell, CA, 1997), 493n11.

Fort Johnston Post Hospital, Smithville, N.C.

(National Archives and Records Administration, Washington, D.C.)

region south of the New River to the South Carolina border. The department's headquarters was located at the strategically important port city of Wilmington.[4]

In May 1861, almost two weeks before North Carolina seceded, the state legislature passed a bill entitled "An Act to Raise Ten Thousand Troops," which, in effect, established a state army. To provide medical care for the state's soldiers, the bill authorized a state medical department administered by a surgeon general. To head the new department, Governor Ellis appointed Charles E. Johnson, a distinguished Raleigh physician, as its first surgeon general. Additionally, to support the regiments in the field, the bill allotted the department "ten surgeons with the assimilated rank of major; and not exceeding ten assistant surgeons, with the assimilated rank of captain; and ten with the assimilated rank of first lieutenant."[5]

Camp and Post Hospitals

Johnson's most pressing tasks at the outset were the appointment and assignment of surgeons to the state's newly formed regiments, as

4. James L. Gaddis Jr., *Richard Gatlin and the Confederate Defense of Eastern North Carolina* (Charleston, SC, 2015), 88-90; New Bern has been spelled a number of ways throughout its history, including Newbern, Newberne, New Berne, and, ultimately, New Bern.
5. Norris, "For the Benefit of Our Gallant Volunteers," *NCHR*, 297-98. Approximately one year later, North Carolina eliminated the lieutenant assistant surgeon position to comply with the Confederate Medical Department's regulation of having only two surgeons per regiment, one surgeon and one assistant surgeon.

Charles E. Johnson served as the surgeon general of North Carolina through the summer of 1862.

(Histories of the Several Regiments and Battalions from North Carolina)

well as providing medical supplies, such as medicines and surgical instruments. Because no military general hospitals existed at the start of the war, nor were these larger institutions an initial concern for either the state or Confederate medical departments, soldiers who became ill frequently received treatment in camp or at post hospitals operated at the local level by military unit or North Carolina Medical Department surgeons.[6]

As militias initially assembled throughout the state, commanders established camp hospitals to care for the sick. Accounts indicate medical officers used a variety of structures for these facilities. Existing buildings, newly-built structures, and sometimes even tents sheltered staff and patients. On Roanoke Island, because no permanent structures were available, the Confederates constructed wooden buildings for use as hospitals. At Garysburg, the trustees from the Methodist Church allowed the use of the sanctuary as a hospital for the units encamped there along the Wilmington and Weldon Railroad. In New Hanover County, when Camp Wyatt became a mustering point for newly formed units in June 1861, there were no barracks for the soldiers, only tents. The camp's sole building was a small slave hut, rented from the property owner for use as a hospital.[7]

Camp hospitals were usually temporary, as military units frequently changed duty stations, whereas post hospitals were normally more permanent, attached to a specific town (or "post"). One of North Carolina's most familiar post hospitals was at the Raleigh

6. Peter E. Hines, "Medical Corps" in Walter Clark, ed., *Histories of the Several Regiments and Battalions from North Carolina in the Great War 1861–'65*. 5 vols. (Goldsboro, NC, 1901), 4:623. Hereafter cited as Clark, *Histories*; Norris, "For the Benefit of Our Gallant Volunteers," *NCHR*, 299, 304. Governor Ellis officially appointed Johnson to the position on May 16, 1861, four days prior to North Carolina officially seceding from the Union.
7. Henry A. Wise to B. Huger, January 15, 1862, *OR*, 9:134; Winfield S. Copeland, CSR, M331, roll 62; Ethel Herring and Carolee Williams, *Fort Caswell in War and Peace* (Wendell, NC, 1983), 37.

Camp of Instruction, located at the state fairgrounds. Named after Governor John W. Ellis, North Carolina military authorities established Camp Ellis in April 1861 to train, uniform, and equip new recruits, as well as provide a rendezvous point for newly mustered companies. On May 1, 1861, Surgeon Peter E. Hines, by authority of Governor Ellis, appointed First Assistant Surgeon Edmund B. Haywood, a Raleigh native and promising medical officer, "to organize a medical staff" for the Camp of Instruction. One Tar Heel soldier remembered the hospital as the former "house of the keeper of the Fair Grounds." With Surgeon Hines accompanying the First North Carolina Volunteers to Virginia about two weeks later, Haywood assumed administrative responsibility for the hospital.[8]

Surgeon Edmund B. Haywood helped establish the Fair Grounds General Hospital in Raleigh. He later served as surgeon-in-charge of General Hospital No. 13, which was one of three pavilion-style hospitals constructed in North Carolina during the war.

(North Carolina Office of Archives and History)

Arguably, Dr. Edmund Burke Haywood is North Carolina's most recognized Confederate surgeon, and rightfully so, considering his distinguished wartime hospital service. Haywood's pre-war professional reputation in the capital city placed him at the forefront in the eyes of the state's executive leadership at the start of the war. Shortly after South Carolina forces fired upon Fort Sumter, Governor Ellis dispatched Haywood, along with two others, on "a tour of observation about military affairs" in Charleston, South Carolina. Before Johnson's selection as the state surgeon general, he actively

---

8. GO No. 4, Executive Department, State of NC, April 24, 1861, see *Our Living and Dead* (New Bern, NC), July 30, 1873; quoted in Norris, "For the Benefit of Gallant Volunteers," *NCHR*, 310; Edmund B. Haywood, CSR, M331, roll 128; Colonel Daniel H. Hill of volunteers, who later became major general, was the camp's first commandant. Daniel H. Hill is commonly referred to as D. H. Hill.

sought Haywood to serve as his chief assistant in the state's medical department—a request Johnson subsequently withdrew upon learning that Haywood's older brother, Fabius J. Haywood Sr., another prominent Raleigh physician, had also sought the state's top medical officer position.[9]

Haywood would remain in Raleigh even while other physicians joined regiments headed for Virginia and elsewhere. Although a year later, at the direction of Governor Clark, he did serve briefly (June – July 1862) at Richmond's Seabrook Hospital in the aftermath of the Seven Days' Battles. A history of health issues may have prevented the 36-year-old physician from performing rigorous field duty. In 1846, for instance, Haywood's medical issues caused him to withdraw from his studies at the University of North Carolina. He subsequently recovered and later graduated from the University of Pennsylvania School of Medicine in 1849, and then returned to Raleigh, where he began a private practice. Fortunately for North Carolina and the Confederate Medical Department, Haywood excelled in hospital administration.[10]

Beyond the Camp of Instruction hospital at Raleigh, separate post hospitals appeared along the coast for infantry and artillery units garrisoned at Forts Caswell, Fisher, and Macon. Each fort contained a small aid station while the post hospitals themselves stood some distance away outside the walls of these installations. At Fort Caswell, the garrison's post hospital was located across the Cape Fear River at Smithville, whereas at Fort Fisher, the post hospital was located a mile north of the fort at the former site of Camp Wyatt.[11]

---

9. J. L. Manning to R. W. Gibbes, April 25, 1861, Haywood Papers, SHC/UNC; C. E. Johnson to E. B. Haywood, April 29 and May 11, 1861, ibid; Doctors Fabius J. Haywood Sr. and W. H. McKee, along with Johnson, served on the medical board appointed by John F. Hoke, North Carolina's adjutant general, on April 25, 1861, to screen potential medical officers for service. Norris, "For the Benefit of Gallant Volunteers," *NCHR*, 298. Norris notes both Johnson and McKee wanted the post of the state surgeon general. However, according to Johnson's letter to Haywood, referenced above, apparently, all three board members sought the position.

10. Marshall De Lancey Haywood, "Edmund Burke Haywood," Powell, William S., ed. *Dictionary of North Carolina Biography*, 6 vols. (Chapel Hill, NC, 1979), 3:83-84; Surgeon General Johnson notes the possibility that Haywood continued to experience lingering health issues. In the document Johnson described Haywood as "unfit for military duty" and that he "has been compelled, for some time past, to withdraw from the active and exposed duties of his profession, on account of his feeble health." Charles E. Johnson, memorandum, August 14, 1861, Haywood Papers, series 4, SHC/UNC.

11. *Wilmington Journal*, August 22, 1861, and September 12, 1861; Fonvielle, *The Wilmington Campaign*, 166.

Hospital Troubles on the Outer Banks

As part of the state's defensive strategy to prevent the use of Pamlico Sound by U.S. naval forces, Governor Ellis ordered forts constructed along the Outer Banks at Hatteras, Ocracoke, and Oregon inlets. The remoteness of these locations posed considerable challenges for military authorities, as these garrisons depended solely upon water transport for written communications, supplies, and evacuation of the seriously ill, if necessary. Officials established a post hospital in the vicinity of Forts Clark and Hatteras to support the units assigned north of Hatteras Inlet. However, authorities initially made no such arrangements at Portsmouth Island for those units assigned to defend Ocracoke Inlet.[12]

The initial operation of the hospital at Portsmouth Island illustrates the various challenges encountered early on in offering adequate medical care for the troops. Unlike Forts Caswell and Macon, which stood within sight of the towns that supported them, a 70-mile boat trip separated the garrison at Portsmouth Island from the two nearest ports, New Bern, and Washington, often referred to as "Little Washington." Furthermore, the commander of the Northern Coastal Defense Department, 59-year-old Brigadier General Walter Gwynn, had established his headquarters at New Bern, making personal hospital visits difficult and causing the delay of written communications by several days. In contrast, the leadership of the Southern Coastal Defense Department could easily access the hospitals under their command at Wilmington and the Lower Cape Fear region.[13]

The Military Board selected Beacon Island, located just inside the inlet between Portsmouth and Ocracoke islands, as the site for Fort Ocracoke. In early May, a company of North Carolina volunteers from Beaufort County, led by Capt. Thomas Sparrow, disembarked at Portsmouth Island to assist in the fort's construction. Sparrow's orders directed him to seize the U.S. Marine Hospital located on the north end of Portsmouth Island for barracks, as it was to become "the nucleus for the encampment of several companies." By the end of June, the force at Portsmouth totaled five companies, with Sparrow designated as the senior captain. Despite the increased troop level, Sparrow's small command had no surgeon on the island to care for an ever-growing number of sick soldiers.[14]

---

12. Barrett, *The Civil War in North Carolina*, 32-33.
13. Ibid.
14. John W. Ellis to Thomas Sparrow, May 6, 1861, E. Morris to Thomas Sparrow, May 16, 1861, Sparrow Papers, ECU; Fort Ocracoke, sometimes referred to as Fort Morris, and erroneously as Fort Morgan, contained 18 guns. Robert K. Smith and Earl O'Neal Jr., ed., *The History of Fort Ocracoke*

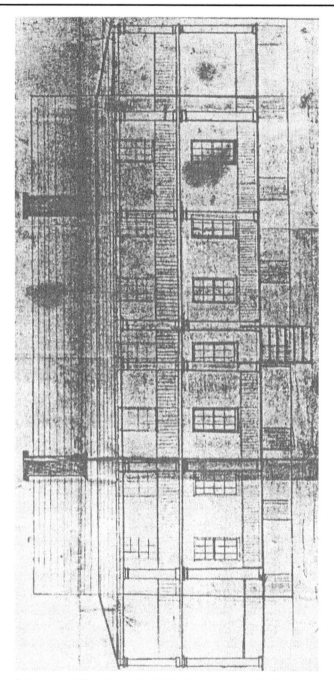

*Architectural Sketch of the U.S. Marine Hospital, Portsmouth
Island, N.C. It was briefly used as a Confederate hospital during
the summer of 1861.*
            (Turned sideways for increased detail)

(National Archives and Records Administration, Washington, D.C.)

On June 20, at the request of Confederate authorities, Dr. William W. Ward, a civilian physician from Washington County, arrived at Portsmouth where he discovered the sick quartered in private residences. Ward's work proved challenging as the individual companies were located at both Portsmouth and Ocracoke islands, as well as at Beacon Island, where soldiers and enslaved laborers were engaged in constructing the fort. Regarding the personnel on Beacon Island, Ward later wrote that without his attention, they "would have suffered greatly."[15]

In late June, First Surgeon Edward Warren, of the North Carolina navy, arrived at Portsmouth and relieved Ward, under orders to provide medical care for the forces stationed in the area. Much to his chagrin, Warren discovered the Marine Hospital was being utilized as barracks, despite the pressing need for a proper hospital. Warren's suggestion to relocate the soldiers to other quarters in order to free up the hospital did little to persuade Capt. Sparrow, who stood fast to his original orders. Undaunted by the post commander's stubbornness, Warren wrote Governor Ellis on June 27 to express his concerns about the medical affairs at Portsmouth, as well as to request permission to impress the Marine Hospital as a hospital.[16]

Only one week later, Private John Wheeler fell victim to measles, the scourge of so many Civil War camps. Alarmed by Wheeler's demise, the officers drafted a pointed letter demanding that Sparrow "surrender for the use of the sick soldiers the hospital now occupied as quarters . . . that we are unable to provide suitable and proper diet, nursing and medical attention for our sick men quartered in our own camps." By not consolidating the sick into one location, the sick remained "scattered on the island," thus preventing "proper care and attention" by the surgeon. "It is large and comfortable. It has a good cistern. Its rooms are so arranged as it separates patients with contagious diseases from all others," the officers wrote.[17]

Sparrow wisely consented and turned the Marine Hospital over to Warren, who informed Governor Ellis on July 20: "As surgeon of this

in Pamlico Sound (Charleston, SC, 2015), 60, 92-93; Fred M. Mallison, *The Civil War on the Outer Banks* (Jefferson, NC, 1997), 27.

15. Ward wrote, "I held the position of Private Surgeon at the insistence of Col. Morris, Genl. Holmes . . ." See Ward to Secretary Board of Claims, November 2, 1861, Sparrow Papers, ECU; Warren W. Ward, CSR, M331, roll 259; Ward Affidavit, December 10, 1861, Sparrow Papers, ECU.

16. Norris, "For the Benefit of Our Gallant Volunteers," *NCHR*, 299-300; Edward Warren to Governor Ellis, June 27, 1861, John W. Ellis, Governors Papers, NCOAH; During the summer of 1861 the state transferred the North Carolina navy to the Confederacy. Barrett, The Civil War in North Carolina, 36.

17. James T. Leith to Thomas Sparrow, July 7, 1861, Sparrow Papers, ECU.

post, it is my duty to inform you, that the Hospital has been taken possession of by me, [and] that it is now open for the accommodation of the sick." After many weeks, the Portsmouth garrison finally had a proper post hospital. The following month, Warren received orders assigning him to duty in Virginia. In a letter to his wife, Annie, Sparrow wrote: "We have a new Hospital Surgeon here, a Dr. West, of the Confederate States, covered all over with gold lace." Clearly still harboring a dislike for Warren, the captain sarcastically wrote, "Dr. Warren left after his Hatteras electioneering tour, and has not since returned."[18]

The situation involving the former Marine Hospital at Portsmouth provides only a snapshot of the many issues that the newly created state and Confederate medical departments confronted regarding the lack of skilled surgeons, shortages of medical supplies, and infighting between commander and surgeon. When Warren penned his announcement regarding the hospital on July 20, he was unaware that in little more than a month, U.S. forces would successfully capture Forts Hatteras and Clark at Hatteras Inlet on August 29, prompting Confederate forces to abandon Fort Ocracoke and, along with it, Portsmouth Island. Perhaps the story of Portsmouth's Confederate hospital is indicative of the Confederate government's failed policy in general concerning the defense of North Carolina. With the loss of Hatteras, Ocracoke, and Oregon inlets, Federal forces now had access to Albemarle and Pamlico sounds, along with a passageway into North Carolina's coastal interior.[19]

North Carolina's First General Hospitals

By the summer of 1861, the number of troops stationed within North Carolina or traveling along the railroads to and from Virginia had increased to levels that required the establishment of general hospitals, which were larger and more complex permanent institutions that admitted soldiers regardless of state or military unit affiliation.

18. Edward Warren to Thomas Sparrow, July 20, 1861, Sparrow Papers, ECU; Sparrow to Annie, August 25, 1861, Joy W. Sparrow, ed., *Sparrow's Nest of Letters* (Wake Forest, NC, 2011), 90. Sparrow is likely referring to Gillespie S. West, who U.S. forces later captured at the battle of New Bern in March 1862. Following a prisoner exchange, West served with the 46th North Carolina. In 1863, Dr. Edward Warren unsuccessfully campaigned for North Carolina's First Congressional District. For a perspective on his political platform, in which he touts the establishment of wayside hospitals while he served as the state surgeon general, see, *Weekly Standard* (Raleigh, NC), October 23, 1863.
19. Barrett, *The Civil War in North Carolina*, 45-47; In July 1862, the Federals established a general hospital in the former U.S. Marine Hospital. *OR*, 9:411.

Documentation indicates that the state's first general hospitals appeared at Smithville and Wilmington as early as June 1861. A request for hospital donations published in the June 18, 1861, edition of Wilmington's *Daily Journal* clearly shows the existence of a general hospital at Smithville. Doctor James A. Miller, the hospital's surgeon-in-charge, wrote, ". . . that a few more cots and mattresses would be highly acceptable as there are two hospitals—a general and a post hospital."[20]

A week later, up the Cape Fear River from Smithville at Wilmington, Brigadier General Richard C. Gatlin, commander of the Southern Coastal Defense Department, issued Special Orders No. 116 on June 24, which designated the former U.S. Marine Hospital as a general hospital. Because units had utilized the building as barracks following its seizure in April, approximately two weeks passed before the hospital admitted its first patients. Gatlin's acting medical director, Dr. James F. McRee, reassigned Surgeon Miller from the Smithville general hospital to take charge of the new hospital. On July 9, Miller proudly announced in the *Daily Journal*, "This Hospital is now ready to receive the sick soldiers of North Carolina, or the Confederate States." Miller's reference to ill soldiers from either "North Carolina, or the Confederate States," highlighted the operating premise of a general hospital, which admitted patients regardless of state or unit affiliation. The Marine General Hospital (later identified as General Hospital No. 5) was Wilmington's first, and within a year, additional hospitals were in operation that established the port city as an important hospital center for the remainder of the war.[21]

Shortly before the defeat at Hatteras Inlet, the Confederate War Department had assumed responsibility for the defense of the state, and appointed Brig. Gen. Gatlin to lead the newly created Department of North Carolina and its subordinate commands: the District of the Cape Fear and the District of the Pamlico. But now, after Federal forces had occupied Hatteras and unlocked a door into the Pamlico Sound, Gatlin had his work cut out for him. Throughout the remainder of 1861, rumors were rampant of an impending follow-on

---

20. *Daily Journal* (Wilmington, NC), June 18, 1861; James A. Miller, CSR, M331, roll 178. The Confederate Medical Department later designated the Smithville General Hospital as General Hospital No. 6. The hospital ceased operations in the summer of 1863, and the No. 6 designation assigned to Fayetteville's newly established general hospital that September.
21. Special Orders (SO) No. 116, Hdqrs. Southern Coastal Defense Dept., June 24, 1861, see the file of James F. McRae, CSR, M331, roll 174; On April 18, 1861, Capt. Edward D. Hall's company took possession of the U.S. Marine Hospital. See "The Rifle Rangers," *Daily Journal* (Wilmington, NC) April 19, 1861, and July 9, 1861; James A. Miller to Hon. Warren Winslow, July 18, 1861, Civil War Collection, NCOAH.

U.S. Marine Hospital, Wilmington. In June 1861, Brig. Gen. Richard C. Gatlin ordered the building designated as a general hospital. Initially identified as Marine General Hospital, Confederate medical authorities later redesignated it as General Hospital No. 5.

(Courtesy of New Hanover County Public Library, North Carolina Room)

invasion along the North Carolina coast. The state's coastal garrisons were on edge, as nervous eyes scanned the ocean horizon from Cape Lookout to Wilmington for signs of an invasion.[22]

As Gatlin prepared the department's coastal defenses against a military threat, a far deadlier menace emerged within the various military camps throughout the state. During the waning days of summer, a "great sickness" prevailed in many of the units located in eastern North Carolina, as cases of measles, mumps, and camp fever (typhus) reached epidemic proportions. The *Weekly Progress* reported that there was "a good deal of sickness" at the New Bern fairgrounds. In the 7th North Carolina camp hospital alone, there were 99 soldiers, "for the most part, afflicted with measles and mumps in mild form." In early September, Assistant Surgeon William E. White supervised the regiment's camp hospital at the fairgrounds. "We rather admire Dr. W's mode of treatment," one newspaper reported, "as we understand he sympathizes with the patients enough not to kill them with

22. *OR*, 4:573-74; Gaddis, *Richard Gatlin*, 96-97; Barrett, *The Civil War in North Carolina*, 62.

medicine and only gives them enough to cure them in the shortest and easiest possible manner."[23]

This wave of illness plagued the troops gathered at New Bern, one of the state's largest cities. The prevailing sickness within the camp hospitals there coincided with an increasing number of units that were either assigned to defend the city or encamped there while awaiting transportation to other points within the newly formed District of the Pamlico. Unlike the general hospitals established several months earlier at Wilmington and Smithville, no such entities would exist at New Bern or anywhere else in the former Northern Coastal Defense Department until September 1861. In fact, it was New Bern's citizens who responded to the crisis by establishing a privately operated institution. Through the generous support of James A. Suydam, who provided the building and assisted extensively in ensuring its "comfortable outfit," what eventually became New Bern's first general hospital was operational by the second week of September. Initially identified as the Suydam Hospital, its location on Hancock Street placed it within proximity to both the riverfront and the railroad depot.[24]

In addition to Suydam's generosities, other New Bern citizens assisted in the wants and cares of the hospital's patients, most notably, the city's women. The ladies formed the Soldiers' Relief Society "to provide proper nourishment for the sick soldiers in the hospital." Consisting of more than 150 members, the society organized New Bern into 15 individual districts, where members "took turns collecting and preparing food for the hospital under the direction of a manager." In expressing his gratitude to the women volunteers, a soldier from the 24th Georgia wrote: "It inspires the soldier with double courage to meet with such hospitality from the fair hands of those heretofore perfect strangers." Equally complimentary, the soldier noted the "able and prompt attendance" that the physician displayed to his patients.[25]

The surgeon-in-charge at the time of the hospital's initial establishment was likely a civilian physician from New Bern, though his name is unknown. However, authority over the hospital eventually transitioned to the military. The Relief Society's minutes from its meeting on October 3 note that Assistant Surgeon Robert S. Halsey, a

23. *Newbern Weekly Progress* (NC), September 10, 1861; Norris, "For the Benefit of Our Gallant Volunteers," *NCHR*, 302.
24. *Newbern Weekly Progress*, October 1, 1861; October 3, 1861, Record Book of Secretary Nannie Daves, 1861–1865, New Bern Soldiers' Relief Society, VMHC. Hereafter cited as New Bern Soldiers' Relief Society, VMHC.
25. New Bern Soldiers' Relief Society, October 3, 1861, VMHC; Hilde, *Worth a Dozen Men*, 114; *Newbern Weekly Progress* (NC), October 1, 1861.

Surgeon Wesley McD. Campbell of the 7th North Carolina. In September 1861, Campbell established a hospital at the former Carolina City Hotel in Carolina City.

(Histories of the Several Regiments and Battalions from North Carolina)

detailed medical officer from the 27th North Carolina, served at the hospital in an official capacity. Halsey's tenure proved brief though, by mid-November Surgeon William H. Moore was in charge, and he remained in the position through the subsequent Confederate evacuation of New Bern in March 1862. Extant documents note that while surgeon-in-charge, Moore formally identified the hospital as either "Neuse General Hospital" or, simply, "General Hospital."[26]

Another hospital appeared to the south in nearby Carteret County. On September 10, coinciding with the establishment of the New Bern hospital, Dr. Wesley McD. Campbell, the regimental surgeon of the 7th North Carolina, occupied the main building of the recently closed Atlantic Scientific and Military Institute, located in the former Carolina City Hotel at Carolina City, for use as a camp hospital for both his unit and the 26th North Carolina. The three-story hotel was located several miles west of Morehead City along Bogue Sound. Adjacent to the Atlantic and North Carolina Railroad depot and its wharf, the hospital was conveniently located to easily support the units stationed across the sound at Fort Macon and Bogue Banks, as well as those on the Carteret County mainland.[27]

26. On June 6, 1861, Halsey received his appointment as an assistant surgeon in the newly formed 27th North Carolina. Robert S. Halsey, Compiled Service Records of Confederate Soldiers Who Served in Organizations from the State of North Carolina, M270, roll 335, RG109, NA. Hereafter, cited as CSR, M270, followed by the roll number; William H. Moore, CSR, M331, roll 181. The patient capacity of the Neuse General Hospital is undetermined.
27. William H. Cuninggin, Confederate Papers Relating to Citizens or Business Firms, 1861–1865, M346, roll 217, RG 109, NA. Hereafter cited as Citizens or Business Papers, M346, and the relevant roll number. The institute held its first session in March 1861, see *State Journal* (Raleigh, NC), March 6, 1861. The April 24, 1861, edition of Raleigh's *North Carolina Standard* reported, "A portion of the citizens of Beaufort, with the Cadets of the A. M. Institute at Carolina City . . . took possession of Fort Macon." The 7th Regiment NC

Beginning in September, both the 7th and 26th North Carolina regiments suffered from "an epidemic of measles and fever." Private William W. Edwards of the 26th served as a detailed nurse at the hospital given his prior exposure to measles. Edwards later recalled, "I never had a harder job in my life; I had 30 cases of measles and 1 of typhoid fever and those all on the second story." As the number of reported cases continued to rise, several Morehead City residents opened their homes for individuals who did not require quarantine. To enable "more efficient aid to the sick and destitute soldiers at the hospital," a group of Morehead City women formed The Ladies Relief Society of Morehead City.

Pvt. William W. Edwards of the 26th North Carolina. Edwards served as a nurse at the Carolina City General Hospital.

(*Histories of the Several Regiments and Battalions from North Carolina*)

A special committee consisting of members from the society met with Surgeon Campbell frequently to better coordinate efforts at the hospital. One of the committee members was Miss Emeline Pigott, perhaps better remembered as one of North Carolina's most noted Confederate spies.[28]

The outbreak of cases at Carolina City had finally subsided by fall, but not before reaping a grim toll. Assistant Surgeon George C. Underwood wrote, "Nine men from one company died in a week." Death claimed not only the lives of the individual rank and file but also those of the attending surgeons. On November 28, Acting Assistant Surgeon Daniel W. Shaw of the 26th North Carolina died of disease in hospital. Assistant Surgeon White, who the *Newbern Weekly Progress* had previously recognized for his exemplary patient care at the

State Troops is not to be confused with the 7th Regiment NC Volunteers, which was later redesignated the 17th Regiment NC Troops to avoid confusion.

28. "Beck's Reminiscences, No. 5," *Siler City Grit* (Siler City, NC), February 12, 1913; The July 1, 1861, edition of the *New Bern Daily Progress* (NC), reported, "Mrs. Granger, Mrs. Duke, Mrs. Arendell . . . made hospitals of their residences;" "Ladies Relief Society," *Newbern Weekly Progress* (NC), October 1, 1861.

Emeline Jamison Pigott, better remembered for her wartime exploits as a Confederate spy, volunteered early in the war as a nurse at the Carolina City and New Bern hospitals.

(North Carolina Office of Archives and History)

camp hospital at New Bern, also died. White contracted typhus while serving at the hospital. He later passed away at his home in Charlotte on November 9, 1861.[29]

It was during this period that Confederate Surgeon General Samuel P. Moore assigned Dr. James J. Waring as medical director for the Department of North Carolina. Up until this point, the department had no assigned director, with only Surgeon McRee in an acting capacity. Waring was a Savannah, Georgia native, who had gained invaluable experience prior to the war as a physician in the North, notably in Washington, D.C. On October 9, Gatlin formally

29. George C. Underwood, "Twenty-Sixth Regiment," Clark, *Histories*, 2:307; Manarin, et al., *North Carolina Troops*, 4:746-47.

James J. Waring, a native of Savannah, Ga., served as the medical director and purveyor for the Department of North Carolina through the battle of New Bern. He was the driving force behind the establishment of the state's early coastal hospitals.

(*Courtesy of Georgia Historical Society, www.georgiahistory.com*)

announced Waring as the department medical director, and wasted no time putting him to work. That same day, Gatlin ordered Waring to Wilmington to "inspect the Hospitals, Forts, and Camps, and Stations" in the District of the Cape Fear. The following month, Waring announced his summarized findings from his inspection in the

Wilmington Journal, and based on its wording, one can surmise that the new medical director was not at all pleased. Waring reported that he "found a large number of sick exposed upon a bleak coast, in tents and badly built cabins." It was clear to Waring that the Marine General Hospital's 51-bed capacity was insufficient to handle the number of personnel assigned to the Wilmington area. To mitigate the problem, Waring began negotiations with the port city's Seaman's Home Society to establish a general hospital in the society's building.[30]

Elsewhere in the Department of North Carolina, the need for a hospital at Washington had become readily apparent. One local resident, Ms. Sallie Gallagher, recalled how "[a]ll vacant houses were used for hospitals, scattered all over town, and there was much sickness among the men. At one time six hundred were down sick." A letter published in the October 10, 1861, edition of the *Wilmington Journal* reported that the Washington Ladies' Relief Society had "established and equipped hospitals for the sick soldiers." According to one officer assigned to Washington at the time, Captain William B. Rodman, the military authorities in the town had "seized Miss Fanny Owen's rooms in the Long Row for a hospital, and drove her off at the point of the bristling bayonet." In describing the suffering at Washington, Rodman further wrote:

> A great many, perhaps 300, of the Georgia regiment are sick with measles and typhoid fever. About six hospitals have been taken charge of by the ladies, who tend the sick and spare no pains. Aunt has taken three into her house, and nurses them constantly. She generally has six soldiers to eat with here—I believe she would give them her last rag of clothes—and the other ladies are not much behind her.[31]

Medical Director Waring responded to the situation by establishing a general hospital, with Dr. John A. Gallagher, a local physician and newly minted army surgeon, assigned as the surgeon-in-charge.

---

30. Biographical information on James J. Waring is from F. T. Hambrecht, and J. L. Koste, "Biographical Register of Physicians who Served the Confederacy in a Medical Capacity." Unpublished database; James J. Waring, CSR, M331, roll 259; "General Hospital," *Wilmington Journal*, November 21, 1861; NC Medical Director Reports, ch. 6, vol. 280, 1, RG109, NA; Thomas R. Micks to Peter E. Hines, November 18, 1863, Letters Sent, General Hospital No. 4, Sept. 12, 1863–Feb. 19, 1865, ch. 6, vol. 399, 23, RG109, NA. Hereafter cited as Letters Sent, General Hospital No. 4, ch. 6, vol. 399, followed by the relevant page number.
31. "For the *Journal*: Hyde and Beaufort Counties," *Wilmington Journal* (NC), October 10, 1861; Wm. B. Rodman to W. A. Blount, October 11, 1861. See Lida T. Rodman, "William Blount Rodman," *Carolina and the Southern Cross* (October 1913), 1:4.

Gallagher's immediate priority was the issue of his dispersed patients. To consolidate the sick scattered about the town, Gallagher had constructed a large frame building near the county bridge. Assistant Surgeon Tandy K. Mitchell, of the 24th Georgia, was likely one of several surgeons detailed from the local units to serve in the temporary hospital. Also, in December, Waring re-designated the former camp hospital at Carolina City as a general hospital, assigning Dr. Spiers Singleton as its surgeon-in-charge. Prior to North Carolina's secession, the 41-year-old Singleton had served as the physician-in-charge of the U.S. Marine Hospital on Portsmouth Island. Once North Carolina seceded, he cast his lot with the Confederacy.[32]

The opening of the general hospitals at New Bern, Carolina City, and Washington significantly improved the Department of North Carolina's overall hospital capability, particularly within the District of the Pamlico. Table 3.1 shows that by year's end the Department had five operational general hospitals, as well as a sixth in the final planning stage, with each located in areas that had the greatest troop concentrations.

Table 3.1: Department of North Carolina General Hospitals, December 1861[33]

Location	Designation	Date Established	Military District
Smithville (Southport)	Smithville General Hospital	June 1861	Cape Fear
Wilmington	Marine General Hospital	June 1861	Cape Fear
New Bern	Neuse General Hospital	September 1861	Pamlico
Carolina City	Carolina City General Hospital	December 1861	Pamlico
Washington	Washington General Hospital	December 1861	Pamlico
Wilmington	Wilmington General Hospital (Seaman's Home)	Planned	Cape Fear

32. John A. Gallagher's service record is filled under the name P. A. Gallager, CSR, M331, roll 101; Gallagher had served briefly as a private with the 1st North Carolina Artillery at Fort Macon prior to his appointment as surgeon on November 16, 1861. Manarin, et al., *North Carolina Troops*, 1:117; Sallie Gallagher, "Dr. John A. Gallagher," *Carolina and the Southern Cross* (October 1913), 1:21-22; Tandy K. Mitchell, Compiled Service Records of Confederate Soldiers Who Served in Organizations from the State of Georgia, M266, roll 358, RG109, NA; SO No. 67, Hdqrs., Dept. of NC, October 23, 1861, directed Waring to inspect the hospitals and camps located in the District of the Pamlico. See file of James J. Waring, CSR, M331, roll 259; Spiers Singleton's service record is filed under the name Seyers W. Singleton, CSR, M331, roll 226.
33. Data from *Daily Journal* (Wilmington, NC), June 18, 1861; SO No. 116, Hdqrs. Southern Coastal Defense Dept., June 24, 1861, ch. 2, vol. 259,

Until December 1861, the hospitals in North Carolina had yet to be tested on a scale like those in Virginia, where the inability of the Confederate government to provide for the army's sick and wounded prompted individual states to take necessary action. Surgeon Edward Warren was one of the first to sound the call for the establishment of a separate North Carolina hospital in Charlottesville, Virginia. Warren's recent service in Virginia allowed him to witness firsthand the successful efforts of South Carolina and Alabama in establishing "large and comfortable Hospitals on their own account." Even North Carolina's new governor, Henry T. Clark, echoed Warren's sentiments by suggesting such a hospital at Richmond.[34]

The North Carolina legislature responded by supporting the establishment and operation of a hospital for its soldiers in Virginia. The funding required that Surgeon General Johnson and his medical department manage the hospital, with executive overwatch by the governor. In October 1861, the state opened the 1st North Carolina Hospital in Virginia close to the Petersburg and Weldon Railroad at Petersburg. Although the hospital was primarily for Tar Heels, it did admit patients from other states "when there are vacant beds, but not to the exclusion from our own State." The spacious three-story brick building was well lighted, heated, and accommodated between 250 to 300 patients. The *Petersburg Express* reported that "it is the most convenient institution of its kind in the South."[35]

The hospital's surgeon-in-charge, Dr. Peter E. Hines, was a rising star among the state's medical officers. Upon graduating from the University of North Carolina in 1852, the Warren County native studied medicine in Philadelphia and later in Paris, before finally settling down in Raleigh with his own practice. In the war's first few months, Hines established a solid reputation as an army surgeon,

---

RG109, NA; *Newbern Weekly Progress*, October 1, 1861; Seyers W. Singleton, CSR, M331, roll 226; SO No. 47, Hdqrs. Dept. of NC, March 10, 1862, ch. 2, vol. 259, RG109, NA; Micks to Hines, November 18, 1863, Letters Sent, General Hospital No. 4, ch. 6, vol. 399, 23, RG109, NA.

34. *Raleigh Register* (NC), August 1, 1861; As early as September 1861, Surgeon General Johnson called upon the North Carolina citizens "to contribute towards furnishing the hospital. See "Military Hospital," *Semi-Weekly Standard* (Raleigh, NC), September 21, 1862. See also, "To the People of North Carolina," *Spirit of the Age* (Raleigh, NC), September 25, 1861; Norris, "For the Benefit of Gallant Volunteers," *NCHR*, 307. Clark had succeeded John W. Ellis after his unexpected death on July 7, 1861, from tuberculosis.

35. *The General Military Hospital for the North Carolina Troops in Petersburg, Virginia* (Raleigh, NC, 1861), 3-4; "North Carolina Hospital in Virginia," *Semi-Weekly State Journal* (Raleigh, NC), November 27, 1861; "The N. C. Hospital," *Spirit of the Age* (Raleigh, NC), October 30, 1861.

having successfully served at the regimental level with the 1st North Carolina Volunteers (Bethel Regiment) and later as chief surgeon of a general hospital at Yorktown, Virginia.[36]

In addition to the hospital's excellent location and accommodations, Surgeon General Johnson also staffed the facility with two assistant surgeons, a hospital steward, and an apothecary. Catherine G. DeRosset Kennedy, of Wilmington, served as the hospital's head matron, with Mary Beasley, Nancy (Nannie) C. Beckwith, and Mary Pettigrew performing assistant matron duties. The hospital's seemingly low death rate during its first month of operation (4 out of the total 269 admitted) is a testament to the quality of patient care that the attending surgeons and female matrons provided.[37] Historian David A. Norris notes that the establishment of the Petersburg hospital "marked a shift in the focus of the state's medical department," as the Confederate Medical Department started to take on more responsibility regarding the units in the field. Johnson already had in the planning stages the establishment of a second state-run general hospital at Petersburg. In December 1861, the state leased "a large and comfortable building lately occupied by Messrs. Riddle and McIlwaine as a Tobacco Factory."[38]

Simultaneous with his efforts in Virginia, Johnson looked to establish a general hospital in Raleigh where a pressing need also existed. By November 1861, an ever-increasing number of soldiers requiring hospitalization in the Raleigh area convinced the state convention of the need "to form a committee of inquiry concerning the sick soldiers." Raleigh had no general hospitals at that time, only three woefully inadequate smaller hospitals operated by the North Carolina Medical Department. By the fall of 1861, there were the two

36. For biographical information on Hines, the author consulted Claiborne T. Smith Jr., "Pete Evans Hines," accessed on January 9, 2021, https://www.ncpedia.org/biography/hines-peter-evans; The "old Nelson house" served as the general hospital for North Carolina troops at Yorktown. Norris, "For the Benefit of Our Gallant Volunteers," *NCHR*, 305-6; The 1st North Carolina Volunteers was later redesignated the 11th North Carolina Troops; Manarin, et al., *North Carolina Troops*, 3:2.

37. "North Carolina Hospital in Virginia," *Semi-Weekly State Journal* (Raleigh, NC), November 27, 1861; The staffing of both an apothecary and a hospital steward was typical for the larger North Carolina Civil War hospitals. In most cases, the hospital steward performed the role of both pharmacist and overseer of property, supplies, and food purchases.

38. Norris, "For the Benefit of Gallant Volunteers," *NCHR*, 312; During the war, several hospitals in South Carolina (three in Charleston and one in Columbia) were designated specifically for North Carolina troops. However, other than the Tar Heel designation, the author found no evidence that the NC Medical Department solely funded and operated these hospitals. See Rebecca B. Calcutt, *South Carolina's Confederate Hospitals* (Self-published, 2015), 24, 27, 41.

Fair Grounds General Hospital (later designated General Hospital No. 7). In December 1861, the North Carolina Medical Department established a general hospital at the State Fairgrounds in Raleigh. C. N. Drie's 1872 engraving depicts the fairgrounds after the departure of Federal troops in 1869.

(Library of Congress)

post hospitals associated with the camps of instruction at Camp Ellis (Fair Grounds) and Camp Magnum, and a third hospital, described as "one comfortable house . . . for the accommodation of sick soldiers in transitu." Extant records indicate the post hospital at Camp Ellis had treated more than 2,700 men since the hospital's establishment in May. Calling for action to alleviate the situation in Raleigh, the *North Carolina Standard* editorialized on November 30, "[O]ught there not to be a hospital here?"[39]

Unbeknownst to the *Standard*, plans had already been in motion for a much larger hospital at the fairgrounds, a point Surgeon General Johnson very quickly fired back at the newspaper. On December 4, Johnson wrote: "Ample and suitable accommodation for two or three hundred sick men will be provided at the Fair Grounds, near this city, in a few days. Carpenters and bricklayers are daily at work on the buildings fitting them up properly for this purpose." He further stressed, "Of course the sick of other States of the Confederacy will be taken care of in this General Military Hospital . . . in consequence of their being detained here by sickness in passing or from the seat of war." The hospital consisted of seven original agricultural exhibition

39. Norris, "For the Benefit of Gallant Volunteers," *NCHR*, 308-10; List of Soldiers Admitted into the Hospital, Haywood Papers, SHC/UNC; *North Carolina Standard* (Raleigh, NC), November 30, 1861.

buildings with large windows and openings in the roof that provided excellent ventilation. The hospital's central location within the state allowed access to the railroads, and, in 1861, removed from the heavy fighting. Governor Clark considered Surgeon Haywood a "competent and faithful officer" who was "meritorious and deserving" of the position, was to remain as surgeon in charge.[40]

In late December, a second general hospital opened in the Piedmont region at Salisbury to support the newly established military prison located there. The Confederate War Department had converted a vacant multistory cotton mill into a prison camp designed to hold approximately 2,500 prisoners. Unlike other general hospitals in North Carolina, the Military Prison Hospital at Salisbury not only supported the prison staff and other Confederate military personnel in the area, but also provided medical care to Federal soldiers, Southern military and civilian prisoners, and Blacks. Salisbury native Surgeon Josephus W. Hall assumed the duties of surgeon-in-charge at the Military Prison Hospital. According to Hospital Steward G. P. Poulson, who served with Hall, the Military Prison Hospital consisted of two separate hospitals. The first hospital was located within the prison and operated solely for the prisoners, while a second structure, located outside the prison wall provided support to Confederate military personnel. The prison's reputation during the first two years of the war was a positive one. Commenting on the favorable conditions at the time, one Federal prisoner wrote that the freedoms at the prison made Salisbury "more endurable than any other point in Rebeldom." However, later in the war, the Salisbury prison would later become infamous for suffering and death.[41]

* * *

As 1861 ended, a viable system of general hospitals was operational in North Carolina. Despite the difficult start, the Confederate government eventually set up such facilities at Carolina City, New

---

40. *Semi-Weekly Standard* (Raleigh, NC), December 4, 1861; R. H. Shield to E. S. Gaillard, December 26, 1862, located in the file of E. Burke Haywood, CSR, M331, roll 123; Norris, "For the Benefit of Gallant Volunteers," *NCHR*, 323-24; Conventional writings often recognize Surgeon Haywood's post hospital at the Raleigh fairgrounds as the first general hospital established in North Carolina during the Civil War. However, David Norris in his superb study, "For the Benefit of Our Gallant Volunteers," argues that the Fair Grounds Hospital originated as a post hospital in May 1861, and authorities did not designate it as a general hospital until after major renovations occurred in December of that year.

41. James S. Brawley, "Hall, Josephus Wells," accessed December 10, 2018, https://www.ncpedia.org/biography/hall-josephus-wells; Louis A. Brown, *The Salisbury Prison: A Case Study of Confederate Military Prisons 1861–1865* (Wendell, NC, 1980), 22.

Bern, Smithville, Washington, and Wilmington, thereby providing essential medical care to both military units assigned to or passing through the state. The newly formed North Carolina Medical Department had proved equally successful regarding the state-operated hospitals, due in large part to the generous financial support of the state legislature. With the necessary funding at hand, Surgeon General Johnson accomplished much in his first eight months in the position. The establishment of the general hospital at Petersburg, Virginia, and a second in the planning stages, demonstrated North Carolina's commitment to its native sons serving out of state. In North Carolina, Johnson's conversion of the post hospital at the Raleigh fairgrounds into one of the largest general hospitals at the time in the state demonstrated his awareness of the increasing importance of the capital city as a medical center. Johnson owed this success in large part to the generous financial support of the state government, various soldier aid societies, and scores of civilian volunteers who bridged the gap while the Confederate Medical Department struggled to establish a proper system for the care of its soldiers. In addition to Johnson's strong efforts, an often-forgotten key element in this early success, particularly at the district and department levels, was excellent leadership on the part of senior officers. Leaders like Brig. Gen. Gatlin, understood the need for a proper medical system. In doing so, Gatlin fostered initiative and success on the part of his medical director and the subordinate surgeons throughout his command. Without Gatlin, the trials of 1861 would have been even harder to overcome.

Because of these efforts, North Carolina accomplished a great deal regarding the care of its soldiers. Although the state's first general hospitals nowhere approached the size and scope of the operations of its later hospitals, the surgeons who oversaw their operation gained invaluable experience. Within a few short years, surgeons Edmund B. Haywood and William H. Moore would advance to operate some of the state's largest hospitals.

Surgeon Peter E. Hines served at the Petersburg and Yorktown general hospitals prior to his assignment as medical director of North Carolina general hospitals in September 1863.

(Histories of Several Regiments and Battalions from North Carolina in the Great War)

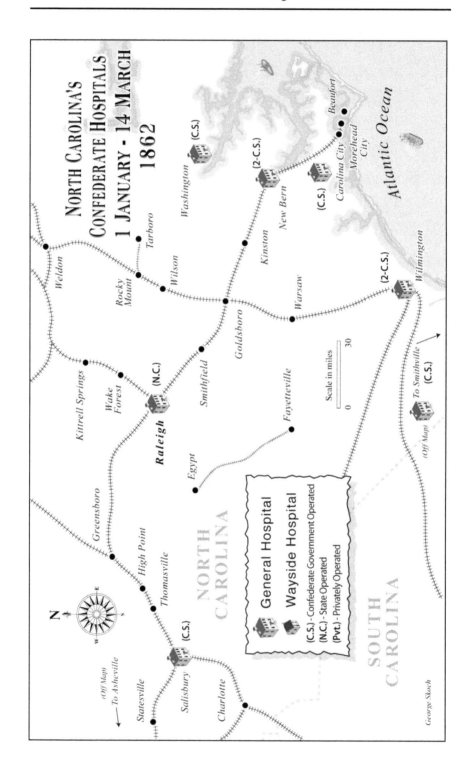

NORTH CAROLINA'S
CONFEDERATE HOSPITALS
1 JANUARY - 14 MARCH
1862

General Hospital

Wayside Hospital

(C.S.) - Confederate Government Operated
(N.C.) - State Operated
(Pvt.) - Privately Operated

Scale in miles

0   30

Atlantic Ocean

Beaufort

Morehead City

Carolina City

New Bern (2-C.S.)

(C.S.)

Washington (C.S.)

Tarboro

Wilson

Kinston

Warsaw

Wilmington (2-C.S.)

Weldon

Rocky Mount

Goldsboro

Smithfield

Fayetteville

Egypt

Raleigh (N.C.)

Wake Forest

Kittrell Springs

Greensboro

High Point

Thomasville

Statesville

(Off Map)
To Asheville

Salisbury (C.S.)

Charlotte

To Smithville (C.S.)

(Off Map)

NORTH CAROLINA

SOUTH CAROLINA

N

George Skoch

Chapter Four

1862: Trying Times along the Coast

"The hospital must be continued."

Hospital Expansion in Eastern North Carolina

Medical Director James J. Waring welcomed the new year by establishing a second general hospital at Wilmington. After several months of negotiation, Charles D. Ellis of the Seaman's Friend Society finally agreed on January 8, 1862, to loan the Department of North Carolina the use of the Seaman's Home as a hospital. Like the former U.S. Marine Hospital at Wilmington, the Seaman's Friend Society built the Seaman's Home with the care and comfort of merchant mariners in mind, which facilitated an easier transition to a military hospital. The building contained a dispensary, dining rooms for convalescents and attendants, storage rooms, and a kitchen. It had gas lighting throughout and an adequate supply of water conveyed by pipes from the city waterworks. The building had a 96-bed capacity, but Waring and his staff would expand that number to approximately 200 beds by leasing several adjacent private residences in the coming months.[1]

Including the newly established Wilmington General Hospital (later designated as General Hospital No. 4), the Lower Cape Fear region now had three general hospitals, reflecting the city's increasing importance as a major blockade running port for the Confederacy. Given the area's crucial role, the Confederate army committed significant resources in both men and material to defend it. Although

---

1. On January 8, 1862, Waring signed a formal agreement with the Seaman's Friend Society for use of the building. See Thomas R. Micks to Peter E. Hines, November 18, 1863, Letters Sent, General Hospital No. 4, ch. 6, vol. 399, 23, RG109, NA; Seaman's Friend Society, Citizens and Business Papers, M346, roll 914, RG109, NA. Although the society initially retained control of two office spaces and a storage room below the main structure, the government agreed to lease the remaining portion within the year, thus lending the department control of the entire structure; General Hospital No. 4 is often described as "the largest and best equipped in the state." See, McKean, *Blood and War at My Door Step*, 1:113. Although the leasing of additional buildings increased the hospital's capacity, other hospitals within the state were larger.

not to the same scale as Raleigh, the Lower Cape Fear region would remain a major hospital center in North Carolina throughout the war.

A need for additional hospital space also existed in New Bern. By January 1862, the District of the Pamlico had the largest concentration of troops, approximately 8,600 soldiers, with the majority located near New Bern. Toward the latter part of the month, Brigadier General Lawrence O'Bryan Branch, commander of the District of the Pamlico at New Bern, notified New Bern's mayor, Frederick Lane, that the "hospital accommodations at this point are found to be altogether insufficient for the Regiments now stationed in this vicinity." According to Branch's letter to the mayor, Medical Director Waring was present in New Bern examining buildings as potential hospital locations, "which can be procured by contract with the owners." A three-story block of brick buildings on Craven Street, known locally as Stephen's Brick Block, caught Waring's attention as suitable for a hospital. However, Branch's quartermaster informed him the building's owner, Mrs. James Riggs, "refused to rent it to him on any terms."[2]

Hoping to avoid seizing the property based on military necessity, Branch asked Mayor Lane to use his influence "with the good lady to induce her to rent it for the purpose indicated." The mayor's assistance proved helpful, and approximately a week later, the *Newbern Daily Progress* reported, "[t]he rooms adjoining the *Progress* building have been taken for a hospital and are being overhauled and refitted for that purpose under the supervision of Dr. W. A. Holt, hospital surgeon." Assistant Surgeon William A. Holt, whom the paper described as "a man of taste, as well as judgment," had previously served in the 27th North Carolina Infantry. The building's condition left much to be desired, so Holt had his work cut out for him. The *Progress* noted that the building required cleaning up, whitewashing, and readjusting the pavement in front of the structure.[3] Officially identified as the Branch

2. The District of the Cape Fear had approximately 4,000 assigned personnel. Return of District of Pamlico, January 1862, *OR*, 9:424; Steve Shaffer, *The Order Book of Brigadier General Lawrence O'Bryan Branch, Confederate Army* (Independently Published, 2021), 106-07; Peter B. Sandbeck, *The Historic Architecture of New Bern and Craven County, North Carolina* (New Bern, NC, 1988), 324-25; Shaffer, *The Order Book of Brigadier General Lawrence O'Bryan Branch*, 107; According to Chris Meekins, from the North Carolina Office of Archives and History, the presence of the *North Carolina Times*' office in the Stephen's Brick Block indicates mid-January 1864 as the earliest possible date for the image. The January 16, 1864, edition of the North Carolina Times is the earliest date the newspaper was published at Craven Street. Beforehand, the office was located at Pollock Street. See the January 2, 1864, edition. Chris Meekins email to author, January 5, 2022.
3. Shaffer, *The Order Book of Brigadier General Lawrence O'Bryan Branch*, 107; "New Hospital," *Newbern Daily Progress*, January 31, 1862; William A. Holt, CSR, M331, roll 131.

Stephens' Brick Block, Craven St., New Bern, ca. 1864–1865.
Confederate Branch General Hospital through the battle of New
Bern.

(*#P0001, North Carolina Collection Photographic Archives,*
Louis Round Wilson Special Collections Library,
University of North Carolina at Chapel Hill)

General Hospital, once readied, the new facility in the Stephen's Brick Block building contained 11 "finely aired, and well-ventilated" wards, capable of handling approximately 240 beds. The opening of the hospital represented a milestone in the short history of North Carolina's Confederate hospitals, marking the first time a Confederate hospital in the state operated with a capacity greater than 200 or more patients.[4]

Along with the Branch General Hospital, Confederate authorities established a smaller third hospital in New Bern, which further increased the city's hospital capacity. The late Stephen B. Forbes home and the adjoining house, both leased by the Department, provided "additional room for some 75 or 80 patients in case that much room

4. Although it is unclear, authorities probably named the hospital for Brig. Gen. Branch; Wm. A. Holt to S. P. Moore, March 21, 1862, Letters Received, AIGO, M474, roll 53, RG109, NA; "New Hospital," *Newbern Daily Progress*, January 31, 1862; S. Kneeland Jr. to Surgeon General, April 19, 1862, in F. E. Oliver, M.D. and S. L. Abbot, M.D., eds. *The Boston Medical and Surgical Journal* (1862), 66:279-80.

should be needed." The Forbes House acquisition highlighted the increasing role that New Bern provided as a hospital center on North Carolina's central coast.[5]

With the establishment of New Bern's additional hospitals, the District of the Pamlico now included four operational general hospitals and, if required, the Forbes Hospital. Evidence suggests this new complex at New Bern impressed observers at the time. As he had previously done at Wilmington, Brig. Gen. Gatlin ordered Waring to inspect the hospitals at New Bern, Carolina City, and Washington. On January 18, Waring started a 10-day visit to each hospital before returning to his post at Goldsboro. By all accounts, Waring was pleased with his tour and, undoubtedly, proud of all that the department had accomplished since taking over as the medical director.[6]

Union Forces Capture Roanoke Island

Although the hospital situation was steadily improving, the overall military situation in the state was on the cusp of disaster. On January 11, a large Federal amphibious force, consisting of approximately 70 warships, troop transports, and other supporting vessels, along with 15,000 soldiers, departed from Fort Monroe, Virginia, heading south toward the Outer Banks. The flotilla's mission was nothing less than an effort to reassert U.S. control over coastal North Carolina. With Brigadier General Ambrose E. Burnside and Flag Officer Louis M. Goldsborough leading, the joint force would use Union-controlled Hatteras Inlet as a doorway to the inland waterways of North Carolina. With the mass armada underway, it soon caught the attention of Ocracoke villagers, who reported "that they could see from the Light House" the Union fleet off Hatteras Inlet.[7]

Supported by naval gunfire, the army planned first to seize

5. *Newbern Daily Progress* (NC), January 17, 1862. Based on the small capacity of the Forbes House, the typhus outbreak in New Bern may have required its acquisition, thereby allowing surgeons to isolate those infected from the two general hospitals. Medical Director Waring noted that typhus patients were present in the hospitals at New Bern before the battle. See James J. Waring to S. P. Moore, March 21, 1862, Letters Received, AIGO, M474, roll 53, RG109, NA.
6. SO, No. 14, Hdqrs. Dept. of NC, January 18, 1862, see the file of James J. Waring, CSR, M331, roll 259.
7. Richard A. Sauers, *A Succession of Honorable Victories: The Burnside Expedition in North Carolina* (Dayton, OH, 1996), 115, 120-21; J. D. Whitford to Gov. Clark, dated, January 17, 1862, North Carolina Digital Collections, accessed on December 9, 2020, https://digital.ncdcr.gov/digital/collection/p15012coll8/id/10553/rec/11.

Roanoke Island and hold it as a base for future operations. At the same time, the navy would conduct further operations in the Albemarle Sound area to effectively close the backdoor to Norfolk, Virginia. Once completed, the amphibious force would move across Pamlico Sound and up the Neuse River to capture the port city of New Bern, where it would sever the rail connection to the port at Morehead City. With New Bern secure, the army would seize Beaufort and Morehead City, thereby isolating Fort Macon. Siege operations would commence forcing the fort's surrender. Follow-on missions included the critical railroad hub at Goldsboro and the port city of Wilmington.[8]

Roanoke Island, the site of indigenous settlements for thousands of years as well as the Roanoke Colony established in 1585, was the key to controlling two main bodies of water covering much of the state's coast—the Albemarle and Pamlico sounds. Like a cork in a bottle, 3-mile-wide by 12-mile-long Roanoke Island separates the two bodies of water, therefore restricting maritime travel between the two. Despite the island's military importance, Confederate authorities had accomplished little in strengthening the island's defenses. In January 1862, four days after assuming his duties as district commander, Confederate Brigadier General Henry A. Wise provided an assessment to his superior about the readiness of the Roanoke Island defenses. A shocked Wise reported on January 15 that he found a total lack of everything, "no adequate preparations whatever to meet the enemy." Wise had a force of 1,400 men on Roanoke Island with 800 in reserve at Nags Head. Unfortunately for Wise and his men, the Union armada was already on the way.[9]

Wise's report noted the presence of a hospital, which he described as "a long wooden building erected for such purposes," though he did not specify its location. He did, however, express concerns about its setting. "The Island is unsafe as a medical depot and hospital, and the spot selected is near a marsh and swamp, which must be, and is reported to be, unhealthy and beset in summer by mosquitoes." Before submitting his report, Wise had already dispatched Surgeon Peter Lyons from his command to conduct a survey of Currituck, about forty miles to the north near the Virginia border, as a suitable location for establishing a permanent hospital for the Confederate forces in the region. Lyons later reported that the town was ideally suited for the construction of a hospital. Although Wise concurred with the surgeon's findings and authorized the requisitioning of the required

8. Barrett, *The Civil War in North Carolina*, 68-69.
9. Michael P. Zatarga, *Battle of Roanoke Island: Burnside and the Fight for North Carolina* (Charleston, SC, 2015), 53. Zatarga's superb study provides the most detailed examination of the battle; Henry A. Wise to Benjamin Huger, January 15, 1862, *OR*, 9:134.

lumber, no documentation indicates that the Confederates ever followed through with Lyon's recommendation.[10]

Before the battle at Roanoke Island in early February, Wise suffered from "pleurisy, with high fever and spitting of blood, threatening pneumonia." Confined to a bed at Nags Head, Wise remained hospitalized until the battle's outcome forced his hurried departure. Although Wise continued to issue orders from his hospital bed, Colonel Henry M. Shaw of the 8th North Carolina commanded the forces on Roanoke Island during the battle. The arrival of the Federal fleet off Roanoke Island on February 7 marked the start of Union operations to seize the island. Beginning at approximately noon, naval gunfire forced the withdrawal of the outmatched Confederate navy, often referred to as the "mosquito fleet," while simultaneously providing supporting fire to enable Burnside to land his forces uncontested upon the island. The Confederate main line of defense was essentially in the middle of the island with swampy marshlands securing its flanks, just north from where the Federals landed.[11]

At dawn the next day, Union forces advanced north on the island's center road, brushing aside the Confederate skirmishers while steadily advancing toward the strength of the defense. The defenders held firm for a short while until elements of the Union force maneuvered through the perceived impenetrable swamps, thus forcing the Confederates to abandon the defensive line. The Southerners retreated to the northern end of the island, at which point, realizing the situation was hopeless, they surrendered. Confederate losses in the brief battle amounted to only 24 killed and 68 wounded. However, a staggering 2,500 Southerners were now prisoners of war, which included five North Carolina surgeons, who likely cared for their wounded compatriots.[12]

Despite Wise's apprehension about Roanoke Island as a suitable hospital location, when Union forces captured the island they discovered favorable living and hospital conditions. One senior Federal commander wrote, "The camps consisted of well-built quarters, store-houses, and hospitals, all newly built." The U.S. troops discovered "unusually large, commodious, and well-ventilated buildings erected upon the island for hospital purposes, which will afford ample accommodation for our sick and wounded. The largest hospital at the

10. Ibid.; Peter Lyons to Henry A. Wise, January 25, 1862, Peter Lyons, CSR, M331, roll 160.
11. Zatarga, *Battle of Roanoke Island*, 62, 79, 85-87.
12. Zatarga, *Battle of Roanoke Island*, 99; *OR*, 9:173, 177-78, 180-81; Sauers, *A Succession of Honorable Victories*, 200.

Surgeon Robert H. Worthington was captured at Roanoke Island and later served in Smithville's General Hospital No. 6 during the 1862 yellow fever epidemic. He spent the remainder of the war as an assistant surgeon in the 7th Virginia.

(Alex Peck Medical Antiques)

north end of the island . . . two hospitals near the fort at the center of the island." According to the Federal reports, it appears the Confederates had constructed two more additional hospitals since Wise had filed his report in January 1862.[13]

In addition to the hospitals on Roanoke Island, several accounts suggest a hospital existed across the water at Nags Head on Bodie Island. Before the war, Nags Head was a popular summer retreat for

13. Report of John G. Foster, February 18, 1862, *OR*, 9:84; Report of Surgeon William H. Church, ibid.; Michael P. Zatarga, email to author, January 5, 2021. Zatarga states that three Confederate camp hospitals were located on Roanoke Island, each associated with one of the island's three significant encampments: the first, established in August 1861, on the island's northern tip, another, a camp hospital, outside of Fort Blanchard, on the northwestern portion of the island, and a third behind Fort Bartow, on the middle of the island. Zatarga states that a fire sparked by naval gunfire consumed the Fort Bartow camp hospital and barracks.

the wealthy, with sound-front cottages and hotels. The Wilmington *Daily Journal* reported that before the battle of Roanoke Island, an unspecified number of the sick soldiers from that island "had been sent off or were at Nags Head in the Hospital." Wise noted in his January report that the "the only quarters yet erected . . . are at Nags Head," suggesting that part of this construction may have included a hospital. A more probable location would have been the "large hotel," which the Confederates later burned during their hasty withdraw after the battle.[14]

With Roanoke Island secure as a base, Burnside was eager to resume operations, but the Union navy first had to destroy its Confederate counterpart. Following the battle, the remnants of the "mosquito fleet" had withdrawn across Albemarle Sound and up the Pasquotank River toward Elizabeth City. On February 10, a Union flotilla located and successfully engaged the Confederate fleet, destroying all but two vessels, which escaped toward the safety of Norfolk. Immediately following their lopsided victory, U.S. sailors disembarked at Elizabeth City, which one sailor described as "a dead town . . . dead as a graveyard." All but a few of the residents had fled, leaving parts of the town in flames.[15]

Having accomplished his first task, Burnside prepared for the next operational phase—the capture of the Confederate base at New Bern. Before doing so, he had to unburden his command of the more than 2,000 prisoners who remained on Roanoke Island. Burnside ordered the prisoners paroled and sent to Elizabeth City, where he had already arranged with Confederate authorities for their delivery. On February 20, the prisoners embarked on naval transports for Elizabeth City, arriving late afternoon.[16]

Two separate newspaper accounts note the presence of a Confederate hospital at Elizabeth City for the sick and wounded prisoners. The February 28, 1862, edition of the Charlotte *Daily Bulletin* reported, "All are doing well in the hospital at Elizabeth City, and will soon return home." A second account published in the *Fayetteville Observer* stated, "All are now in a hospital at Elizabeth City; but will be removed to Norfolk as soon as proper transportation can be provided. Medical supplies and medicine have been sent down from Norfolk, and every possible attention given to relieve their

14. Mallison, *The Civil War on the Outer Banks*, 175; A. E. Burnside to Lorenzo Thomas, February 20, 1862, *OR*, 9:365; As early as 1838, a large hotel operated at Nags Head capable of accommodating 200 guests. See Catherine W. Bishir, *The "Unpainted Aristocracy"* (Raleigh, NC, 1983), 6.
15. Cited from Barrett, *The Civil War in North Carolina*, 87. Union forces would not occupy Elizabeth City permanently until the following April.
16. A. E. Burnside to Lorenzo Thomas, February 20, 1862, *OR*, 9:365.

sufferings." These two accounts aside, a Confederate hospital at Elizabeth City is somewhat of a mystery. It is uncertain whether the hospital was in place before the battle of Roanoke Island; Union accounts from the earlier naval expedition to the town do not mention a hospital. Additionally, other than brief mentions in newspaper accounts, no extant Confederate reports suggest that a hospital existed before the battle of Roanoke Island. Based on the scarcity of information, the surgeons who were prisoners or those who escaped capture from within Wise's command most likely established the hospital. In any case, by March 11, the Confederates had successfully evacuated all their sick and wounded to Norfolk.[17]

Closure of Carolina City and Washington General Hospitals

The fall of Roanoke Island created a desperate situation for Confederate North Carolina as it exposed the inner-coastal region of the state to possible further Federal attacks. Instead of reinforcing Brig. Gen. Gatlin's Department of North Carolina with additional forces, Confederate President Jefferson Davis chose an entirely opposite course of action. On March 2, President Davis ordered the abandonment of Washington so "that the troops be withdrawn . . . and sent immediately . . . to Suffolk [Virginia] to aid in the defense of that place." In obedience to orders, Gatlin immediately complied. Two days following President Davis' order, a group of concerned North Carolinians wrote to Confederate Secretary of War Judah P. Benjamin, "The State has been invaded and the enemy has taken possession of a large portion of her territory, and the State has not now an adequate organized force to drive the invaders from her soil."[18]

The Confederate withdrawal from Washington led to the closure of its general hospital. Despite ordering the immediate transfer of Washington's garrison, Gatlin recognized that closing the hospital would not be that simple. On March 4, he wired Brigadier General Branch at New Bern, asserting, "The hospital must be continued at Washington until the medical director can make other arrangements." Gatlin provided his medical director almost a week to plan accordingly, but unfortunately for the Confederates, time had run out. The Union preparations at Roanoke Island for continuing operations

17. *Daily Bulletin* (Charlotte, NC), February 28, 1862; "The Killed and Wounded at Roanoke," *Fayetteville Observer* (NC), March 3, 1862; "Elizabeth City," *Newbern Weekly Progress* (NC), March 11, 1862.
18. J. P. Benjamin to Gatlin, March 2, 1862, *OR*, 9:442. Although President Davis issued the order on March 2, 1862, Gatlin did not receive the order until the following day; B. S. Gaither to J. P. Benjamin, March 4, 1862, *OR*, 51, pt. 2, 485-86.

had not gone unnoticed. Astute to the threat, Gatlin formally ordered Surgeon Gallagher on March 10 to break up the general hospital at Washington, N.C. and remove the sick as well as "the stores and property pertaining to the same." Gatlin informed Gallagher that the hospital's senior medical officer would transfer that material to Goldsboro.[19]

In early March, Waring also directed the closure of the Carolina City General Hospital, located across from Fort Macon. But first, the patients required transfer to the general hospitals in New Bern. William Robinson, a civilian traveling on the railroad to the coast to visit one of his sons at Fort Macon, described the process as "arduous work," as the medical director labored for two days, around the clock, before successfully removing the sick. In describing Waring's relief upon completing the task, Robinson observed that he "seemed as delighted as a father who had removed his children from danger when the work was accomplished." The closure of both the Washington and Carolina City general hospitals was the first time that a Confederate general hospital in North Carolina was either closed or relocated on account of the enemy. Unfortunately for Waring, this was just a prelude to things to come.[20]

Disaster at New Bern

The day after Gatlin ordered the closure of the Washington General Hospital, Burnside's soldiers embarked from Roanoke Island for a short journey to Hatteras as part of the final preparations for the movement toward New Bern. On March 12, Burnside's transports departed Hatteras, escorted by 14 naval gunboats. By evening, the amphibious task force had completed the crossing of Pamlico Sound and traveled 25 nautical miles up the Neuse River to the vicinity of Slocum Creek, where the vessels weighed anchor 18 miles south of New Bern. The following morning, under naval gunfire cover, Burnside's infantry landed, secured a foothold, and began their movement toward New Bern. The small Confederate force sent to

19. Gatlin to Branch, March 4, 1862, *OR*, 51, pt. 2, 486-87; SO No. 47, Hdqrs. Dept. of NC, March 10, 1862, see file of P. A. Gallagher, CSR, M331, roll 101; Gallagher died on July 31, 1862, from an infection caught while assisting Surgeon S. S. Satchwell at Wilson General Hospital.

20. Wm. Robinson to S. P. Moore, March 21, 1862, Letters Received, AIGO, M474, roll 53; Before the closure of the Carolina City General Hospital, Branch had ordered the garrison force stationed on Harker's Island relocated back to Fort Macon. With the abandonment of the island, the small camp hospital operated by Assistant Surgeon Richard G. Barham ceased operations. Paul Branch, *Fort Macon a History* (Charleston, SC, 1999), 123. See also, Report of Brig. Gen. Richard C. Gatlin, March 19, 1862, *OR*, 4:577.

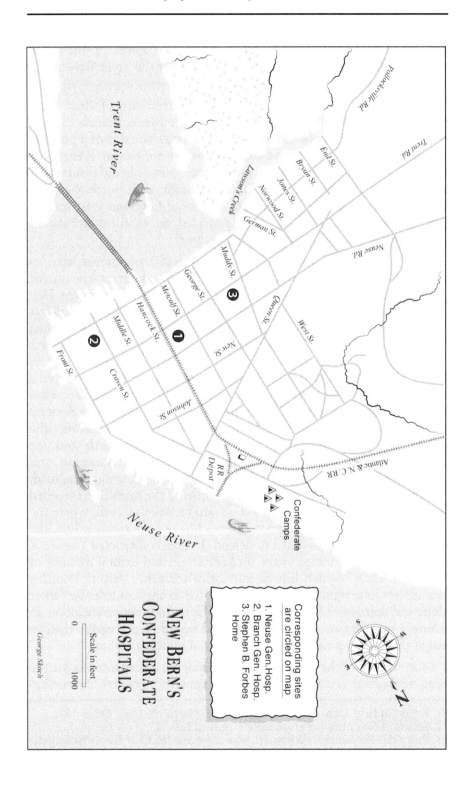

Trent River

Paducksville Rd.

Trent Rd.

End St.

Bryan St.

Jones St.

Norwood St.

German St.

Lawson's Creek

Neuse Rd.

Muddy St.

George St.

Metcalf St.

Hancock St.

Middle St.

Front St.

Craven St.

Johnson St.

Queen St.

New St.

West St.

①
②
③

R R Depot

Atlantic & N.C. RR

Confederate Camps

Neuse River

Corresponding sites
are circled on map

1. Neuse Gen. Hosp.
2. Branch Gen. Hosp.
3. Stephen B. Forbes Home

NEW BERN'S CONFEDERATE HOSPITALS

Scale in feet

0   1000

George Skoch

contest the Federal landing hastily withdrew back toward New Bern. By nightfall, Union infantry had arrived just south of the main Confederate defensive line, several miles south of the Trent River from New Bern, where they encamped.[21]

The defense of New Bern was the responsibility of Brig. Gen. Branch. But despite the recent loss of Roanoke Island, Branch had not received reinforcements—Confederate authorities worried of a possible attack against Norfolk. More so than the authorities in Richmond, Burnside recognized New Bern's importance. Not only did it serve as a port city, but it also sat athwart the Atlantic and North Carolina Railroad, which ran to the coast at Morehead City and west toward Kinston and Goldsboro and thus provided an excellent avenue of advance for any push into the state's interior.[22]

On March 13, Branch's approximately 4,000 troops prepared to face a force of more than 11,000 Federals. The Confederate strategy for defending New Bern focused on opposing the superiority of the U.S. Navy on the Neuse River and defeating an attack by land. To defeat the naval threat, the Confederates had constructed a series of earthen forts along the Neuse. Approximately five miles below New Bern was the 13-gun Fort Thompson, the main fortification on the Neuse. Between Fort Thompson and New Bern, the Confederates employed a series of smaller river batteries in the event the Federal "fleet succeeded in passing Fort Thompson." To counter an attack against New Bern by land, prior to Branch assuming command at New Bern, the Confederate authorities had constructed continuous earth and log breastwork, which anchored on the left at Fort Thompson and extended for about a mile to the Atlantic and North Carolina Railroad. Several days prior to the battle, Branch ordered the main line extended on the opposite side of the railroad toward to Brice's Creek, where the terrain greatly aided the defender. Instead of one continuous line, the Confederate infantry assigned to defend the area constructed a series of redans to take "advantage of the broken terrain and natural defenses of Bullen's Branch," which flowed into Brice's Creek." Despite Branch's best efforts, one significant weakness existed in the Confederate center along the railroad at Wood's Brickyard. Here, in order to maintain an infantry regiment in reserve, Branch had no other alternative than to assign this critical point in the line to a local militia battalion.[23]

On the eve of the battle, as Branch made final preparations for the pending Federal assault, Gatlin had "reluctantly" granted his medical

21. Report of Brig. Gen. Ambrose E. Burnside, March 16, 1862, *OR*, 9:197.
22. Sauers, *A Succession of Honorable Victories*, 220-21.
23. Ibid., 250-52; James E. White, III, *New Bern and the Civil War* (Charleston, SC, 2018), 40-41.

director's request to travel to New Bern, where he might render assistance. Catching the first available train from Goldsboro to New Bern, Surgeon Waring arrived later that evening on March 13 and then proceeded to Neuse General Hospital to meet with William H. Moore, the hospital's surgeon-in-charge. Upon discovering many sick at the hospital, Waring soon departed for Branch's headquarters located south of New Bern, across the Trent River. Waring sought to gain the commanding general's authorization for rail transportation to enable the immediate transfer of the sick to Goldsboro. As medical director, Waring clearly understood that the presence of several hundred sick limited the hospital's ability to handle the wounded from the pending battle properly.[24]

Waring found little time for sleep that night. According to the father of Lieutenant Colonel Wm. G. Robinson of the 2nd North Carolina Cavalry, who was traveling to the field to see his son, Waring arrived at the railroad depot shortly after midnight seeking passage to Branch's headquarters. Robinson described Waring as "incessant and importunate in his entreaties to be sent forward." At some point before 2 a.m., the two men departed by train for the front, where after a short journey, they arrived and headed off on foot, "in mud and water to the knees," toward the general's headquarters. Robinson wrote that it was a "raw and miserable night," and they were forced to travel "[s]uch a road I never walked before." After receiving Branch's authorization to start clearing the hospitals, Waring proceeded back across the Trent to New Bern.[25]

After a miserable wet night, dawn broke on the morning of March 14 "raw and cold," with a dense fog blanketing the area. One Confederate soldier remembered, "we could not see fifty yards beyond our works." At approximately 7:30 a.m., the Federal attack began. The Federal plan for capturing New Bern employed both naval and land forces. With naval gunfire in support, Burnside ordered one brigade to advance up the Beaufort Road and assault Fort Thompson, while a second brigade used the railroad as an avenue of approach to turn the supposed right flank of the Confederate line in the vicinity of Wood's Brickyard—the Federals were unaware that the Confederate line extended beyond the railroad. Burnside kept his remaining brigade as a reserve ready to exploit any successes by the attacking two brigades.[26]

24. R. C. Gatlin to S. P. Moore, March 19, 1862, Letters Received, AIGO, M474, roll 53, RG109, NA; Wm. H. Moore to S. P. Moore, March 21, 1862, ibid.
25. Wm. Robinson to S. P. Moore, March 21, 1862, Letters Received, AIGO, M474, roll 53, RG109, NA; Branch stated in his official report that his headquarters was located "200 yards in the rear of the entrenchment at the railroad." *OR*, 9:244.
26. John A. Sloan, *Reminiscences of the Guilford Grays, Co. B, 27th N. C.*

The brigade assigned to capture Fort Thompson struck first, but the Confederates successfully turned back the assault with minimal loss. At approximately the same time the opening shots of the battle occurred, Waring arrived back at New Bern, where he visited Assistant Surgeon Holt at Branch General Hospital. According to Holt, Waring issued instructions to evacuate the sick from Branch General Hospital to the railroad depot. A train stood ready to transport the soldiers out of New Bern. Waring then returned to Neuse General Hospital, whereupon he issued the exact instructions to Surgeon Moore. Meanwhile, the first of the wounded had begun to arrive in the hospital from the battle, and Waring took time to assist Moore in a leg amputation. After completing the procedure, Waring was eager to return to the front to assess the situation. He and Moore quickly departed, leaving Assistant Surgeon Thomas D. Martin at the hospital busy "making preparations to remove the sick in pursuance to orders."[27]

Shortly after the Federals initiated the attack on Fort Thompson, the lead regiments of Burnside's other brigade attempted to turn the supposed Confederate right flank near the railroad. Near the brickyard, despite an initial good showing, the local militia became unsettled, and some broke to the rear as "panic took hold," however, a successful counterattack by other Confederate units stabilized the situation momentarily. The fight in the center soon transpired into a see-saw fight, with one side momentarily gaining the upper hand. With one brigade stalled in front of Fort Thompson, Burnside ordered his reserve brigade into the fray along the railroad. By 11:00 a.m. two Union regiments had effectively "penetrated the Confederate center," which reverberated all down the Confederate line back toward Fort Thompson. The presence of Federal infantry in their former works and the likelihood of confronting an enemy possessing far greater numbers convinced the regiments nearby to withdraw. In response, the Confederate regiments positioned on the left back toward Fort Thompson began to withdraw. Noticing a definite slackening in the fire from the Confederate line, the Union brigade opposite Fort Thompson unleashed an all-out assault, successfully capturing the position. Realizing the situation hopeless, Branch attempted to organize a rearguard to protect his line of retreat over the two bridges across the Trent, however, the situation only worsened, and any hope

Regiment (Washington, D.C., 1883), 28-29; *OR*, 9:198, 202-03, 221, 224; White, *New Bern and the Civil War*, 45-46; Sauers, *A Succession of Honorable Victories*, 271-72.

27. White, *New Bern and the Civil War*, 45-46; W. A. Holt to S. P. Moore, March 21, 1862, Letters Received, AIGO, M474, roll 53; T. D. Martin to S. P. Moore, March 21, 1862, ibid.

the Confederate commander had of continuing the fight on the opposite bank of the Trent quickly turned into a rout. Once safely on the opposite shore, many demoralized Confederates "did not stop running" until they were safely beyond New Bern.[28]

Surgeon Holt from the Branch Hospital witnessed firsthand the withdrawal by Confederates back toward New Bern. Earlier that morning, after "seeing the sick under my charge safely placed upon the train," Holt departed the hospital for the battlefield. A short while later, he met surgeons Waring and Moore on the New Bern side of the Trent River Bridge, where Holt commented to the medical director "that all the excitement and confusion he saw was due to the fact that the army was retreating." The medical officers proceeded to go some distance beyond the Trent River, and "found everything in great confusion . . . and running in every direction in the panic." Back at the Neuse General Hospital, Assistant Surgeon Martin was still laboring to remove the sick when he observed "the Militia and 35th North Carolina" flee past the hospital, moving toward the train depot located several blocks north of the hospital. Martin had witnessed part of the ensuing rout following the engagement which resulted in the loss of approximately 400 captured or missing, along with 64 killed and 101 wounded.[29]

During the ensuing chaos in the Confederate rear area, Surgeon Moore separated from the others, and he and Waring would not reunite until several days later at Goldsboro. According to Assistant Surgeon Martin, Waring and Holt arrived back at Neuse General Hospital with some wounded men, at which point Waring "ordered them dressed and put on the train." Meanwhile, Holt hurried back to Branch General Hospital to assess the status of his patients.[30]

With the loss of Fort Thompson and the subsequent abandonment of the remaining river batteries by the Confederates, the commander of the naval element, Commodore Stephen Rowan ordered his vessels "to rapidly steam upriver toward New Bern." The U.S. sailors had a perfect view of the ensuing chaos occurring at New Bern. As Rowan's vessels approached New Bern they observed the 1,340-foot covered railroad bridge consumed in flames. The flagship *Delaware* began to

28. *OR*, 9:203; W. A. Holt to S. P. Moore, March 21, 1862, Letters Received, AIGO, M474, roll 53; Sauers, *A Succession of Honorable Victories*, 283-86; White, *New Bern and the Civil War*, 49-51.
29. W. A. Holt to S. P. Moore, March 21, 1862, Letters Received, AIGO, M474, roll 53, RG109, NA; T. D. Martin to S. P. Moore, March 21, 1862, ibid.; W. H. Moore to S. P. Moore, March 21, 1862, ibid.; Barrett, *The Civil War in North Carolina*, 95-98; White, *New Bern and the Civil War*, 51.
30. Wm. A. Holt to S. P, Moore, March 21, 1862, Letters Received, AIGO, M474, roll 53, RG109, NA.

shell the city in the direction of the railroad depot, adding further stress to an already desperate situation. During this period, Waring informed several of the remaining surgeons that he could not afford capture because of his position as department medical director. Therefore, he needed to leave immediately. Surgeon Holt later wrote, "I afterward met Dr. W[aring] at the Railroad depot, when the enemy were shelling the town. The shelling became more violent and the trains moved off. We then rode away . . . [and] had not gone far from the town when the last locomotive departed without any trains."[31]

Some perceived Waring's decision to avoid capture when all seemed lost at New Bern as cowardice, notably Dr. Edward Warren of the state medical examination board, who had arrived at the port city the night prior to the battle from Goldsboro, along with two other board surgeons. On the morning of the battle, Warren and his companions had volunteered their services at the Neuse General Hospital, where they heard Waring state his desire to avoid capture. According to Warren the naval gunfire "showered the roof" of the hospital with fragments, alarming Medical Director Waring to the point, he threw up his arms and cried: "My God, the fleet has passed the obstructions and is shelling the town; we shall all be killed." Waring "immediately fled" the hospital for safety, Surgeon Warren later wrote, and that in his absence, he solely coordinated the evacuation of the wounded, and if not for his actions, the situation would have been worse.[32]

The withdrawal west toward Kinston was anything but organized for Branch's defeated Confederates, and cohesion proved challenging to maintain in many of the units. Throughout several days, those who were lucky enough to have escaped arrived at Kinston sporadically—some by rail, others by foot—including the sick and wounded, who the surgeons placed on whatever transportation means available.

Because the Confederates destroyed both the draw and rail bridges across the Trent, Burnside chose to have Brigadier General John G. Foster's brigade ferried across the river to New Bern and the other two to remain on the opposite shore. The navy ferried some of Foster's

31. Sauers, *A Succession of Honorable Victories*, 295-96; Barrett, *The Civil War in North Carolina*, 105; Wm. A. Holt to S. P. Moore, March 21, 1862, Letters Received, AIGO, M474, roll 53, RG109, NA.
32. Warren, *A Doctor's Experiences in Three Continents*, 287, 289; Ed. Warren and W. W. Gaither to Branch, March 23, 1862, Lawrence O. Branch Papers, University of Virginia, Charlottesville; Sauers, *A Succession of Honorable Victories*, 296. Sauers mistakenly relies solely on Warren's account in *A Succession of Honorable Victories*. The written testimonies of the other surgeons who were present in New Bern raise doubts about the validity of Warren's account.

Doctor Edward Warren began the war as First Surgeon in the North Carolina navy, before accepting a commission in the Confederate army. In September 1862, Warren accepted the position of surgeon general of North Carolina, a role he held for the remainder of the war.

(*Engraving from Edward Warren, A Doctor's Experience in Three Continents*)

soldiers to the wharf at the foot of Craven Street, while others arrived at the docks, opposite the abandoned Confederate camp at the fairgrounds. As smoke filled the sky from the burning war material intentionally set afire by the retreating Rebels, scores of Blacks welcomed the blue-clad soldiers.[33]

According to Medical Director Waring, he coordinated the evacuation of approximately 200 men via the railroad before his departure. However, sources indicate the Federals accounted for

33. Sauers, *A Succession of Honorable Victories*, 299-300.

approximately 100 sick and wounded Rebels left behind in the hospitals or later recovered from the battlefield. Among the Confederate prisoners were surgeons William A. Blount and Gillespie S. West, Hospital Steward B. A. Edwards, and several soldiers detailed as nurses, all of whom had volunteered to remain behind with those soldiers left at the Neuse and Branch general hospitals. The final tally of prisoners also included Surgeon Richard B. Baker of the 33rd North Carolina, who the Federals likely captured south of the Trent River with the wounded from his command. Federal authorities relocated the sick and wounded Confederate prisoners to two private residences across the street from the New Bern Academy, where the captured surgeons cared for them. Vincent Colyer, Superintendent of the Benevolent Association of New York, provided critical supplies to the prisoners located in the two makeshift hospitals, thus ensuring that they were "seen to with as much attention as we have bestowed upon our own sick and wounded."[34]

The day after the battle, Dr. Samuel E. Kneeland of the 45th Massachusetts received orders to prepare the former Confederate Branch General Hospital on Craven Street for the reception of the Federal wounded. In a later report to the surgeon general, Kneeland later described his work at the hospital, providing a revealing glimpse at the final moments before the Confederate evacuation. Kneeland first occupied the building on March 16, when he discovered all that remained were "about one hundred bedsteads, with beds and coverings in a most filthy condition; one man dead, and another dying, left by the rebels in their hurried flight."[35]

Shortly after the battle of New Bern, Union and Confederate authorities reached an agreement to transfer the sick and wounded Confederates still at New Bern to Washington and then forwarded on

34. James J. Waring to Sir, April 2, 1862, Letters Received, AIGO, M474, roll 53, RG109, NA; Not counting the surgeons and hospital attendants, a parole list dated March 15, 1862, noted a total of 99 sick or wounded Confederate prisoners. See Muster Rolls and Lists of Confederate Troops Paroled in North Carolina, M1761, RG109, NA; William A. Blount, CSR, M331, roll 25; Two days before the battle, Medical Director Waring assigned Blount to Branch's District of the Pamlico. See SO No. 49, Hdqrs., Dept. of NC, March 12, 1862, filed in Blount's service record; "Hospitals," *Newbern Daily Progress*, March 29, 1862. Academy Green was the name for the small park-like campus area surrounding the New Bern Academy; Kearns, *Sanatoriums and Asylums of Eastern North Carolina*, 52. See also, Report of Lt. Col. Wm. Clark, March 16, 1862, *OR*, 9:227; S. Kneeland Jr. to Surgeon General, April 19, 1862, in Oliver and Abbot, eds., *The Boston Medical and Surgical Journal*, 279; "Report of the Superintendent of the Poor," *Newbern Weekly Progress* (NC), May 10, 1862.
35. S. Kneeland Jr. to Surgeon General, April 19, 1862, in Oliver and Abbot, eds., *The Boston Medical and Surgical Journal*, 279.

*Union surgeon Samuel E. Kneeland Jr. of the 45th Massachusetts.
Kneeland utilized the former Confederate Branch General Hospital
for Federal wounded following the battle of New Bern.*

(Wade Sokolosky Collection)

Surgeon Richard B. Baker of the 33rd North Carolina was captured at the battle of New Bern. He later helped establish the hospital at Tarboro to care for the paroled sick and wounded Confederate soldiers from the battle.

(Histories of the Several Regiments and Battalions from North Carolina)

to Tarboro. On March 20, a Federal expedition arrived at Washington with 27 wounded prisoners on board the vessel *Albemarle*. Unfortunately, the transfer did not happen without incident, as a near-fatal mishap involving the *Albemarle* occurred as it approached the wharf. According to one Union account, the vessel's master, "by stupidity or accident[,] . . . ran her on the piles," causing the *Albemarle* to take on water immediately. The proximity of other Union ships enabled a quick rescue.[36]

Surgeons Baker and Blount, who were among the released prisoners, had the prisoners offloaded, and in obedience to orders, transferred approximately 50 miles to the small river town of Tarboro, where the medical officers were "to select a building for a hospital." Twelve-year-old Joseph B. Cheshire, who later became Episcopal bishop of North Carolina, recalled when the sick and wounded arrived from New Bern, "[t]here were no provisions of hospital supplies of any kind" available in the town, the patients being wholly dependent upon the good graces of the townspeople. "For several weeks . . . I carried meals three times a day to the good Iredell County man, who had been assigned to our care." Cheshire noted the surgeons used the Tarboro Female Academy, located behind his house, as a temporary hospital. The two-story brick

---

36. A. E. Burnside to E. M. Stanton, March 27, 1862, *OR*, 9:372; S. C. Rowan to L. M. Goldsborough, April 2, 1862, *Official Records of the Union and Confederate Navies in the War of the Rebellion*, Series 1, vol. 7, 203-204. Hereafter cited as *ORN*. All references are to series 1, unless otherwise noted. See also, Report of Lt. Col. Wm. Clark, March 16, 1862, *OR*, 9:227; The April 9, 1862, edition of the *Semi-Weekly Standard* (Raleigh, NC) reported, "We learn that 27 of our wounded have been removed to Washington, and would be carried up to Tarboro."

structure was located on the east end of the town common, standing approximately seven blocks north of the Tar River.[37]

Francis L. Bond, a Tarboro furniture and mattress manufacturer, witnessed the arrival of the wounded soldiers from New Bern and how they "received the very kindest treatment" at the Female Academy. "They are not left to the usual Hospital treatment," wrote Bond, "but each housekeeper in town takes 2 of them as their regular patients, has their victuals sent regular to them 3 times a day, wash for them, indulge them in any little notion that they may need [and] they seem to be so grateful for this."[38]

The Waring Controversy

As Baker and Blount carried out their duties in Tarboro, controversy swirled at Department of North Carolina headquarters in Goldsboro regarding the conduct of Medical Director Waring. In the days immediately following the Confederate exodus from New Bern, Waring found himself embroiled in a separate battle for his reputation, based on his decision to avoid capture. Regrettably for Waring, authorities dismissed him as medical director five days later, pending further disciplinary action. The man behind Waring's dismissal was more than likely William T. Dortch of Wayne County, a North Carolina senator, who on March 19 had written Surgeon General Moore in Richmond requesting an investigation into the former medical director's actions on the day of the battle. It is unclear who informed Senator Dortch about Waring's supposed cowardice.[39]

---

37. Joseph B. Cheshire Jr., "Some Account of My Life for My Children," 46-47, Joseph B. Cheshire Jr. Memoirs, Mfp.161, NCOAH. Cheshire said Surgeon Blount resided in his home during the doctor's temporary duty at Tarboro; SO, No. 70, Hdqrs. Dept. of NC, April 3, 1862, see file of William A. Blount, CSR, M331, roll 25; Monika Fleming notes that the Confederates first used the all-male Tarboro Academy, adjacent to Hendricks Creek, on the western edge of Tarboro, as a military hospital, and only after "[t]he war had progressed, the Female Academy . . . was also turned into a hospital." Unfortunately, Fleming does not reference the source for this information. Monika Fleming, *Edgecombe County: Along the Tar River* (Charleston, SC, 2003), 2003. For the purposes of this study, the author chose to rely upon Cheshire's and Bond's written accounts, in particular the latter, dated from April 1862, which notes the use of the Female Academy.

38. F. L. Bond to Capt. Garrett, April 11, 1862, Civil War Collection, NCOAH; The April 5, 1862, edition of the *Fayetteville Semi-Weekly Standard* incorrectly reported that "27 of our wounded have been removed to Washington and would be carried up to Tarboro."; Private Richard Vance of the 7th North Carolina, who had previously served as a nurse at the Washington General Hospital, was detailed as a nurse at Tarboro through May 28, 1862. Vance received an additional 25-cent per day for his service as a nurse. Robert Vance, Civilians and Business Papers, M346, roll, 1,050.

39. W. T. Dortch to S. P. Moore, March 19, 1865, Letters Received, AIGO, M474, roll 53; Dr. Nathaniel S. Crowell, Waring's replacement as medical

Confederate authorities later dropped the charges against Waring on the technicality that he still required confirmation as a surgeon in the Provisional Confederate States Army. For Waring, his service in North Carolina had come to a close. But despite the stain of the charges, one thing is sure: both superiors and subordinates alike respected him. Surgeons Holt, Martin, and Moore wrote strong statements in Waring's defense and Brig. Gen. Gatlin, who praised Waring's service as the department medical director. In a letter to the surgeon general, Gatlin wrote, "He has worked with untiring energy and with a zeal which cannot be too highly commended."[40]

The circumstances surrounding Waring's departure are suspect. On the same day of Waring's dismissal, Warren took over as acting medical director for the department. Although he only held the position for a brief while, interestingly, Waring understood that Warren had "been striving to get my place." The Waring controversy is one of the few instances in North Carolina Confederate hospitals when one individual surgeon questioned the actions, leading to the other's dismissal. Historians have correctly noted Warren's outstanding war record, however, incidents such as the Waring controversy are noticeably absent that cast doubt about Warren's selfless service as a military officer. Nine months later, Warren's behavior during the battle of Goldsboro Bridge would again raise questions about his professionalism.[41]

In the aftermath of the Confederate disaster at New Bern, Waring was not the only senior officer out of a job. On March 15, authorities relieved Gatlin as department commander and Major General Joseph R. Anderson replaced him in the interim. The desperate situation in North Carolina forced the Confederate leaders in Richmond to reexamine the level of military support provided to the Old North State. With Burnside's force at New Bern seemingly poised to push farther into the state, thereby threatening the vital railroad hub at Goldsboro and even Raleigh, the War Department transferred

---

director and who was also present at New Bern during the battle, informed Surgeon General Moore, "Surgeon Waring did not leave the hospital at New Bern until sometime after the issue of the action was known." Furthermore, "while [Waring] remained in the hospital, he was actively engaged attending the wounded." See N. S. Crowell to S. P. Moore, March 22, 1862, Letters Received, AIGO, M474, roll 53. See Appendix A for the complete transcribed statements submitted during the course of the investigation into Waring's alleged misconduct.

40. R. C. Gatlin to S. P. Moore, March 19, 1865, Letters Received, AIGO, M474, roll 53, RG109, NA.
41. James J. Waring to S. P. Moore, April 1, 1862, ibid.; One only needs to read Warren's autobiography, *A Doctor's Experiences in Three Continents*, to gain an appreciation for his inflated ego.

additional forces immediately from Virginia to North Carolina. By the end of March, the total number of personnel in the state surpassed 24,000. For the Confederates though, Burnside's eyes were set upon his following objectives: occupying the port cities of Beaufort and Morehead City, along with their guardian, Fort Macon.[42]

Jarvis Farm Hospital

PLATE XX

Confederate field hospital at the Jarvis Farm during the battle of Roanoke Island.

(The Long Roll, by Charles F. Johnson)

---

42. *OR*, 9:445; Gadis, *Richard Gatlin*, 140; Barrett, *The Civil War in North Carolina*, 107-08; *OR*, 9:352-53; Following the battle of New Bern, Col. Moses White, commander of Fort Macon, knew that it was only a matter of time before Union forces besieged his fort. On March 18, 1862, a raiding party from the fort burned the Carolina City General Hospital to deny the Federals any future use of the structure. Branch, *Fort Macon a History*, 126; After a 33-day siege of Fort Macon, the Confederate defenders capitulated and surrendered on April 26, 1862; On July 6, the U.S. War Department transferred Burnside, along with 7,000 of his men, to Virginia. Barrett, *The Civil War in North Carolina*, 129.

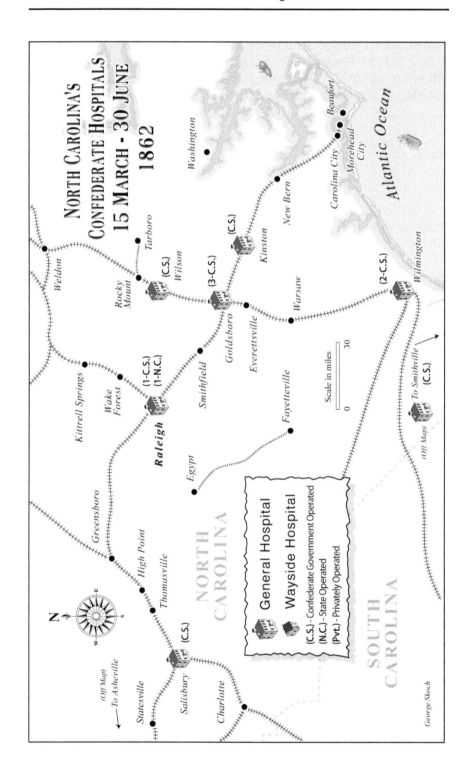

CHAPTER FIVE

1862: Hospital Expansion along the Railroad

"[T]he old Dr. is a snappish old cock."

General Hospitals at Kinston and Goldsboro

Burnside's successful offensive had wreaked havoc on the Confederate hospital operations in North Carolina. To the south, the Confederates still occupied Wilmington. However, further north along the coastal region, the loss of the general hospitals in Carolina City, New Bern, and Washington, along with a decision by the Confederate War Department to reinforce the Kinston-Goldsboro region with additional forces, created a severe shortfall in hospital capacity within eastern North Carolina. On March 24, 1862, Major General Theophilus H. Holmes, the newly appointed military commander of the Department of North Carolina—the third department commander in ten days—initiated actions that not only regenerated the department's diminished hospital capability but further expanded it. Three days following Holmes' appointment, Dr. Nathaniel S. Crowell replaced acting medical director Surgeon Edward Warren as the new medical director for the department.[1]

Crowell immediately went to work to mitigate the hospital shortfall created by the Federal victories. Beginning in the latter part of March, the Department of North Carolina issued a flurry of special orders to establish temporary and permanent hospitals in the Kinston and Goldsboro areas. Fearing a possible Union advance along the railroad from the coast, Maj. Gen. Holmes hurried reinforcements to Kinston. A small farming and railroad town on the banks of the Neuse River approximately 35 miles west of New Bern, Kinston would become, in essence, the forward base for Confederate operations in the eastern portion of state after the Federals gained control of New Bern and other posts in the coastal region. On March 29, Surgeon William J. Blow of the 27th North Carolina received orders "to immediately proceed to Kinston and organize a hospital for the sick."[2]

---

1. *OR*, 9:450-51; SO No. 70, AIGO, March 27, 1862, Nathaniel S. Crowell, CSR, M331, roll 66; Warren served as the medical purveyor until his appointment as Surgeon General of North Carolina in September 1862.
2. SO No. 65, Hdqrs. Dept. of NC, March 29, 1862, located in the file of William J. Blow, CSR, M331, roll 25.

It is unclear which site Blow selected in the town; however, sources indicate that Kinston was home to several Confederate hospitals throughout the war. The first was the partially constructed Methodist Episcopal Church, at the corner of Caswell and Independence streets. Although the war halted construction, the Confederates were able to convert the unfinished church into a hospital. A second facility occupied the Nicols Store on the corner of Queen and Caswell streets, and a third reportedly existed in the Wood and West General Store, at the intersection of Queen and King streets. Because of the pressing need for bed space following New Bern's evacuation, the Confederates probably utilized all three known hospital sites, as well as private residences such as the Peebles House (also known as Harmony House) and Dr. A. R. Miller's house, a Kinston physician and Confederate surgeon, to shelter the sick and wounded at least until the situation stabilized. Although extant records indicate the presence of only one general hospital at Kinston, it is unclear which of the above-identified locations served that function.[3]

In early April, Surgeon Richard H. Shields replaced Blow as the surgeon-in-charge of the Kinston General Hospital. Aid for the hospital came from as far away as Charlotte, where the women from the Soldiers' Aid Society appealed for donations of furniture or other articles necessary for the "sick in the Hospital at Kinston." Records show that the Kinston General Hospital closed mid-June, by order of the department commander. Two factors drove the decision to close the hospital at Kinston. First, the previously perceived Federal threat to the state's interior following New Bern's fall had never materialized; subsequently, Confederate authorities began to transfer many of the units back to the Virginia battlefront, where a far greater need existed. Secondly, the minimal forces that remained in Kinston did not justify operating a general hospital there, especially given the presence of several general hospitals only 25 miles to the west at Goldsboro. On June 14, department headquarters ordered Surgeon Shields to have "those of the sick who are in condition to travel sent to the Goldsboro hospitals." The order further directed Shields to transfer all the remaining medicine, stores, and other properties belonging to the

3. Heritage Sunday Committee, "Our Christian Heritage: Faith through the Ages," Queen Street United Methodist Church, November 19, 2006, 3, accessed on September 8, 2018, https://nccumc.org/history/files/Queen-street-UMC-history; G. B. W. and Mrs. F. H., "Kinston in the Sixties," *Carolina and the Southern Cross* (November 1913), 1:2; The March 12, 1895, edition of the *Raleigh News & Observer* (NC) reported, "The old building, corner of Queen and King Streets, once a Confederate hospital, is now the headquarters for the Oettinger Bros."; Tom J. Edwards and William H. Rowland, *Through the Eyes of Soldiers: The Battle of Wyse Fork* (Kinston, NC, 2006), 134.

Confederate General Hospital No. 3 (first wartime location). In March 1862, Confederate authorities established a hospital in the Wayne Female College building.

(*Wayne County Library, Goldsboro, N.C.*)

medical department to the medical purveyor in Goldsboro. For the military remaining in the area, all future "cases of sickness occurring among the troops at Kinston" required evacuation to the hospitals at Goldsboro for treatment.[4]

Goldsboro was a key north-south, east-west transportation hub for three major railroads: the Atlantic and North Carolina, the Wilmington and Weldon, and the North Carolina. In the days following the battle of New Bern, the railroads at Goldsboro transformed the town seemingly overnight into an important hospital center. Records indicate that beginning in mid-March, the Department

4. SO No. 72, Hdqrs. Dept. of NC, April 5, 1862, Orders and Circulars Issued, 1861–1865, ch. 2, vol. 259, RG109, NA; SO No. 130, Hdqrs. Dept. of NC, June 14, 1862, ibid.; "To the Ladies of Mecklenburg," *Daily Bulletin* (Charlotte, NC), April 14, 1862; On April 18, Charlotte's Soldiers Aid Society donated $100 in support of the Kinston Hospital. See Drury Lacy Papers, SHC/UNC; On July 6, the U.S. War Department transferred Burnside, along with 7,000 of his men, to Virginia. Barrett, *The Civil War in North Carolina*, 129.

of North Carolina attempted to establish no less than five individual hospitals in and around the Goldsboro area. Unfortunately, other than the original orders directing their establishment and a few extant documents, little information exists about the day-to-day operations for three of these hospitals. In any case, the Confederates discontinued operations at most of these hospitals by early summer. However, two hospitals at Goldsboro, the Female College General Hospital and the Fair Grounds Hospital would operate throughout most of the war.

Authorities opened Goldsboro's first military hospital, the Female College General Hospital (later designated as General Hospital No. 3), on March 15, 1862, the day after the Confederate defeat at New Bern. The medical staff occupied the college's relatively new multistory building situated in Goldsboro's suburbs on the southeast of town. Despite encountering stiff opposition from school administrators, military authorities impressed the property based on the premise that the officials "were obliged to submit to dire necessity." Seeking to ease tensions with both local leaders and school officials, Maj. Gen. Holmes appointed surgeons Benjamin F. Fessenden and Wyatt M. Brown to "appraise the movable property of the college needed for medical purposes, to assess damages to the same . . . used by the Confederate States for hospital purposes."[5]

An inspection conducted later in 1862 found the hospital's location "healthy" with "able grounds for exercise." The "well ventilated" three-story brick building contained a basement above ground, with the "apothecary room, clerk's office, linen room, dining room, and matron's room" all located within the main building. The hospital's surgeon-in-charge, Goldsboro native, Dr. William H. Moore, organized the hospital into eight wards of varying sizes allowing for a total capacity of 200 beds. Moore, who had just days prior superintended the Neuse General Hospital at New Bern, undoubtedly welcomed the hometown assignment, especially considering his recent narrow escape from New Bern. Hospital Steward Jesse A. Jones, from Greene County, assisted Moore. Two weeks after the hospital's opening, the *Goldsboro Tribune* reported that approximately a dozen wounded from

5. School Officials to Governor Jonathan Worth, May 8, 1866, Governor John Worth Papers, SHC/UNC; E. S. Gaillard to Richard S. Shield, December 27, 1862, see the file of John S. Murphy, CSR, M331, roll 184; SO No. 85, Hdqrs. Dept. of NC, April 19, 1862, Orders and Circulars, ch. 2, vol. 259, RG109, NA; SO 85, April 19, 1862, ibid; S. Milton Frost, Citizens or Business Papers, M346, roll 327; Wayne Female College, ibid., roll 1,081; Wayne Female College, formerly the Goldsboro Female College, was founded in 1854, but it had held classes in the Borden Hotel until the building's completion in 1857, at which time the school's name was changed to Wayne Female College. See William S. Powell, *Higher Education in North Carolina*, 2nd ed. (Raleigh, NC, 1964), 71.

the battle of New Bern were still present in the hospital under Moore's care. However, his tenure at the Female College General Hospital proved brief with the assignment of Surgeon Benjamin Fessenden as his replacement in late March."[6]

Moore's departure from the hospital is one of several unknowns regarding names and locations that occurred with Goldsboro's hospitals in the immediate weeks following the battle of New Bern. Two days after the *Tribune* noted Moore's presence at the Female College General Hospital, on March 29, department headquarters ordered Moore "to take charge of the Branch Hospital" (this is not the former Branch General Hospital at New Bern). Other than Special Orders No. 65, no further information regarding Branch Hospital exists. Adding yet more mystery, several weeks later in April, Moore submitted a fuel requisition for three cords of wood for use at the Blount Hospital. As with the Branch Hospital, no documentation other than the supply requisition exists relating to the Blount Hospital. Were these two hospitals the same hospital? Unfortunately, a lack of documentation prevents determining an answer.[7]

Additionally, medical authorities obtained the Wayne County fairgrounds to house and care for the Confederate wounded from New Bern. Ideally situated near the Wilmington and Weldon Railroad, surgeons used a small wooden structure located on the fairgrounds as a hospital. The former surgeon-in-charge of the Carolina City General Hospital, Dr. Spiers Singleton, superintended the hospital aided by nurse Miss Jenney McCallum. With a capacity of approximately only 40 beds, the Fair Grounds General Hospital was small in comparison to the Female College General Hospital. Surgeon Singleton's subsequent transfer to the Fort Fisher Post Hospital and a "Report of Sick and Wounded" from September 1862 by Assistant Surgeon Edward B. Haughton of the 1st North Carolina Artillery, which he identifies his hospital as the "Fair Grounds Barracks Hospital," suggests that by late summer, the Fair Grounds General Hospital had transitioned to a more traditional camp hospital. Conventional writings traditionally recognize the hospital at the fairgrounds as a wayside; however, the Confederate Medical Department did not convert Haughton's camp hospital into a wayside until July 1863.[8]

6. E. S. Gaillard to Richard S. Shield, December 27, 1862, see the file of John S. Murphy, CSR, M331, roll 184; Jesse A. Jones, CSR, M331, roll 144; *Goldsboro Tribune* (NC), March 27, 1862. The newspaper reported that a total of 24 wounded soldiers from New Bern were still present at the College Hospital (13 men) and Fair Grounds Hospital (11 men).
7. SO No. 65, Hdqrs. Dept. of NC, March 29, 1862, Orders and Circulars, ch. 2, vol. 259, RG109, NA; "Requisition for Fuel," April 28, 1862, see the file of William H. Moore, CSR, M331, roll 181.
8. Seyers W. Singleton, CSR, M331, roll 226; Jenney McCallum, Civilians and Business Papers, M346, roll 614; Edward B. Haughton, CSR, M331, roll 121.

Confederate surgeon Edward B. Haughton of the 1st North Carolina Artillery. Haughton superintended the Fair Grounds Barracks Hospital at Goldsboro before its conversion to a wayside hospital in the spring of 1863.

(Courtesy of Robin Oldham)

The occupation of the Women's College by the Medical Department was not the only action that rankled civilian leaders in Goldsboro. Special Orders No. 70 directed Surgeon Thomas A. Hill, who had recently arrived at Goldsboro from Fredericksburg, Virginia, to "take possession of the Court House at Goldsboro and without delay organize a hospital there." The department's attempted impressment of the courthouse caused an outcry of objections from local leaders. But unlike the Female College, the town's leadership refused to compromise, prompting the immediate cancellation of Hill's order. The following day, Medical Director Crowell ordered Hill "to take immediate possession of the Glass House in the vicinity of Goldsboro and fit it up as a hospital."[9]

Like the Branch Hospital, the Glass House is also a bit of mystery. Other than Crowell's special order directing Hill to utilize the "Glass House," no further documentation exists on this location. However,

9. Thomas A. Hill, CSR, M331, roll 127; N. S. Crowell to "Sir," April 4, 1862, Henry T. Clark, Governor Papers, NCOAH; Norris, "For the Benefit of Our Gallant Volunteers," *NCHR*, 318; SO No. 70 (April 3, 1862) and SO No. 71, (April 4, 1862), Hdqrs. Dept. of NC, Orders and Circulars, ch. 2, vol. 259, RG109, NA; During the battle of Wise's Forks (March 7 to 10, 1865) near Kinston, the Wayne County Court House served as a temporary hospital for the wounded evacuated to Goldsboro. See Wade Sokolosky and Mark A. Smith, *To Prepare for Sherman's Coming: The Battle of Wise's Forks, March 1865* (El Dorado Hills, CA, 2015), 137.

both Hill's and Hospital Steward John H. Crawford's names appear on several period documents associated with the Webbtown General Hospital. It is unclear whether the Glass House and Webbtown General Hospital are the same; however, based on the April documents found in both Hill and Crawford's service records and the presence of their names on the muster rolls for Webbtown, likely, the two were probably the same hospital. According to the muster rolls, the Webbtown General Hospital operated between April and June 1862. In June, the hospital's apparent closure coincided with Hill and Crawford transferring to Raleigh, where Crowell assigned the two the responsibility for putting the Peace Institute General Hospital into operation.[10]

Another reported hospital nearby was located at Everettsville, approximately nine miles south of Goldsboro, along the Wilmington and Weldon Railroad. On April 14, department headquarters ordered Surgeon Benjamin F. Cobb "without delay proceed to establish a general hospital at Everettsville." Special Orders No. 80 directed Cobb to "take possession of Mr. Coble's and other buildings in that town suitable for Hospital purposes." Other than the extant department order, the lack of further documentation prevents confirming whether Cobb successfully placed the hospital into operation.[11]

Despite establishing half-dozen hospitals in the Goldsboro area, Medical Director Crowell thought the requirements for hospital space still exceeded the present capability. With the medical emergency behind him regarding the wounded from New Bern, by mid-April, Crowell became increasingly concerned regarding the rising reported cases of sickness within the local camps. In the 26th North Carolina alone, the *Fayetteville Observer* reported the deaths of five of its soldiers to disease, four of them under the age of twenty. By April, the number of Confederate troops assigned just in the Goldsboro-Kinston area totaled approximately 17,000, consisting of veteran units from the battle of New Bern, recently arrived forces from Virginia, and several newly organized North Carolina and Georgia regiments. It was the latter group of soldiers, fresh off the farms and from rural parts, that proved the most vulnerable to the various communicable diseases typically associated with the large Civil War camps. Indeed, illness

10. John H. Crawford, CSR, M331, roll 65; Thomas A. Hill, CSR, M331, roll 127; Webtown (the conventional spelling) is a neighborhood located in the southern area of Goldsboro.

11. SO No. 80, Hdqrs. Dept. of NC, April 14, 1862, Orders and Circulars, ch. 2, vol. 259, RG109, NA; Prior to the Civil War, plantation families predominantly made up Everettsville. The small community supported two churches, a Masonic Lodge, and an academy. Marie Lewis, "Wayne's Early History Swirls about Old House," https://files.usgenarchives.net/wayne/history/overet30.tx.

descended on many of these men. One North Carolinian, Private Benjamin E. Stiles, echoed Crowell's concerns in a letter to his mother, describing the prevailing illness in the camps as "dreadful times." To add further worry to an already concerned mother, he unknowingly informed her: "Men are dying every day."[12]

Exhausting his options for further expansion of hospitals in the Goldsboro area, Crowell informed Maj. Gen. Holmes of the "urgent necessity of providing, at this point [Goldsboro], liberal accommodations for the sick and wounded of the army." With all the "suitable" buildings in Goldsboro now occupied as hospital space, Crowell recommended to the commanding general that "arrangements be made at once to erect suitable hospital buildings for summer use." Although extant records indicate that the Confederates never proceeded with any major new construction, Crowell's uneasiness with the situation at Goldsboro set in motion plans for establishing general hospitals at Wilson and Raleigh.[13]

Wilson General Hospital

The Federal victories along the coast also spurred department officials to open a general hospital at Wilson, 24 miles north of Goldsboro, along the Wilmington and Weldon Railroad to Weldon. On April 1, the government obtained the two-story Wilson Female Institute and supported outbuildings from the school's trustees as a hospital.[14] Completed in 1859, the school's proximity to the railroad made it a perfect hospital location. In 1862, there was a "large, well-landscaped lawn between the front of the building" and the railroad. The structure's interior allowed for 220 beds, a large capacity comparable to the Female College General Hospital at Goldsboro. A hospital visitor praised the selection of the building, writing it was "large, airy and admirably adapted for its present purpose . . . the long wards of comfortless looking rows of cots that are seen in other Hospitals replaced by much smaller rooms containing at most six or

---

12. N. S. Crowell to "Sir," April 4, 1862, Henry T. Clark, Governors Papers, NCOAH; Norris, "For the Benefit of Gallant Volunteers," *NCHR*, 320; *Fayetteville Semi-Weekly Observer* (NC), April 21 and May 1, 1862; *OR*, 9:451, 456, 459-60; Benjamin F. Stiles to Mother, April 4, 1862, McKay-Stiles Papers, SHC/UNC.
13. N. S. Crowell to "Sir," April 4, 1862, Clark Papers, NCOAH; Norris, "For the Benefit of Gallant Volunteers," *NCHR*, 320.
14. Joshua Barnes, Citizens or Business Papers, M346, roll 43. Although the government acquired the building in April 1862, it was not until September 1863, 17 months later, that the school board presented a bill for approximately $2,500 to the government to use the building and its furnishings. Moving forward, the government agreed to pay $143.75 per month for continued use of the building as a hospital.

Post-Civil War lithograph of the Wilson Female Institute. In March 1862, Confederate authorities established General Hospital No. 2 in the building.

(Wilson County Public Library, Wilson, N.C.)

eight beds, presenting a warm-like, quiet appearance infinitely agreeable to the way-worn soldiers." Such praise at the time was a testament to the professionalism of the hospital's surgeon-in-charge, Dr. Samuel S. Satchwell.[15]

Satchwell, a native of Beaufort County, attended Wake Forest College and received his medical degree from New York University. Before studying abroad in Europe, he spent nearly a decade practicing medicine in eastern North Carolina. At the start of the war, Satchwell gained valuable experience as the regimental surgeon for the 25th North Carolina. But it is Satchwell's subsequent reassignment to hospital duty at Wilson, where he remained for the war's duration, that his service is most recognized. The *Wilmington Journal* praised Satchwell as "one of the most accomplished and skillful surgeons in the Confederacy, and is withal a gentleman of high character." However, not everyone showered praise upon Satchwell. Private Peyton A. Cox

15. Patrick M. Valentine, *The Rise of a Southern Town: Wilson, North Carolina 1849–1920* (Baltimore, MD, 2002), 34; Hugh Buckner Johnston Jr., "The Wilson Confederate Hospital 1862–1865," *United Daughters of Confederacy Magazine* (October 1989), 52:37; A November 23, 1862, letter was written to the editor by the penname "Cape Fear." See *Wilmington Journal* (NC), December 4, 1862. Surgeon Satchwell served at the hospital for the duration of the war.

Dr. Samuel S. Satchwell, surgeon-in-charge of General Hospital No. 2 throughout the entire war.

(Pender County
Historical Society)

of Forsyth County, who served as a nurse at the hospital, characterized the doctor as an "old coon." He informed his brother, "Everything seems to be well managed, but the old Dr. is a snappish old cock [and] blisters a great deal though. They say he is not a bad man after all, which I hope to find true, for I never fancied his looks from my first sight."[16]

Peace Institute General Hospital

Medical officials looked for more capacity further in the state's interior. In addition to the Wilson General Hospital Medical Director Crowell considered it "very important that a large General Hospital should be established at or near Raleigh." The state capital offered a logical spot for such a facility. It was a center of military activity with its garrisoning troops, camps of instruction, and served as a railroad hub for units and personnel traveling to and from the Virginia front. It also made perfect sense from a medical planning perspective. Siting a new facility there would further expand the department's hospital system west along the railroad into the Piedmont region of the state,

16. W. Conrad Gass, "Solomon Sampson Satchwell," in Powell, *Dictionary of North Carolina Biography*, 5:284-85; *Wilmington Journal*, August 22, 1861; P. A. Cox to Dear Brother, September 17, 1863, "1862–64: Peyton Alexander Cox to His Siblings," Spared and Shared, accessed on November 11, 2021, https://sparedshared22.wordpress.com/2021/10/22/1862-64-peyton-alexander-cox-to-john-henderson-cox/.

thereby providing a contingency if the Federal's advanced from New Bern, possibly threatening the general hospitals at Goldsboro or Wilson.[17]

Crowell dispatched Surgeon Wyatt M. Brown to identify a suitable site in Raleigh for the new hospital. Brown recommended the "Female Seminary" as the best location; however, obtaining use of the school by the government proved challenging. Having learned a valuable lesson at Goldsboro in dealing with civilian authorities, Crowell recognized the sensitivity of impressing the school's building out of military necessity. In an April 4 memorandum to the department commander, Crowell summarized his plan for using the Female Seminary. Major General Holmes forwarded Crowell's assessment with his written endorsement to Governor Clark. Holmes stressed to the governor of the "indisputable necessity" of establishing a general hospital in the capital city while acknowledging the sensitivity of the circumstances. "It gives me great pain to interfere with the excellent female school there." wrote Holmes. "I have no alternative . . . and unless his Excellency the Governor can make some other arrangements for the accommodations of my sick [and] wounded, I shall be obliged to take the academy; paying however full compensation for the use of it."[18]

Through Governor Clark's assistance, Medical Director Crowell obtained the main building at Peace Institute as the site for the new general hospital. Unlike the move-in-ready female schools at Goldsboro and Wilson, the main building at Peace Institute had two significant issues. The framed structure had a roof, but no floors or glass in its windows. In mid-May, Surgeon Hill departed the Webbtown General Hospital in Goldsboro for Raleigh, where he began managing the necessary work required to enable the building's use. Hill later recalled, "General Holmes' orders were to hurry up matters, and if necessary, to impress every able-bodied man in Raleigh and put him to work." Impressment proved unnecessary, as Major W. W. Pierce of the Quartermaster Department hired Thomas H. Briggs

---

17. *The State Journal* (Raleigh, NC), August 13, 1862; Norris, "For the Benefit of Gallant Volunteers," *NCHR*, 318; The Fair Grounds Hospital in Raleigh was still a state-operated institution, and the Confederate Medical Department had not yet acquired it.

18. N. S. Crowell to "Sir," April 4, 1862, Clark Papers, NCOAH; Norris, "For the Benefit of Gallant Volunteers," *NCHR*, 318; Hill's postwar "Sketch" notes that authorities first "proposed to take the St. Mary's School," instead of the Methodist Female Seminary as reported by Crowell on April 2, 1862. See Thomas Hill, "Sketch of General Hospital No. 8, Peace Institute, Raleigh," 1, Confederate States of America, Archives, 1861-1865, Perkins Library, Duke University (DU), Durham, NC; Peace Institute is now present-day William Peace University.

Peace Institute General Hospital (later designated General Hospital No. 8). In mid-May 1862, Confederate authorities established a hospital in the semi-complete Peace Institute building.

(North Carolina Office of Archives and History)

and James Dodd, a local construction partnership, to complete the construction. Within a month, the workers had the floors installed, however, due to a shortage of window glass, Briggs & Dodd substituted painted white "domestic" (i.e., canvas) to keep the weather out. Work had progressed well enough that by late May Surgeon Hill placed wanted ads in the local Raleigh newspapers for hospital attendants. One such ad, titled, "Nurses, Cooks, and Waiters Wanted," Hill sought for hire, "White men over 35 years old, and persons having experienced negro cooks and waiters."[19]

Despite the building's semi-complete state, necessity drove Hill to begin admitting patients on the 6th of June. Hill's requisition for 100 bedsteads in June indicates that initially, the facility operated at only one-third total capacity. The fact the Peace Institute General Hospital

19. Hill departed Goldsboro on May 12 and began work in Raleigh the following day. Thomas A. Hill, CSR, M331, roll 127; Hill, "Sketch of General Hospital No. 8, 1, DU; "Main Building, Peace College Raleigh, NC," *The Journal of Presbyterian History* (2011), 89:98, accessed January 1, 2021, http://www.jstor.org/stable/23338049; Angie Clifton, "Thomas Henry Briggs Sr. (1821–1886)," accessed on February 6, 1861, https://ncarchitects.lib.ncsu.edu/people/P000037; Briggs and Dodd, Citizens or Business Papers, M346, roll 97, RG109, NA; *Semi-Weekly State Journal* (Raleigh, NC), May 21, 1862.

(later designated as General Hospital No. 8) treated 675 patients within the first six weeks of operation, validates the need for the hospital. Once appropriately resourced, the Peace Institute General Hospital operated at a 300-bed capacity, making it the largest hospital within North Carolina until authorities introduced the larger pavilion-style hospitals in 1864. By August 1862, Hill's staff included three assistant surgeons and Chief Matron Miss Jessie McCallum, who supervised three other matrons.[20]

Simultaneous with the establishment of the Confederate government's Peace Institute General Hospital, the North Carolina Medical Department opened the Baptist Grove Hospital on Raleigh's east side. Authorities established the hospital in an area known locally as the "Baptist Grove," because of a small church that stood on the property amidst magnificent oak trees that lined the entire city block. The hospital's account ledger is the only known extant record that provides a glimpse into its day-to-day operations. According to the ledger, the hospital operated for a brief two-month period (May to June 1862), under the supervision of Surgeon Edmund B. Haywood from the Fair Grounds Hospital. The Reverend James F. W. Freeman served as both acting steward and ward master for the hospital.[21]

North Carolina's Virginia Hospitals

As officials in North Carolina scrambled to open new facilities after the Federal occupation of key locations along the coast, they also looked to the care of the thousands of Tar Heel troops serving the Confederate cause in Virginia. On March 21, 1862, the Surgeon General of North Carolina, Charles E. Johnson, opened a second state-operated general hospital in Petersburg, Virginia. Officially identified as the 2nd North Carolina Hospital, the 250-bed facility occupied the former Riddle and McIlwain Tobacco Factory. Period documents indicate the business partners leased the building at a cost of $100 per month. Like its sister hospital, the 1st North Carolina, the state of North Carolina operated the facility independent from the Confederate Medical Department. Surgeon General Johnson selected a fellow North Carolinian, 62-year-old Surgeon William C. Warren, a

20. In Hill's "Sketch" Thomas A. Hill, CSR, M331, roll 127; Hill, "Sketch of General Hospital No. 8," 1, DU; *Semi-Weekly State Journal* (Raleigh, NC), May 21, 1862; Pollitt and Reese, "When One Goes Nursing, All Things Must Be Expected," *CV*, 29.
21. Baptist Grove Hospital Ledger, Haywood Papers, SHC/UNC; Reverend Freeman later served in the Confederate army as a chaplain at Virginia and North Carolina hospitals. James W. F. Freeman, CSR, M331, roll 98.

prominent Edenton physician, and father of Surgeon Edward Warren, to oversee the new institution.[22]

The elder Warren's service record indicates that he periodically suffered from ill-health, necessitating leaves of absence from the hospital. In September 1862, an anonymous individual, probably a patient at the hospital, complained in writing to the Raleigh *Standard* about the poorly run state of the hospital. It is not surprising, considering the prominence of Warren in Raleigh's social and medical circles, that the newspaper came to his defense. The *Standard* printed, "The bare announcement of the name Dr. W. C. Warren . . . is a sufficient guarantee . . . that no blame could be attached to him or to any institution or subordinate under his immediate care." Despite the newspapers' strong defense of Warren's reputation, Medical Director and Inspector of Virginia Hospitals Thomas H. Williams reassigned Warren the following month to the Ladies Relief Hospital in Lynchburg, Virginia, replacing him with another North Carolinian, Surgeon John G. Brodnax.[23]

The North Carolina Medical Department purportedly opened a hospital at Richmond in May, the Moore Hospital, named in honor of Confederate Surgeon General Samuel P. Moore. Assistant Surgeon Thomas Fanning Wood of Wilmington, who briefly served at the hospital, recalled that Surgeon Moore "disliked the compliment expecting to have a larger one named after him." The Moore Hospital (officially designated as General Hospital No. 24) occupied a large three-story brick building, "with a considerable basement," leased by Harwood's Tobacco Factory. Located a few blocks north of the James River on Richmond's east side, the hospital had a 120-bed capacity. The hospital's first floor provided room for administrative offices, staff sleeping quarters, and a large dining room for the patients. The patient care occurred on the second and third floors in "large open wards," with space allocated for "dispensary, linen and bath rooms."[24]

---

22. Peter E. Hines to Thomas H. Williams, November 26, 1862, CSR, M331, roll 128; Norris, "For the Benefit of Gallant Volunteers," *NCHR*, 312; McIlwain and Riddle, Citizens or Business Papers, M346, roll, 632; William C. Warren, CSR, M331, roll 260, RG109, NA.

23. In October 1862, the Confederate Medical Department reassigned the elder Warren to the Ladies Relief Hospital at Lynchburg, Virginia, where he served for the remainder of the war. Warren's service record indicates that his frequent incidents of ill-health continued during his assignments at Lynchburg. William C. Warren, CSR, M331, roll 260; *Semi-Weekly Standard* (Raleigh, NC), October 1, 1862; John G. Brodnax, CSR, M331, roll 34.

24. Norris, "For the Benefit of Gallant Volunteers," *NCHR*, 312; Koonce, ed., *Doctor to the Front*, 36; Calcutt, *Richmond's Wartime Hospitals*, 139; Koonce, ed., *Doctor to the Front*, 36.

Moore Hospital (later designated General Hospital No. 24), Richmond, Va., April 1865

(*Library of Congress*)

The narrative held by contemporary historians is that the North Carolina Medical Department established the Moore Hospital—a thought probably influenced by the post-war writings of Confederate Surgeon Peter E. Hines—however, "period accounts suggest a more reactive role by the state," and that North Carolina merely adopted an already functioning hospital that happened to contain primarily Tar Heel soldiers. A letter from Dr. Otis F. Manson, the hospital's surgeon-in-charge, to Confederate Secretary of War James A. Seddon, raises doubt as to the state's role in solely establishing the Moore Hospital. "In May 1861, I was placed in charge of this Confederate Hospital by Surg. Genl. Moore," Manson wrote. "From the fact that I am the only surgeon hailing from N.C. in charge of a hospital here it became filled with N.C. sick & wounded from its opening." According to Manson, the hospital "was set apart for the N.C. troops" immediately following the passage of the "An Act to Better Provide for the Sick and Wounded of the Army in Hospitals," in September 1862 by the Confederate Congress. Manson's letter clearly notes that the Moore Hospital operated for almost a year prior to the claimed May 1862 date.[25]

25. Norris, "For the Benefit of Gallant Volunteers," *NCHR*, 312; Hines, "The Medical Corps," Clark, *Histories*, 4:624; Hasegawa argues that the state

Manson was a Richmond native who moved to Granville County, North Carolina, in 1841 to practice medicine. Following North Carolina's secession, Manson received an appointment in the North Carolina Medical Department, where he first served as an acting medical agent in Richmond, visiting the various hospitals daily "to supply the wants" of sick and wounded Tar Heel soldiers. Even after Manson's later appointment as a surgeon in the Provisional Confederate States Army in 1863, he continued to serve as the state's agent for the remainder of the war while performing the duties of the surgeon-in-charge. In explaining his unusual duty arrangement to the Secretary of War, Manson wrote, "I am therefore a Virginian, adopted by North Carolina as her son."[26]

Although North Carolina regarded the Moore Hospital "as under her peculiar protection," and as such, provided much-needed commissary, medical supplies, and other necessary sundries, the hospital staff still depended on the support of generous individuals and various benevolent organizations to mitigate critical government shortages. Both Manson's North Carolina and Richmond connections proved beneficial in acquiring critical hospital donations. In publicly thanking the Ladies' Soldiers Aid Society of Oxford, North Carolina, Surgeon Manson expressed his "warmest thanks" for the articles that the women had donated but at the same time appealed for continued support. Manson specifically noted that the hospital required various supplies, "as they are not furnished by the government at all, or insufficient quantities, or of inferior quality." In addition to food donations, he requested "100 soft mattresses," along with "a soft pillow for the head of each wounded soldier, and some to place under their wounded limbs." Manson noted that the mattresses and pillows "made of shucks and cotton" were preferable to the government-issued "straw sack and straw pillow." Ice was one of the more unique items Manson requested, suggesting it be "packed in saw dust in barrels." In one month alone in 1862, the hospital received monetary donations totaling almost $600, along with necessary hospitals items from 16 individual North Carolina charitable organizations.[27]

The Moore Hospital would not lack for patients in the summer of 1862. At the end of May 1862, the Union Army of the Potomac, 100,000 strong, threatened the Confederate capital at Richmond.

      merely adopted an already functioning hospital. See, Hasegawa, *Matchless Organization*, 112-13. Otis F. Manson to Hon. James A Seddon, October 22, 1863, CSR, M331, roll 163.
26. Norris, "For the Benefit of Gallant Volunteers," *NCHR*, 312n43; "Report of the Surgeon General," Daily Progress (Raleigh, NC), December 2, 1864; Otis F. Manson to Hon. James A Seddon, October 22, 1863, CSR, M331, roll 163.
27. *Weekly State Journal* (Raleigh, NC), August 13, 1862; "Moore Hospital," *Richmond Dispatch* (VA), September 4, 1862.

Beginning with the battle of Seven Pines, on May 31, and concluding with a series of engagements outside Richmond, commonly referred to as the Seven Days' Battles, by July 1, the Confederates had prevailed against the Federal threat. Unfortunately, success came at a heavy cost, resulting in approximately 20,000 Confederate casualties, which quickly overwhelmed the nearby Richmond hospitals. A relief worker from Franklin County, North Carolina, wrote that the state's "sick and particularly wounded can be found in almost every hospital and many private houses." Sergeant Joseph S. Dunn of the 46th North Carolina, which had just arrived at Richmond by train from Goldsboro, described the scene in the capital as "awful to behold." Marching along Main Street, Dunn observed filled "wagons hauling the wounded: the sidewalk almost impassable, the wounded standing and lying in every direction." Surgeon Manson noted that the Moore Hospital alone "received 332 officers and soldiers, 272 of whom were North Carolinians." Because Richmond's hospitals lacked adequate space to care for the many wounded, medical authorities distributed the Tar Heel wounded throughout Richmond hospitals, as well as evacuating patients south by rail to Petersburg, where the 1st and 2nd North Carolina Hospitals, as well as the South Carolina Hospital Aid Society facility, treated the wounded.[28]

The adoption of the Moore Hospital by Surgeon General Johnson increased the total number of general hospitals operated by North Carolina in the Old Dominion State to three. Considering that the majority of North Carolina's regiments throughout the war served in Virginia, it is logical that three-quarters of the North Carolina-operated hospitals resided to the north in the Commonwealth. Additionally, it demonstrated North Carolina's commitment to its soldiers serving in the Army of Northern Virginia. As the state focused its efforts in Virginia, the Confederate government proved equally busy in North Carolina during the first half of 1862—best described as a period of ups and downs. The new year saw the Department of North Carolina expand its hospital capacity to seven general hospitals, only to lose four of them by March, due to the Federal invasion of coastal North Carolina. With only the general hospitals remaining at Wilmington, Medical Director Crowell proved resilient, and by June had increased the total number of government-operated general hospitals within the Old North State to 11, while also

---

28. Doug Crenshaw, *Richmond Shall Not Be Given Up: The Seven Days' Battles*, June 25–July 1, 1862 (El Dorado Hills, CA, 2017), xxi, 126; *Semi-Weekly Standard* (Raleigh, NC), July 12, 1862; "From the North Carolina Soldiers," *Fayetteville Semi-Weekly* (NC), June 26, 1862; *The State Journal* (Raleigh, NC), July 2, 1862; Norris, "For the Benefit of Gallant Volunteers," *NCHR*, 321.

expanding the department's hospital footprint into the Piedmont region (see table 5.1).

Table 5.1: North Carolina General Hospitals, June 1862[29]

Location	Designation	Authority
Charlotte	Charlotte General Hospital	Department of North Carolina
Goldsboro	Female College Gen. Hospital	Department of North Carolina
Goldsboro	Fair Grounds General Hospital	Department of North Carolina
Goldsboro	Webbtown General Hospital	Department of North Carolina
Kinston	Kinston General Hospital	Department of North Carolina
Raleigh	Peace Institute General Hospital	Department of North Carolina
Wilmington	Marine General Hospital	Department of North Carolina
Wilmington	Wilmington General Hospital	Department of North Carolina
Wilson	Wilson General Hospital	Department of North Carolina
Salisbury	Military Prison Hospital	Department of North Carolina
Smithville (Southport)	Smithville General Hospital	Department of North Carolina
Raleigh	Fair Grounds General Hospital	N.C. Medical Department
Petersburg	1st North Carolina Hospital	N.C. Medical Department
Petersburg	2nd North Carolina Hospital	N.C. Medical Department
Richmond	Moore Hospital	N.C. Medical Department

The State's First Wayside Hospitals

The effusion of blood resulting from the recent fighting in Virginia forced the furlough from the army of many convalescing Confederate soldiers that otherwise would have remained in the Petersburg and Richmond hospitals. Although not ideal, "it was frequently necessary to furlough large numbers . . . to provide beds for new battle

29. Data from *Daily Bulletin* (Charlotte, NC), January 22, 1863; SO No. 85, Hdqrs. Dept. of NC, April 19, 1862, ch. 2, vol. 259, RG109, NA; Seyers Singleton, CSR M331, roll 226; John H. Crawford, CSR, M331, roll 65; SO No. 65, Dept. of NC, March 29, 1862. ch. 2, vol. 259, RG109, NA; Hill, "Sketch of General Hospital No. 8," 1, DU; SO No. 116, Hdqrs. Southern Coastal Defense Dept., June 24, 1861; Micks to Hines, November 18, 1863, Letters Sent, General Hospital No. 4, ch. 6, vol. 399, RG109, NA; Valentine, *The Rise of a Southern Town*, 34; Brown, *The Salisbury Prison*, 22; *Daily Journal* (Wilmington, NC), June 18, 1861; *North Carolina Standard* (Raleigh, NC), November 31, 1861; *Semi-Weekly State Journal* (Raleigh, NC), November 27, 1861; Norris, "For the Benefit of Gallant Volunteers," *NCHR*, 312. Due to its brief two-month existence, the Baptist Grove Hospital is not included.

casualties." The terrible condition of the men as they traveled along the railroads shocked observers. Sadly, transient soldiers, alone and far from home, often lingered for days awaiting a connection to another railroad. During this dark period, a local grassroots effort emerged within the Confederacy to create wayside hospitals.[30]

The wayside hospital concept in North Carolina came to fruition in the summer of 1862, as private organizations from across the state followed the lead of Confederate women in South Carolina, the first to pioneer the idea earlier that spring. Wayside hospitals cared for transient Confederate soldiers who might require limited medical attention, meals, or places to stay overnight. Years after the war, Surgeon Peter E. Hines, in his short piece, "The Medical Corps," recalled, "Wayside Hospitals . . . were established in the summer of 1862 at Weldon, Goldsboro, Tarboro, Raleigh, Salisbury, and Charlotte." Hines' statement is only partially correct, as not all of North Carolina's wayside hospitals existed by the summer of 1862. The process occurred over several years, beginning with Charlotte, Salisbury, and Wilmington in July 1862 and concluding with the opening of the Greensboro wayside in May 1864.[31]

During these two years, private organizations, the state, and the Confederate government operated individual wayside hospitals in North Carolina. Also, a hospital's designation, wayside or general, may have changed at some point in the war. For example, the hospital at Weldon began as a state-operated wayside in December 1862, however, three months later, the Confederate Medical Department assumed responsibility for the hospital and re-designated it as a general hospital, only to convert back to a wayside two months later. However, in the beginning, neither the state nor the Confederate governments initiated the wayside concept in North Carolina but, instead, its citizens.[32]

The Hospital Committee at Salisbury, a local benevolent organization, established the Rowan Wayside Hospital near the railroad depot. The committee president, Mr. James C. Smyth, formerly opened the hospital on July 14, and within a few hours, "some 18 or 20 persons found it a most welcome retreat," one newspaper reported. The committee appointed Dr. Marcellus Whitehead, a practicing physician in Salisbury since 1835, head

---

30. Cunningham, *Doctors in Gray*, 41. The Confederate army's issues from furloughing soldiers go well beyond the scope of this study. See Cunningham's *Doctors in Gray* for an excellent analysis.
31. Pollitt and Reese, "War Between the States, Nurses in North Carolina, *CV*, 24; Hines, "The Medical Corps," Clark, *Histories*, 4:624.
32. Paul S. Carrington, CSR, M331, roll 49.

surgeon, and Ms. Jesse McCallum, a 34-year-old Scottish immigrant, as the hospital matron. As matron, McCallum was responsible for the "domestic management of the hospital" and all the property. The property management was usually the hospital steward's responsibility in a government institution, but in private privately owned waysides, the matron carried out such duties.

The Hospital Committee also set strict guidelines regarding hospital visitation. The "Rules and Regulations" specified, "No person shall be admitted to the Hospital except such as have relatives among the patients, or go to render assistance, and such persons . . . in taking care of the sick and wounded shall be under the direction of the Matron." A team of seven local physicians and more than 100 women volunteers assisted Whitehead and McCallum. The hospital's first month of operation cared for "87 wounded and 47 sick soldiers." Soldiers from as far away as Texas and Florida sought care at the wayside, which validated the necessity of caring for transient patients. The hospital's 45-bed capacity was typical of most waysides operating in North Carolina.[33]

The hospital depended much upon the generosity of others. The July 21, 1862, edition of the *Carolina Watchman* reported that Salisbury's Gun Boat Fund Committee had recently decided to transfer monies already raised for ship construction to the wayside hospital. Two months later, the Hospital Committee appealed to the generosities of neighboring counties because three-quarters of the soldiers cared for at the hospital were from Iredell, Catawba, Burke, Davie, Yadkin, and Wilkes counties. The announcement, published in the *Carolina Watchman*, read: "The good people of those counties should note the fact, and recollect that it is not a government establishment, but is sustained by private liberality; and as such, appeals to them for such assistance as they can spare from abundance."[34]

Whitehead and his Rowan County volunteers successfully operated the wayside hospital until its takeover by the Confederate government in June 1863. During this brief one-year period, the hospital welcomed more than 1,400 soldiers through its doors, a testament to its volunteer

33. Salisbury Hospital Committee, "An Appeal for the Sick and Wounded Soldiers," May 7, 1863, accessed on March 12, 2021, http://docsouth.unc.edu.imls/salisbury/salisbury.html; "Way-side Hospital," *Carolina Watchman* (Salisbury, NC), July 21, 1862. For a report noting bed capacity, see the file of M. Whitehead, CSR, M331, roll 266. See also NC Medical Director Reports, ch. 6, vol. 280, RG109, NA.

34. "The Gun Boat Fund," *Carolina Watchman* (Salisbury, NC), July 21, 1862; "Way-Side Hospital," *Carolina Watchman* (Salisbury, NC), September 1, 1862.

staff, the Hospital Committee's excellent oversight, and, more importantly, its fundraising efforts. Arguably, the Rowan Wayside Hospital proved the most successful of the state's privately operated hospitals established in July 1862. Upon assuming control, the government renamed it Way Hospital No. 3 and retained Whitehead as the surgeon-in-charge on a $100-per-month contract. Whitehead proved quite capable, remaining in the position for the duration of the war.[35]

Wayside hospitals appeared elsewhere as well. Along the coast at Wilmington, a collaborative effort between the Wilmington and Weldon Railroad and local citizens helped place the port city's first wayside hospital into operation. By the summer of 1862, Wilmington had become a central stopover point for furloughed soldiers traveling south from Virginia to other locations within the Confederacy. In early August, the *Wilmington Journal* reported that a "way-side hospital has been fitted up at the Wilmington [and] Weldon Railroad depot, for the relief of sick and wounded soldiers going through."[36]

Private donations helped outfit rooms with cots within the depot, along with several rooms for transient soldiers to bathe. Local physicians volunteered their services at the hospital to address any medical concerns that the soldiers may have had. The heart and soul of the operation rested with the members from the Ladies' Aid Society who volunteered "their kind and generous attention to the wants of the soldiers," which included making them home-cooked meals. The *Wilmington Journal* reported, "The soldiers say that this is the first point where such provision is found on the whole route from Richmond." The society's president, Mrs. Armand J. DeRosset, described her work at the wayside in a letter, "I have been up all morning at the wayside hospital. Some poor fellows wounded ever since June, others sick for three or four months, it is delightful to see the pleasure they express and many of them so grateful for every act of kindness," she informed one family member. DeRosset explained the invaluable service she and the other ladies provided to the transient soldiers, writing, "their wounds are dressed, their faces washed and fed,

35. *Semi-Weekly Standard* (Raleigh, NC), September 6, 1862; "A Card," *Carolina Watchman* (Salisbury, NC), July 6, 1863; Norris, "For the Benefit of Our Gallant Volunteers," *NCHR*, 319-20; M. Whitehead, CSR, M331, roll 266.

36. After arriving at the port city on the Wilmington and Weldon Railroad soldiers from the Deep South traveling home on furlough might continue onward on the Wilmington and Manchester Railroad. The 173-mile-long railroad operated between Wilmington and Manchester, South Carolina. The Wilmington and Manchester Railroad was established initially to transport South Carolina cotton to the port at Wilmington; "Wayside Hospital," *Wilmington Journal* (NC), August 7, 1862.

Mrs. Armand J. DeRosset

(Confederate Veteran)

with little delicacies to those who cannot eat substantially. DeRosset stated that it cost the society approximately $25 a day to provide for the soldiers, "A great deal too much I think," she wrote.[37]

Unlike the Rowan Wayside Hospital, which continued operations until the government assumed control in June 1863, the Wilmington Wayside Hospital closed its doors. The exact date and reason for the closure are unclear, but operations likely ceased because of Wilmington's yellow fever epidemic, which ravaged the city from September through December 1862. Because the wayside depended solely on local physicians and citizen volunteers, much of the volunteer workforce probably evacuated the city out of fear or too engaged caring for ill family and friends. Additionally, authorities quarantined Wilmington, preventing the arrival of troop trains from South Carolina and Virginia. Finally, in March 1863, Governor Zebulon B. Vance ordered a new state-run wayside established at Wilmington.[38]

---

37. "Wayside Hospital," *Wilmington Journal* (NC), August 7, 1862; Jim McCallum, "Hospitals in Wilmington 1861–1865," Robert Cooke Research Files, 2; Mrs. Armand J. DeRosset Jr. to Unknown Family Member, [September 1862], DeRosset Family Papers, SHC/UNC. Mrs. DeRosset wrote the undated letter prior to the battle of Antietam (Sharpsburg), which occurred on September 17, 1862. During the battle, one son, Col. William L. DeRosset, suffered a severe wound in the thigh and hip, and another son, Lt. Armand L. DeRosset, was wounded as well. See Manarin et al., *North Carolina Troops*, 3:487, 566.

38. SO [no number], North Carolina Surgeon General's Office, March 24, 1863, Civil War Collection, Medical Corps, NCOAH; The May 14, 1863, edition of the *Wilmington Journal* reported that the Wilmington Wayside officially reopened on March 31, 1863.

North Carolina Military Institute, Charlotte. The institute's bathhouse served as General Hospital No. 10 until the opening of the larger pavilion-style hospital in Charlotte during the spring of 1864.

(*North Carolina Office of Archives and History*)

Charlotte's First Hospitals

In addition to the Salisbury and Wilmington wayside hospitals, the ever-increasing number of sick and wounded soldiers passing through Charlotte along the railroad spurred the Ladies Hospital Association into action. In early July, the women put into operation Charlotte's first hospital in the washroom of the former North Carolina Military Institute, which at the time the Confederate Medical Purveyor's Department controlled. The July 8, 1862, edition of the Charlotte *Daily Bulletin* reported: "that the proper authorities had granted permission to use the Laboratory connected with the Military Institute . . . as a Soldiers Hospital." The Association used locally raised funds for the "comfort of sick and wounded soldiers" to help set up the hospital.[39]

39. The Ladies Hospital Association of Mecklenburg County, formed in July 1861, originated out of concern for the sick and wounded at Yorktown, Virginia. The organization later changed its official title to Soldiers Aid Society of Charlotte. Hardy, *Civil War Charlotte: Last Capital of the Confederacy*, 25-26, 35; "The Hospital," *Daily Bulletin* (Charlotte, NC) July 8, 1862; In the 1850s a group of Charlotte businessmen founded the North Carolina Military Institute, modeling it after the U.S. Military Academy at West Point. The Institute stood on the site of today's Dowd YMCA, near the rail line that ran parallel to South Boulevard and South Tryon Street.

The establishment of the Charlotte hospital occurred when Surgeon General Samuel P. Moore began to exert greater control over non-Confederate-operated facilities. On July 11, the Confederate Medical Department contracted Dr. Richard K. Gregory, a Charlotte physician and former assistant surgeon in the U.S. Army, to assume responsibility for the new hospital. Gregory's orders specified that he was "assigned to duty with the transient sick of the C.S. Army at Charlotte, N.C. and will without delay take charge of the hospital at that place." Within days of his appointment, Gregory announced the hospital's establishment at the institute in the local newspapers. Short on medical supplies, Gregory requested the local women "send bandages, lint and old linen, as large quantities are necessary" to help alleviate his shortages. "Every day, two members of the Hospital Association went there with supplies of all necessary articles and gave their time and strength to nursing and caring for our men," Lily Long recalled.[40]

The women's invaluable assistance, ministering "to the comforts and necessities of the soldiers," along with the kind donations from others, enabled Gregory to operate the hospital successfully. A reporter from the *North Carolina Whig*, who visited the hospital in late July, wrote, "We were pleased to find everything as well as could be expected under the circumstances, the sick and wounded, are doing well . . . Dr. Gregory deserves great credit, for his untiring devotion to make them comfortable." The hospital located at the military institute was one of two separate hospitals established in Charlotte that July.[41]

Along with the government-operated hospital at the military institute, the town of Charlotte established a privately operated institution. Thomas Dewey, treasurer for the town, announced in the July 7, 1862, edition of the *Daily Bulletin*: "Buildings have been obtained near the Depot for the Hospital and will be in readiness in a few days for the reception of those who may be compelled to lie over in their passage through Charlotte." A closer examination of Dewey's announcement, specifically his reference to "near the Depot for the Hospital," shows it coincided with a report that Dr. Gregory submitted at the end of the year. In January 1863, Gregory published detailed information regarding the hospital's first six months of operation (July to December 1862), as shown in table 5.2. In his report, Gregory distinguished permanent versus transient soldiers admitted to the military institute hospital. Regarding transient soldiers, Gregory

40. Robert K. Gregory, CSR, M331, roll 111; Hines, "Medical Corps," Clark, *Histories*, 4:624; "Notice," *Daily Bulletin* (Charlotte, NC), July 16, 1863; Lily W. Long, "The War Hospitals and the Memorial Association," *Charlotte Observer* (NC), May 20, 1896.
41. *North Carolina Whig* (Charlotte, NC), August 5, 1862.

wrote that they were "received into the Hospital, their wounds attended to and they [were] properly cared for during their stay, varying from one to ten days." Additionally, he included a third category, "Received at the Depot," which were soldiers treated at his office, conveniently located within the Quartermaster Building at the North Carolina Railroad Depot. Gregory noted 814 soldiers "had their wounds dressed at the depot and at my office, and they [were] supplied with fresh bandages and lint." In addition to providing limited medical care, the soldiers at the wayside received a meal and a place to rest overnight.[42]

Table 5.2: Charlotte Hospitals, July–December 1862[43]

Received into Hospital as Permanent Patients	126
Received into Hospital as Transient Patients	183
Received at Depot	814
Total	1,223

Gregory supervised two separate hospitals based on the report—a cause for his abrupt resignation in 1863. The main hospital, located at the North Carolina Military Institute, was the Charlotte General Hospital, later designated as General Hospital No. 10 in April 1863. The buildings near the depot that the town of Charlotte had obtained constituted the wayside hospital. It was the latter hospital, near the depot, that Lily Long references in her 1896 treatise, "The War Hospitals and the Memorial Association." Long remembered, "After a while, the Confederate government took charge of the Wayside hospital and placed it under the care of the Medical department, utilizing the buildings of the Carolina Fair Association." These changes occurred in June 1863, under the authority of then Surgeon Edward N. Covey, Medical Director of North Carolina General Hospitals, when

42. "Acknowledgements," *Daily Bulletin* (Charlotte, NC), July 7, 1862; "Report of Charlotte Hospital," ibid., January 22, 1863. Gregory's report is a few known examples of the patient workload at government-operated hospitals in North Carolina prior to 1863. Salisbury's *Carolina Watchman* periodically published the monthly patient figures for the privately operated Rowan Wayside Hospital.
43. *Daily Bulletin* (Charlotte, NC), January 22, 1863

he began instituting government-operated wayside hospitals within the state.[44]

Because the Confederate Medical Department did not recognize the Charlotte Wayside Hospital, the privately operated institution received no additional funding and relied solely on donations and volunteers to remain operational. By year's end, the hospital struggled to stay open. In early January 1863, Dewey published an announcement in the local newspapers titled, "Appeal to the Chartable." Dewey was pleading for civilian aid, stating, "The funds for the support of the Charlotte Wayside Hospital are exhausted." According to Dewey, the wayside had been "sustained during the year under the supervision of the Board of Commissioners of the Town by donations from our citizens." Dewey's request is important; it proves the existence of a second hospital, separate from the general hospital. Aside from tending to financial worries, the hospital nearly burned in a structure fire. The January 26, 1863, edition of the *Daily Bulletin* reported, "A fire broke out this evening . . . in the Wayside Hospital, but by the timely assistance of the citizens was put out. At any other time of the day or night, it would have consumed several houses."[45]

It is unclear how long the hospital continued to operate before its eventual government takeover. However, a "Business Directory of the City of Charlotte," published in the June 5, 1863, edition of the *Daily Bulletin*, listed only one hospital: "General Hospital No. 10 on the grounds of North Carolina Institute." It is probable that the Confederate Medical Department had already taken over the wayside but had not yet officially opened it. The Confederate government reopened the wayside by the end of June, designating it "Way Hospital No. 4."[46]

The Confederate Medical Department's takeover of the Charlotte Wayside Hospital demonstrated the government's effort beginning the summer of 1862 to institute "a more centralized administration" regarding North Carolina's private and state-operated hospitals. Up to

44. Robert K. Gregory, CSR, M331, roll 111; Lily W. Long, "The War Hospitals and the Memorial Association," *Charlotte Observer* (NC), May 20, 1896. After the war the Mecklenburg Agricultural Society morphed into the Carolina Fair Association. It was in summer 1863, that the society granted the government use of 12-acres at the fairgrounds for the construction of the new pavilion-style hospital. See Chapter 7 for further discussion.
45. "Appeal to the Charitable," *Daily Bulletin* (Charlotte, NC), January 30, 1863; ibid., January 26, 1863.
46. "Business Directory of the City of Charlotte, N.C.," ibid., June 5, 1863; The Confederate government briefly used the No. 4 designation for the Charlotte wayside through August 1863, and monthly returns note the hospital's new identification as No. 6 thereafter. The change was probably necessary to eliminate confusion with Goldsboro's Way Hospital No. 4.

that point, these various institutions existed across the state and Virginia with little to no governmental oversight. Despite the perceived benefits of having a centralized system regarding military hospitals, this transition did not occur seamlessly, as it coincided with a change in the state's executive leadership. North Carolina's newly elected governor, Zebulon B. Vance, believed the state had a fundamental obligation to ensure its soldiers received the best possible health care. A war of ideas soon transpired over ownership of the hospitals; one represented states' rights, and the other stood for the Confederate government's centralized control.[47]

---

47. Pollitt and Reese, "War Between the States, Nursing in North Carolina," *CV,* 27.

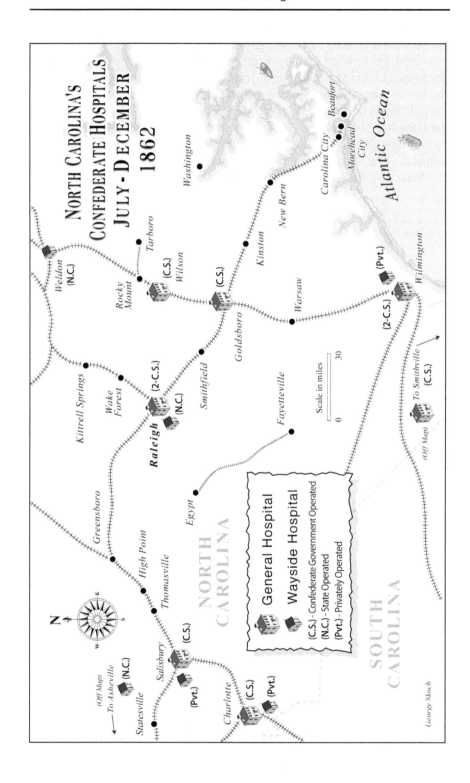

NORTH CAROLINA'S
CONFEDERATE HOSPITALS
JULY - DECEMBER
1862

Atlantic Ocean

Beaufort

Carolina City

Morehead
City

Washington

New Bern

Tarboro

Wilson
(C.S.)

Rocky
Mount

Weldon
(N.C.)

Kinston

Warsaw

Goldsboro
(C.S.)

(Pvt.)
Wilmington

(2-C.S.)

Smithfield

Kittrell Springs

Wake
Forest

Raleigh
(2-C.S.)
(N.C.)

Fayetteville

To Smithville
(C.S.)

(Off Map)

Scale in miles
0   30

Egypt

Greensboro

NORTH
CAROLINA

High Point

Thomasville

N

General Hospital

Wayside Hospital

(C.S.) - Confederate Government Operated
(N.C.) - State Operated
(Pvt.) - Privately Operated

SOUTH
CAROLINA

Salisbury
(C.S.)

(Pvt.)

(Off Map)
To Asheville

Statesville

Charlotte
(C.S.)
(Pvt.)

George Skoch

Chapter Six

1862: Fever, Raids, and Further Growth

"We certainly have a need of something of the kind here."

Summer of Change

During the summer of 1862, the Confederate government began instituting "a more centralized administration" in military hospitals. Up to that point, various hospitals had existed across the Confederacy with little to no governmental oversight. In July, Charles E. Johnson, North Carolina's surgeon general, met with Governor Henry T. Clark to discuss the Confederate War Department's request to transfer all state-operated hospitals in Virginia and North Carolina to the Confederate Medical Department. Clark agreed to the transfer but stipulated that Surgeon Edmund B. Haywood and his two assistants, Dr. William Little and the other identified only as "Miller," would remain at Raleigh's Fair Grounds Hospital once the Confederate government assumed control. Additionally, the Moore Hospital at Richmond would stay under the state's "peculiar protection," ensuring the well-being of the state's soldiers.[1]

Shortly after transferring the state-run hospitals to the government, Surgeon General Johnson tendered his resignation on September 4 to the governor. Johnson believed that "such an officer is no longer needed in the service of the state," considering the recent transfer of the state's military hospitals. According to a colleague,

---

1. Pollitt and Reese, "War Between the States, Nursing in North Carolina, *CV*, 27; Charles E. Johnson to E. N. Covey, June 22, 1862 [3], Vance Papers, NCOAH; Clark further stated that he directed the Peace Institute General Hospital turned over as well. See H. T. Clark to E. B. Haywood, July 11, 1863, NCOAH; Norris, "For the Benefit of Gallant Volunteers," *NCHR*, 323-24; William Little served with Haywood through the Union occupation of Raleigh in April 1865. According to Haywood, Dr. Miller resigned in September 1862. Haywood does note Miller's first name. In all probability, Dr. Miller was William R. Miller, who received a state appointment as assistant surgeon on January 8, 1862. In June 1863, he was appointed as a surgeon in 38th N.C. Militia. Manarin, et al., *North Carolina Troops*, 20:80. See file of E. B. Haywood, CSR, M331, roll 123.

Johnson considered the position "useless in the supposed perfected condition of the Confederate medical organization." Historian David A. Norris suggests, "perhaps the increasing number of Confederate army hospitals in North Carolina and Virginia, where most of the state's soldiers were, made a state-run medical department seem redundant."[2]

Johnson's accomplishments during his time as the state's surgeon general are worthy of praise. Although he served for only 18 months, it was, arguably, the most trying period during the war; Johnson and the North Carolina Medical Department labored to adequately staff and supply the state's newly formed regiments. Johnson established the state-run depot at Richmond and the general hospitals at Raleigh, Petersburg, and Richmond.

In September 1863, Zebulon B. Vance, the former commander of the 26th North Carolina and veteran of the battle of New Bern, began his term as North Carolina's 37th governor. Governor Vance strongly maintained that the surgeon general's position was necessary, so on September 13, he appointed Dr. Edward Warren to fill the vacancy. But because the Provisional Confederate army did not acknowledge the role of North Carolina's surgeon general, Warren had to first resign from the army before accepting a governor's commission with the rank of colonel. The Tyrrell County native felt much "gratification" on his selection. Years later, he wrote, "To be thus elevated to the highest medical position known to my native State, filled my bosom with peculiar pride and exultation." For the duration of the war, Warren faithfully served Governor Vance in carrying out the duties of the surgeon general.[3]

Eight days following Warren's appointment, Governor Vance abruptly changed course. In a brash effort to reassert state control, he ordered his surgeon general to Richmond to secure "the transfer of the hospitals belonging to the state to the state." Vance's decision to retake possession of the hospitals occurred less than a month after Gen. Robert E. Lee's victory at Second Manassas (Second Bull Run) in Virginia. During the two days of heavy fighting, Lee's army suffered

2. *The State Journal*, (Raleigh, NC) September 10, 1862; Warren, *A Doctor's Experiences in Three Continents*, 308; Norris, "For the Benefit of Gallant Volunteers," *NCHR*, 323-24. Surgeon Peter E. Hines, who later became Director of North Carolina General Hospitals, recalled years later that Johnson "resigned because in his judgment there was nothing more for him to do." Hines, "The Medical Corps," Clark, *Histories*, 4:624; Johnson returned to practicing medicine but remained active in soliciting funds and supplies for the North Carolina depot in Richmond.
3. Norris, "For the Benefit of Gallant Volunteers," *NCHR*, 323-24; Warren, *A Doctor's Experiences in Three Continents*, 308.

Zebulon B. Vance, Representative from North Carolina, 35th Congress, 1859. Vance commanded the 26th North Carolina prior to taking office as governor in September 1862.

(*Library of Congress*)

approximately 7,000 wounded. In the battle's immediate aftermath, once again, the Confederate government proved incapable of adequately caring for the wounded.[4]

But Vance's effort did not go over well with Confederate officials. In obedience to Governor Vance's order, Warren appealed to the Surgeon General of the Confederacy, Samuel P. Moore, to restore his authority over the hospitals to North Carolina. According to Warren, Surgeon General Moore "promptly re-transferred them to the state, and formally withdrew all claims to them and to their stores and furniture." However, a few months after North Carolina's repossession of the hospitals, Moore reneged on the agreement by notifying Warren that "he regarded this re-transfer as null and void, and that he did not recognize the right of North Carolina to them, in any manner or form."[5]

These differences between Warren and Moore regarding ownership of the state's former hospitals continued throughout the rest of the year—as the two tangled over whether North Carolina or the Confederate government would ultimately control the hospitals. Raleigh's *Weekly Standard* stated, "This man Moore, we understand, entertains a peculiar dislike for North Carolina." After much debate, Warren, who had apparently met his match in Moore, proposed that North Carolina withdraw the claims, "provided the property was fairly assessed and paid for." Regarding the care of North Carolina's soldiers, Warren further requested that "the privilege of being treated in them was extended to all troops exclusively engaged in the service of the State." Negotiations continued into the spring of 1863, when, finally, Surgeon General Moore agreed to Warren's proposal.[6]

Yellow Fever Epidemic

Unfortunately for Vance, there would be no easy transition into the gubernatorial position. In addition to dealing with the stress of

4. Zebulon B. Vance to Edward Warren, September 22, 1862, Civil War Collection, NCOAH; A. Wilson Greene, *The Second Battle of Manassas* (Fort Washington, PA, 2006), 54. The battle of Second Manassas (Second Bull Run) occurred August 29–30, 1862. Less than three weeks later, Lee's army suffered another 7,750 wounded at the battle of Sharpsburg (Antietam). "Casualties of Battle," Antietam, accessed on February 25, 2021, https://www.nps.gov/anti/learn/historyculture/casualties.htm.
5. "Report of the Surgeon General of North Carolina," November 21, 1864, 13-14, Civil War Collection, NCOAH; Hasegawa, *Matchless Organization*, 119.
6. "Office-Holders—Who Are They?" *Weekly Standard* (Raleigh, NC), March 11, 1863; "Report of the Surgeon General of North Carolina," November 21, 1864, 14, NCOAH; Warren reported that as late as November 1864, the Confederate government had yet to reimburse North Carolina, as agreed upon between Moore and Warren.

governing in wartime, a new type of enemy emerged in the state's largest city, Wilmington. The city's first yellow fever epidemic in 41 years swept down on the port city from September to December 1862. The crisis had reached a dire point by October, necessitating outside medical intervention. Confederate General Pierre G. T. Beauregard, commander of the Department of South Carolina, Georgia, and Florida, volunteered the services of several army surgeons from Charleston, South Carolina. Surgeon William T. Wragg, who authorities considered "the highest living authority on yellow fever," headed the medical team. In addition to the surgeons, four Charleston nurses from the Convent of Our Lady Mercy arrived to render assistance.[7]

The results of the outbreak were devastating. One local newspaper reported that Wilmington was "one vast fever hospital," as the epidemic had spread throughout the city by mid-October. In Company A, 10th Battalion North Carolina Heavy Artillery, the fever claimed the lives of 29 Confederate soldiers. Authorities closed the general hospital located in the former Seaman's Home to any further military use. They transferred patients not infected with the disease to other military hospitals in the area. This enabled doctors to consolidate the ill, both military and civilian, into one hospital. The change created a much more efficient system compared to the "house call" conducted previously by the physicians. Because the number of sick exceeded the hospital's capacity, the Seaman's Society rented out the storage room beneath the hospital to the Medical Department to allow for more patients. To assist in consolidation efforts, the local quartermaster provided two ambulances for transporting the sick to the army hospital.[8]

---

7. SO No. 176, Hdqrs. Dept. of South Carolina, Georgia, & Florida, dated September 28, 1862, see file of William T. Wragg, CSR, M331, roll 274; Leora H. McEachern and Isabel M. William, comps., "The Prevailing Epidemic—1862," *LCFHSB* (November 1967), vol. 11, no. 1, 18. The Sisters of Mercy's work at Wilmington during the epidemic is the only documented instance of the Catholic nurses serving in a North Carolina Confederate hospital. However, from July 1862 through May 1863, a New York convent did serve briefly in the Union hospitals located at Beaufort and New Bern. See Phillip Gerard, "During the Civil War, Sisters of Mercy Provide Medical Attention," accessed on December 1, 2020, https://www.ourstate.com/sisters-mercy/. Also see, *OR*, 9:410, for Sisters of Charity at Beaufort.
8. "The Hospital," *Wilmington Journal* (NC), October 21, 1862; Jim D. Brisson, "City of the Dead: The 1862 Yellow Fever Epidemic in Wilmington, North Carolina," 17, accessed on November 1, 2019, http://commons.lib.jmu.edu/cgi/viewcontent.cgi?article=1022&context=mhr; Seaman's Society, Citizens or Business Papers, M346, roll 914, RG109, NA; F. C. Frazier, "Additional Sketch Tenth Battalion," Clarks, *Histories*, 4:326.

Throughout the epidemic, the hospital was under the direction of Surgeon Wragg. A reporter from the *Wilmington Journal*, who visited the hospital shortly after Wragg's arrival, found "the wards clean, airy, and comfortable, and the bedding and other things in the purest condition." Impressed by the hospital's favorable conditions, the newspaper echoed the authorities' plan of using the hospital to consolidate the ill into one location, writing, "[T]he majority of the sick in town would be better off at the Hospital than home."[9]

As authorities in Wilmington confronted the epidemic, yellow fever spread down the Cape Fear River to Smithville. Doctor William G. Curtis, a local physician there, wrote years later, "During the prevalence of Yellow Fever in Smithville nearly all the troops were ordered to leave town and camp outside in the forest and there to await orders." On October 6, Dr. Ashton Miles, senior staff surgeon for the District of the Cape Fear, notified Medical Director Crowell at department headquarters in Goldsboro: "The Fever is on the increase here, and the inhabitants say the first time in the memory of many." The deadly disease had incapacitated several of the area's assigned surgeons. At the Smithville General Hospital, the fever had stricken both the surgeon-in-charge, Dr. Milton W. Ritenour, and his assistant, Dr. Robert H. Worthington. Surgeon John F. Heath, surgeon-in-charge of the Fort Caswell Post Hospital, lay near death, and Surgeon William S. Strudwick was absent without leave, presumably ill as well. Only Surgeon Miles at Smithville, who served as the staff surgeon for Brigadier General Gabriel J. Rains, and Assistant Surgeon Robert F. Lewis, stationed on Oak Island at Fort Caswell, remained to care for the infected soldiers in the area.[10]

Desperately short on medical officers, Surgeon Miles temporarily stepped down from his staff duties and took charge of both the general hospital and Fort Caswell Post Hospital in Smithville. Committed to the care of the sick, Miles informed Medical Director Crowell, "If Gen. Rains moves his headquarters from here, I shall be obliged to remain as I would not leave the hospital without attendance." Miles requested Crowell send two additional surgeons, emphasizing "acclimated officers," meaning he required only physicians previously exposed to the fever.[11]

---

9. "The Hospital," *Wilmington Journal* (NC), October 13, 1862.

10. Ashton Miles to Nathaniel S. Crowell, October 6, 1862, Ashton Miles, CSR, M331, roll 177; Strudwick submitted his resignation on January 1, 1863, by reason of ill health. The War Department approved his request two weeks later. See William S. Strudwick, CSR, M331, roll 238. See also, William S. Stradwick, CSR, M331, roll 238.

11. Ibid.

The situation worsened for Surgeon Miles in Smithville during the following days. On October 7, the fever claimed the life of Surgeon Heath. In October, Assistant Surgeon Lewis reported 69 cases of varying degrees of fever at the Fort Caswell Post Hospital. On October 11, Private William B. B. Thompson, who the doctor noted "was convalescing from Typhoid fever, but think he died from Yellow fever . . . he had black vomit," a sign of stomach bleeding caused by the illness.[12]

In addition to devastating the medical staff, the epidemic had disrupted the normal supply requisition process, thus creating a critical shortage of medicines and other necessities. On October 14, Miles notified Crowell of the desperate need at Smithville. The departure of Medical Purveyor Thomas J. Boykin at Wilmington and the subsequent death of the individual left in charge of the medical stores to yellow fever exacerbated the supply issues. Miles reported, "Major Young has by order of Gen. Rains taken possession of the storehouse and contents, but there is no one to issue medicines, etc." Anxious for assistance, Miles wrote, "What am I to do in the matter? The Fever shows no abatement."[13]

Surgeon Ashton Miles began the war as a surgeon in the 1st Louisiana Zouave Battalion and later served as the senior staff surgeon for the District of the Cape Fear. Miles died of yellow fever in Smithville on November 2, 1862.

(From the collection of Jonathan O'Neal, MD)

Miles' October 14 correspondence proved his last, as he too became stricken with the fever. For almost two weeks he lay bedridden

12. "Report of Sick and Wounded," October 1862, CSR, John F. Heath, M331, roll 123. Lewis' reference to typhoid stems from the fact that in addition to yellow fever, he treated eight members of the garrison on Oak Island for typhoid.
13. Ashton Miles to Nathaniel S. Crowell, October 14, 1862, Ashton Miles, CSR, M331, roll 177.

in the hospital, finally succumbing to the deadly illness on November 2. With Miles' death, the remaining surgeon in the Smithville area, Dr. Lewis, crossed over from Oak Island and assumed senior staff responsibilities for the various Smithville hospitals. A soldier from Fort Caswell, Sergeant John N. Bennett, recalled years later the final day of Surgeon Miles' life. Bennett's commander on Oak Island had ordered his transfer to the Smithville hospital due to him suffering a relapse of typhoid fever. Bennett remembered when he first arrived at the hospital "there were several cases of yellow fever in the place." The hospital steward ordered Bennett to report to Miles, who he discovered bed-ridden. In recalling Miles' semi-conscious state, Bennett wrote, "I do not suppose that he knew what ailed him as he was taken that day." But before his death, Miles sent word to Bennett "to not stay there but to go home," an order the sergeant quickly obeyed. "I immediately set about making ready, but as all were trying to take care of themselves, there was no chance to get any assistance from any of them." As Bennett departed the hospital he observed: "three or four cases of yellow fever within forty yards of the Hospital and one lady died with it before I left."[14]

The onset of cooler temperatures by late November brought an end to the deadly epidemic. On December 1, David G. Worth of Wilmington informed Governor Vance: "The health of Wilmington is good, there are no traces of yellow fever left." In the end, the yellow fever epidemic of 1862 proved quite deadly, of the 1,550 reported cases, an estimated 654 Wilmington citizens died. Included in the death toll was Julia E. Capps, a nurse at General Hospital No. 4. The mother of a small child, Capps had contracted the deadly disease in October while working in the hospital. At Smithville, a reported 18 individuals died of the disease. In addition to the cost of lives, the secondary effects of the epidemic had a detrimental effect on Confederate military logistics, as the late Surgeon Miles had earlier reported. With the port of Wilmington closed to blockade runners, the critical Confederate supply lifeline to Virginia, the Wilmington and Weldon Railroad, had all but ceased to operate.[15]

14. John N. Bennett, 13, Confederate Veteran Talks, Latimer House Archives, Lower Cape Fear Historical Society, Wilmington, North Carolina.
15. Nurse Capps' mother later applied for her back pay due. See file of B. L. Capps, Citizens or Business Papers, M346, roll 140; The total number of deaths that occurred during the epidemic remains unclear. *The Wilmington Journal* estimated that 654 people died, but according to Jim D. Brisson, that figure "is certainly a conservative estimate because they based their estimates almost solely on the number of internments at Wilmington's local Oakdale Cemetery." To further complicate matters, the cemetery's overseer, Charles Quigley, died on October 17, and his assistant contracted yellow fever shortly thereafter, so the records of Oakdale became unreliable. Brisson, "City of the Dead: The 1862 Yellow Fever Epidemic in Wilmington, North Carolina," 7.

Foster's Raid

More than disease occupied North Carolina Confederate officials in late 1862. In December, Maj. Gen. John G. Foster, the Union commander at New Bern, set out on a raid toward Goldsboro, with nearly 10,000 men and 40 artillery pieces. Foster's movement coincided with Maj. Gen. Ambrose E. Burnside's attack on the Confederate position at Fredericksburg, Virginia, and thereby prevented either Confederate force from reinforcing the other. Foster sought to sever the critical supply link between Virginia and the port of Wilmington by destroying the Wilmington and Weldon Railroad Bridge spanning the Neuse River at Goldsboro. After destroying the bridge over the Neuse, Foster proposed a follow-on attack on Wilmington with the cooperation of the U.S. Navy.[16]

Foster's first serious action occurred at Kinston, where Confederate commander, Brigadier General Nathan G. Evans had established a main defensive line just south of the Neuse River across from the town. On December 14, the Federals attacked the Confederate position with an overwhelming force of more than five to one. The brief battle came to an end when Confederate units occupying the left of the line suddenly withdrew toward Kinston, and after crossing the Neuse River Bridge, mistakenly set it on fire. In doing so, they effectively cut off the remaining Confederate forces, and consequently, the Federals captured approximately 400 Southerners. Foster's men crossed the river and entered Kinston, where they discovered the town's remaining defenders had unceremoniously withdrawn. Evans withdrew his remaining Confederates two miles beyond Kinston where he briefly established a new battle line, before continuing toward Goldsboro.[17]

On the eve of the battle, North Carolina Surgeon General Edward Warren had gained Governor Vance's permission to leave for Kinston, where he might render assistance as needed. Warren arrived just in time to witness the Confederates withdraw. After learning of the presence of wounded at a house on the main road beyond Kinston, Warren "hastened to it, hoping to be able to render assistance to the surgeon in charge." When he arrived at the home, Warren discovered that a "Mississippi surgeon" had taken the abandoned house to use as a temporary hospital. According to Warren, the two surgeons "worked harmoniously together until every wounded man had been properly

16. J. G. Foster to H. W. Halleck, December 10, 1862, *OR*, 18:476-77; Newsome, The Fight for the Old North State, 13. Foster was promoted to major general of volunteers in July 1862.
17. *OR*, 18:55-56; Barrett, *The Civil War in North Carolina*, 144.

attended to" and sent toward Goldsboro in wagons and ambulances. The two medical officers discovered a horse and buggy at the home, which they used to hasten in the direction of Goldsboro.[18]

With the Confederates in retreat toward Goldsboro, Foster paused for the night at Kinston to allow time to care for his wounded, parole the Confederate prisoners, and either destroy or send back to New Bern captured Confederate war material. The Federal surgeons established a temporary hospital in the unfinished Methodist Episcopal Church building, as well as the Nicols Store, where one local "witnessed hundreds of hands and feet already severed from the bodies standing in buckets at this hospital." It was during the night that Foster received word of the Federal defeat at Fredericksburg and that Confederate reinforcements were en route to eastern North Carolina.[19]

Despite the troubling news from Virginia, Maj. Gen. Foster decided to continue the march toward Goldsboro and "do as much damage to the railroad as possible before returning to New Bern." Late on December 15, a small Federal cavalry contingent encountered an enemy force at Whitehall (present-day Seven Springs) under the command of Brigadier General Beverly H. Robertson. After a spirited engagement, Robertson withdrew into Whitehall destroying the bridge across the Neuse River. The Federal contingent returned to the main column encamped several miles away, but not before unsuccessfully trying to destroy the ironclad *Neuse* under construction at Whitehall.[20]

---

18. Warren, *A Doctor's Experience*, 323-25. The author used Warren's timeline noted in his autobiography for when he arrived at Kinston (December 14). Governor Vance issued an executive order on December 15, the day after the battle, directing Warren to "immediately visit Goldsboro and Kinston for the purpose of giving such attention to the wounded." Vance's order conflicts with Warren's statement that he arrived on the day of the battle. It is probable that Vance first gave the order verbally and Warren acted upon it, and a written order was issued the following day. Zebulon B. Vance to Edward Warren, December 15, 1862, Civil War Collection, Medical Corps-N.C. Troops, NCOAH.

19. *OR*, 18:56, 110; Committee, "Our Christian Heritage: Faith through the Ages," Queen Street United Methodist Church, November 19, 2006, 3; "The Methodist Episcopal Church," *Kinston Free Press* (NC), September 2, 1899; W. and H., "Kinston in the Sixties," *Carolina and the Southern Cross*, 2; The March 12, 1895, edition of the *Raleigh News & Observer* reported, "The old building, corner of Queen and King Streets, once a Confederate hospital, is now the headquarters for the Oettinger Bros."; Cliff Tyndall, *Threshold of Freedom: Lenoir County, NC During the Civil War* (Kinston, NC, 2005), 66; Barrett, *Civil War in North Carolina*, 144; R. V. Archbell, "Whitfield House," *Carolina and the Southern Cross* (November 1912), vol. 1, no. 1 , 2; After Foster's departure from Kinston, Col. Sion H. Rogers returned to the town, discovering the paroled soldiers and wounded prisoners. *Weekly State Journal* (Raleigh, NC), December 24, 1862.

20. *OR*, 18:56; Barrett, *The Civil War in North Carolina*, 144.

The following day, Foster resumed the march, where he encountered the Confederates again at Whitehall, but this time, "in force, with infantry and artillery" posted on the opposite side of the river. To deceive Robertson that he intended to rebuild the bridge and cross, Foster deployed an infantry brigade "to make a strong fight." However, Foster's subsequent decision to overwhelm the Confederate defenders with artillery, enabled the main column of Federal infantry to continue its movement toward Goldsboro unmolested, whereby the night of December 16, the Federals encamped eight miles shy of their objective. Early the next morning, Foster renewed his movement toward the railroad bridge at Goldsboro, while sending detachments to destroy key points along the Wilmington and Weldon Railroad at Mount Olive, Dudley Station, and Everettsville.[21]

Meanwhile, Surgeon General Warren and his Mississippi companion arrived at Goldsboro. Weary from the events of the previous 24 hours, the two physicians retired to the Gregory Hotel for some needed rest. After a restful slumber, Warren awoke to the town "in a state of great confusion," and his "old and valued friend," Maj. Gen. Gustavus W. Smith, commander of the Department of North Carolina and Southern Virginia, had recently arrived from Virginia with reinforcements. Eager to report the situation to Governor Vance, as well as begin preparations for the reception of sick and wounded, Warren hurriedly caught a train to Raleigh.[22]

On the afternoon of December 16, Warren, along with Raleigh's mayor, W. H. Harris, met to discuss plans "for the purpose of receiving and providing for the comfort of the wounded at the battle of Kinston." Mayor Harris appointed a committee of 50 citizens to coordinate all the necessary actions. Confident the mayor had affairs in order, Warren immediately returned to Goldsboro. The next day in Raleigh, the mayor, and the group met again to formalize their plan for the pending arrival of the wounded. The group designated four primary subcommittees, each with a key task necessary to carry out the plan. The group assigned the First Committee with the task of acquiring "a Depot for the wounded, to provide homes and accommodations for the same." The remaining three committees were responsible for the reception of the wounded, supplying ambulances, and providing nurses.[23]

Upon arriving back at Goldsboro, Warren sought a meeting with Maj. Gen. Smith. After a "warm reception and exchange of pleasantries," Warren later recalled the general said to him, "You are

21. *OR*, 18:57; Barrett, *The Civil War in North Carolina*, 145-46.
22. Warren, *A Doctor's Experience*, 326-27.
23. "Public Meeting," *Weekly State Journal* (Raleigh, NC), December 24, 1862.

the very man I was looking for. You must serve as my medical director. Get to work at once, and make arrangements for a severe fight tomorrow." Because Warren held a state commission and was not an officer in the Confederate army, Smith's unorthodox directive created an uncomfortable situation for Warren as North Carolina's surgeon general. According to Warren, he conveyed to the general that his proposal was "out of the question," based on his state commission and that "the Confederate surgeons would reject my authority and hate me for the remainder of their lives." Warren was correct in his assumption in that it did seemingly question the competence of the attending surgeons in Goldsboro. It is understandable why these army officers would have questioned Smith's directive subordinating them to Warren.[24]

Warren later noted that "certain of my confrères" protested Smith's decision, but the department commander quickly silenced them. Warren recalled how the general verbally disciplined them, writing: "I am here in the interest of North Carolina, and I shall exercise the discretion of utilizing the best materials which I find around. You must either resign or submit to my orders. I shall arrest the first man who manifests the slightest spirit of insubordination." The commanding general's "decided words had the desired effect," ending the matter. Smith dismissed all concerns regarding military protocols and immediately appointed Warren as medical director.[25]

Warren did not disclose in his autobiography his preparations with the mayor of Raleigh nor what actions he undertook regarding Goldsboro's hospitals prior to the battle, electing instead to summarize the circumstances in one sentence. He stated, "I devoted myself diligently to the work of preparing the medical department for its expected labors." However, Warren used no such brevity when it came to expressing how he abused his authority to personally humiliate a Confederate surgeon. On the day of the battle, Warren crossed over the Neuse River with Maj. Gen. Smith and other members of his staff "to be better able to take in the whole situation and to act intelligently in regard to it." Warren remembered, "As we rode along, I met one of the

24. Warren, *A Doctor's Experience*, 326–27; Warren failed to mention that Major General Smith already had a medical director, Dr. Edwin S. Gaillard. Gaillard, who had contracted smallpox on December 10, was in Richmond's Howard's Grove General Hospital at the time of the battle of Goldsboro Bridge for treatment. Gaillard resigned the following year on account of his "protracted absence . . . on an extended furlough for sickness." In the interim, Surgeon Thomas H. Williams was the acting medical director. See the file of E. S. Gaillard, CSR, M331, roll 100.
25. Warren, *A Doctor's Experience*, 326-27. Based on extant records, no such written order exists appointing Warren as the medical director. If Warren's account is correct, then likely, Smith's order was only verbal.

surgeons who had shown so rebellious a spirit in regard to my appointment, and, by way of testing his metal as well as of making him useful, I ordered him to follow me." According to Warren, the unidentified surgeon "bowed in acquiescence, and turned his horse toward the expected battlefield." [26]

As the party advanced toward the sounds of battle the Confederate line soon appeared, which Warren later described as "one of the most magnificent panoramas . . . that can be conceived of." The Confederate infantry stood at the ready, "their battle flags floating in the wind, and in the distance were large masses of the enemy with the 'star-spangled banner' waving over them." The infantry battle line Warren observed was that of Brigadier General Thomas L. Clingman's brigade, tasked with defending the important railroad bridge over the Neuse. Colonel Stephen D. Pool supported Clingman's infantry from the opposite side of the river with a mixture of red infantry (artillery serving as infantry) and a battery of artillery.[27]

According to Warren, Maj. Gen. Smith was so "impressed by the spectacle" that he paused to observe the moment, unknowingly placing himself and the other staff officers in danger with their exposed position and his "conspicuous" uniform. The situation soon became a little too unnerving for Warren's fellow surgeon. In a comical flair, Warren later wrote: "I turned to observe its effects upon my ambitious confrère, but only in time to catch a glimpse of his horse's tail as he disappeared . . . Whether his nerves were too weak for the racket or important business called him to the rear, I never knew, but I could not refrain from directing the attention of my comrades to his disappearance and joining in the hearty laugh with-which they greeted it."[28]

Clingman's infantry engaged the advancing Federals, and despite offering stiff resistance, the attackers forced the Confederate defenders to withdraw to the opposite bank, and soon thereafter, succeeded in setting fire to the bridge. Considering the mission accomplished, Foster ordered his force to begin their return march back to New Bern. Fortunately for the Confederates, the bridge received minimal damage,

26. Ibid. It is unclear who the surgeon was that Warren was referring to in his short passage. In the absence of the department medical director, Dr. Benjamin F. Fessenden, chief surgeon of Brig. Gen. Nathan G. Evans' division, would have been the next senior-ranking Confederate medical officer. However, it is unknown whether Fessenden was present on the day of the battle.
27. Warren, *A Doctor's Experience*, 326-27; Barrett, *The Civil War in North Carolina*, 146-47.
28. Warren, *A Doctor's Experience*, 327-28.

and within several weeks, trains were once again crossing the Neuse River.[29]

Both during and after the battle of Goldsboro Bridge, the Confederates evacuated the wounded to the hospitals at Goldsboro. Although the Female College General Hospital was capable of caring for up to 200 patients, Surgeon Richard H. Shields, who inspected the hospital shortly after the battle, noted, "[T]here are now 273 in Hospital, which crowds these wards . . . large number of these patients are from the battlefield near this place." The unexpected influx of wounded men required Assistant Surgeon John S. Murphy, who had just recently been assigned as the surgeon-in-charge, to submit an emergency requisition for needed medical supplies "in consequence of there not being sufficient quantities on hand." To compensate for the hospital's crowded conditions, the surgeons transferred a dozen patients to private residences. In addition to overcrowding, the inspection found the hospital's overall sanitary conditions lacking, suffering from what Surgeon Shields described as "a want of cleanliness." However, Shields' report noted neither Surgeon Murphy nor his staff was responsible for the hospital's poor state, as "the hospital is so much crowded with wounded men."[30]

To alleviate the situation, the medical officers at Goldsboro evacuated an undetermined number of wounded to Raleigh. The *Weekly State Journal* reported a train arrived at Raleigh from Goldsboro with 60 Rebels, and later, another carried 23 wounded. The reception and admittance to the city's hospitals without issue is a testament to the prior planning of Surgeon General Warren and Mayor Harris. Although the number of evacuated wounded received at Raleigh following the battles of Kinston and Goldsboro Bridge were slight, far greater casualty numbers would tax these facilities later in the war. Accordingly, the operations in 1862 provided a vital dress rehearsal in civil-military cooperation.[31]

29. Don Blair, "Foster's Raid," accessed on January 4, 2021, https://www.ncpedia.org/fosters-raid.

30. "Requisition for Medical and Hospital Supplies," December 25, 1862, John S. Murphy, CSR, M331, roll 184. Murphy's request included 50 spittoons, which indicates he allowed patients to chew tobacco while in the hospital; Richard S. Shields to Edwin S. Gaillard, December 27, 1862, see the file of John S. Murphy, CSR, M331, roll 184. Major General Smith later reported a combined total of 268 wounded from the engagements at Kinston, Whitehall, and Goldsboro Bridge. *OR*, 18:110.

31. "Affairs at Goldsboro," *Weekly State Journal* (Raleigh, NC), December 24, 1862; The December 20, 1862, edition of Raleigh's *Daily Progress* reported, "A number of our wounded have since arrived, and been properly cared for, the most of them being accommodated at the hospitals."

Second Round of Wayside Hospitals

Earlier in November, Governor Vance approved Surgeon General Warren's initiative to establish a series of state-run wayside hospitals "in the immediate neighborhoods of the principal lines of travel." Warren envisioned the state-run waysides as more than just a location for the sick and wounded. The surgeon general wanted the state's facilities "thrown open" to also permit friends and family members. In his report to the governor, Warren noted the excellence of North Carolina's state-run waysides compared to others within the Confederacy. Warren wrote, "[T]he immediate friends of soldiers who come to nurse their stricken relatives or to bear their dead bodies homeward are permitted to enjoy the advantages of these institutions upon the daily payment of a moderate sum—such as would not procure a single scanty meal elsewhere."[32]

Warren selected Raleigh as the location for the North Carolina Medical Department's first wayside. The surgeon general's choice pleased many of the city's residents, who had expressed a need for such a hospital for quite some time. One such resident, Ms. Louisa Hill, a member of the DeRosset family, was intrigued upon reading her sister's account about the success of Wilmington's wayside. In August, wishing that Raleigh had something similar, she had written: "Your account of the wayside hospital was especially interesting. We certainly have need of something of the kind here." Because Raleigh served as a key railroad center in the state, transient soldiers often lingered awaiting further transportation. It was "good Samaritans in the neighborhood of the depot" that tended to the needs of these soldiers. "Br[other] John Palmer's kind wife [and] others have taken seven or eight at a time kept them as long as they chose to stay [and] nursed them most kindly," Hill wrote. "But sometimes we would hear there were soldiers there detained without food . . . my sister C. would send off dinner as soon as possible."[33]

Warren's decision to establish a wayside at Raleigh also pleased the editor of city's *Standard*, William W. Holden, who "had urged the necessity of this more than a year ago." The newspaper formally announced in its December 3, 1862, edition that Warren had "determined to establish a wayside hospital at the place near the

32. Warren, "Report of the Surgeon General of North Carolina," November 21, 1864, 6, NCOAH.
33. Louisa Hill to My Dear Sister, August 11, 1862, DeRosset Family Papers, SHC/UNC.
34. "Way Side Hospital," *Weekly Standard* (Raleigh, NC), December 3, 1862; "Mechanic's Association," *Daily Standard* (Raleigh, NC), March 27, 1866; "The Ladies Wayside Hospital," *Weekly Raleigh Register* (NC), January 28, 1863.

Central Depot [North Carolina Railroad Depot], and the ladies of the City are busily engaged in aiding him to raise the funds." Warren acquired the use of the John W. Williams & Co. Building and assigned Assistant Surgeon Richard Anderson to superintend the required work to convert it into a hospital. Reporters from the *Weekly Raleigh Register* visited the hospital shortly after its opening. They "were pleased to see that the ladies were manifesting a good deal of interest in the hospital" and that there were "admirable arrangements made for the sick and wounded travailing soldiers." In honor of these women, the hospital was unofficially known as the Ladies Wayside Hospital.[34]

On December 5, Assistant Surgeon William C. Roberts replaced Anderson as the surgeon-in-charge. Roberts, a close associate of Warren from the start of the war, had previously served with him in the North Carolina navy. At that time, former Hospital Steward Roberts served at the navy's hospital on Ocracoke Island. Good fortune followed Roberts' association with the future state surgeon general. He later received a state commission and an assignment at the Raleigh wayside, a position he held for the remainder of the war. Hospital Steward E. J. Purifoy assisted Roberts at the Ladies Wayside Hospital.[35]

With the Raleigh wayside proceeding to plan, Surgeon General Warren selected Weldon, a stop on the much-traveled Wilmington and Weldon Railroad, as the site for the next state-run wayside hospital. On December 5, Warren relieved Dr. Anderson of his duties at the Ladies Wayside Hospital, ordering him to Weldon where he was to identify "a proper place for a Way Side Hospital." Anderson selected the Weldon Methodist Church as the location for the hospital. At the time, the small wooden chapel was located on a grassy square between the Weldon Hotel and the banks of the Roanoke Canal, conveniently located near the railroad depot. Once the hospital's staff removed the benches from the little church, the new wayside had a patient capacity of approximately 50 beds.[36]

In late November 1862, the Asheville Town Board called to the attention of Mayor E. J. Ashton the "importance of establishing a

---

35. "Wayside Hospital," *Daily Progress* (Raleigh, NC), March 9, 1863; William C. Roberts, CSR, M331, roll 213; E. J. Purifoy, CSR, M270, roll 88. Prior to serving at the wayside hospital, Purifoy served in the 13th Battalion Light Artillery.

36. SO [no number], NC Surgeon General's Office, December 5, 1862, Civil War Collection, Medical Corps-N.C. Troops, NCOAH; Mrs. Ida Wilkins, "History of the Weldon Methodist Church," 4, accessed on October 4, 2019, https://nccumc.org/history/files/Weldon-UMC-History.pdf; Weekly hospital reports submitted to the medical director's office in Raleigh note that throughout the period, April 1863–March 1865, the capacity at Weldon Wayside fluctuated between 30 and 50. NC Medical Director Reports, ch. 6, vol. 280, RG109, NA.

wayside hospital for the sick and wounded soldiers at this place." The Asheville Wayside Hospital was atypical of others in North Carolina during the Civil War because there was no railroad, only dirt roads that connected the small mountain town with the rest of the state. However, it was along those roads that soldiers, some of whom were sick or recovering from wounds, traveled while on furlough. Additionally, despite Asheville's seemingly remoteness from the remainder of the state, the town was important to Confederate interests in western North Carolina.[37]

A postwar article titled, "First Army Hospital Established in 1862," notes Asheville authorities obtained the use of the building previously "operated as a boarding house in connection" with the women's college in the town. It is unclear whether the authorities acted on their own initiative or worked in conjunction with Surgeon General Warren. The fact, Warren notes the presence of the wayside hospital in his "Report of the Surgeon General of North Carolina" to Governor Vance later in 1864, suggests that if the state did not originally open it, at an undetermined date Asheville authorities turned over control to the North Carolina Medical Department.[38]

Warren, in just a few short weeks, had established two, three if you count Asheville, wayside hospitals, with plans for more in the works. Justifiably, Warren wrote with pride, "I claim for North Carolina the credit, if not of originating this admirable system, at least so of amplifying and perfecting it." He had taken an already successful idea and improved upon it, not just for individual soldiers but also their families. The addition of the Asheville, Raleigh, and Weldon hospitals increased the total number of wayside and general hospitals in North Carolina to 14, with slightly more than half being Confederate government institutions, as displayed in table 6.1. Although the government established no new hospitals in North Carolina during the latter half of 1862, during that same period, both private organizations and the state government opened hospitals to fill the void the struggling Confederate Medical Department had left.

---

37. Warren, "Report of the Surgeon General of North Carolina," November 21, 1864, 6, NCOAH.
38. During the Civil War, the closest railroad to Asheville was located at Morganton, approximately 60-miles away; "First Army Hospital Established in 1862: Confederate Soldiers Treated in Present Cherokee Inn," *Asheville Citizens-Times* (NC), February 1, 1919. At some point after the opening of the wayside hospital, probably, late 1863 or early 1864, the army established a second hospital, the Sorrel General Hospital, on the south side of Asheville's Public Square, known today as Pack Square. Existing documents refer to it as a general hospital, not a wayside. The Sorrel General Hospital operated for the duration of the war until Federal raiders destroyed it in April 1865.

Table 6.1: North Carolina General and Wayside Hospitals, December 1862[39]

Location	Designation	Authority
Charlotte	Charlotte General Hospital	Dept. of N.C. and So. Virginia
Goldsboro	Female College Gen. Hospital	Dept. of N.C. and So. Virginia
Raleigh	Fair Grounds Gen. Hospital	Dept. of N.C. and So. Virginia
Raleigh	Peace Institute Gen. Hospital	Dept. of N.C. and So. Virginia
Wilmington	Wilmington General Hospital	Dept. of N.C. and So. Virginia
Wilmington	Marine General Hospital	Dept. of N.C. and So. Virginia
Salisbury	Military Prison Hospital	Dept. of N.C. and So. Virginia
Smithville (Southport)	Smithville General Hospital	Dept. of N.C. and So. Virginia
Wilson	Wilson General Hospital	Dept. of N.C. and So. Virginia
Asheville	Asheville Wayside Hospital	N.C. Medical Department
Charlotte	Charlotte Wayside Hospital	Privately Operated
Raleigh	Ladies Wayside Hospital	N.C. Medical Department
Salisbury	Rowan Wayside Hospital	Privately Operated
Weldon	Weldon Wayside Hospital	N.C. Medical Department

In addition to his successful opening of the waysides, Warren received an early Christmas present from the North Carolina General Assembly, which passed "An act for the relief of our sick and wounded soldiers" on December 22. Under the direction of Surgeon General Warren, the bill authorized Governor Vance to act in several key areas deemed essential to improving the medical care provided to the soldiers. To enable these efforts the legislature appropriated $300,000 annually to the governor for use at his disposal.[40]

The December 22 act required the appointment of an officer, with the rank of major, who was to reside at Richmond to assess the needs

39. Data from *Daily Bulletin* (Charlotte), July 7, 1862; SO No. 85, Hdqrs. Dept. of NC, April 19, 1862, ch. 2, vol. 259, RG109, NA; *North Carolina Standard* (Raleigh, NC), November 31, 1861; Hill, "Sketch of General Hospital No. 8," 1, DU; Micks to Hines, November 18, 1863, Letters Sent, General Hospital No. 4, ch. 6, vol. 399, RG109, NA; SO No. 116, Hdqrs. Southern Coastal Defense Dept., June 24, 1861; Brown, *The Salisbury Prison*, 22; *Daily Journal* (Wilmington, NC), June 18, 1861; Valentine, *The Rise of a Southern Town*, 34; Crews and Bailey, eds., Records of the Moravians in North Carolina, 12:6,488; *Asheville Citizen-Times*, February1, 1919; *Daily Bulletin* (Charlotte), July 7, 1862; *Weekly Standard* (Raleigh), March 27, 1862; *Carolina Watchman* (Salisbury, NC), July 21, 1862; SO [no number], NC Surgeon General's Office, December 5, 1862, Civil War Collection, NCOAH.

40. "Captions, of the Acts and Resolutions passed by the General Assembly of North Carolina, December 22, 1862," *Weekly Standard* (Raleigh, NC), December 31, 1862.

of the state's sick and wounded soldiers and provide them with supplies. The officer was responsible for also assisting deserving soldiers in obtaining furloughs or discharges, as well as managing the North Carolina Depot of Medical Stores. Additionally, the legislation authorized the appointment of "two or more surgeons" to visit the camps and hospitals in North Carolina and Virginia hospitals, both within and outside of Richmond.[41]

To address the shortage of medical officers within the state's regiments, the bill authorized the governor to fill existing vacancies until Confederate authorities selected permanent appointees. It also required the surgeon general to establish a depot at Raleigh or elsewhere "for the collection of medical supplies, hospital stores, clothing, etc." To confront smallpox, especially considering the recent epidemic at Wilmington, the legislature directed the surgeon general "to provide proper medical attention for soldiers returning to State, afflicted with smallpox or other communicable diseases." The December 22 act's final directive "empowered" Surgeon General Warren with the authority to establish waysides where he deemed necessary.[42]

The North Carolina General Assembly's strong actions, not only with words but with money, demonstrated the state's commitment to the welfare of its soldiers. The backing of both the governor and legislature, and a strong operating budget, allowed Surgeon General Warren to implement initiatives he considered necessary. And Warren would do just that during the first months of 1863, as he sought to expand the network of state-run waysides. However, the winds of change would once again blow when the Confederate War Department would consider further regulations in 1863 designed to improve the army's hospital situation, thereby granting Confederate Surgeon General Samuel P. Moore more centralized control. Despite the forthcoming positive changes, the power struggle between two surgeon generals—Warren and Moore—would only continue as the latter began to exercise even more control of the Old North State's hospitals.

---

41. Ibid.
42. Ibid. Warren's establishment of the two waysides during the first week of December suggests that he may have been aware of the pending legislation, thus providing him the driving force to execute his wayside hospital initiatives.

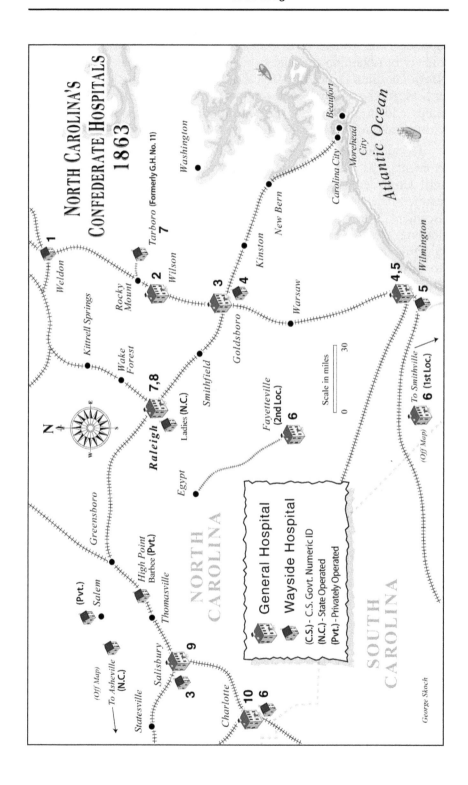

North Carolina's Confederate Hospitals 1863

General Hospital
Wayside Hospital

(C.S.) - C.S. Govt. Numeric ID
(N.C.) - State Operated
(Pvt.) - Privately Operated

Scale in miles
0   30

N

NORTH CAROLINA

SOUTH CAROLINA

Atlantic Ocean

George Skoch

Chapter Seven

1863: A Busy New Year

"Let the soldiers be cared for."

On December 31, 1862, the Union Army of the Cumberland and the Confederate Army of Tennessee clashed at the battle of Stones River, at Murfreesboro, Tennessee. The bloody three-day engagement (December 31, 1862 – January 2, 1863) resulted in an estimated 24,000 casualties. Although the Federal commander, Major General William S. Rosecrans, controlled the battlefield in the end, his army paid a heavy price for victory. The nearly 13,000 dead and wounded left the Union army battered, and months would pass before Rosecrans would once again begin active campaigning. For the struggling Confederacy, the defeat at the battle of Murfreesboro was just one more disaster that had befallen Confederate forces in the final quarter of 1862. General Robert E. Lee's costly Maryland campaign the previous September resulted in more than 10,000 dead and wounded while failing to accomplish anything strategically.[1]

However, the fortunes of war had not yet abandoned the Confederate cause, and despite significant setbacks in the west, Lee's resounding victory at Fredericksburg in December 1862 sparked a glimmer of hope and gave a much-needed morale boost for Confederate forces in the east. While Lee's Army of Northern Virginia may have had a renewed vigor, several weeks had passed since the Confederate success at Fredericksburg, and by early January, the human cost of the victory—more than 4,000—lay wounded in the Petersburg and Richmond hospitals. North Carolina Surgeon General Warren reported that in Richmond's Chimborazo Hospital No. 3 alone 279 Tar Heels were recovering from the battle. Although North Carolina was no longer responsible for the hospitals in Virginia housing Tar Heel patients, Warren felt compelled to aid the state's wounded. He responded by dispatching a team of physicians from the North Carolina Medical Department to Virginia to seek out "wherever

---

1. American Battlefield Trust, "Stones River," accessed on December 16, 2021, https://www.battlefields.org/learn/civil-war/battles/stones-river; National Parks Service, "Antietam," accessed on December 16, 2021, https://www.nps.gov/anti/learn/historyculture/casualties.htm.

the sick and wounded were to be found and services could be rendered." Warren's team ensured the distribution of the food items and medical supplies that the state and its generous civilians provided to various hospitals caring for North Carolina soldiers.[2]

Tarboro General Hospital

As Warren focused on relief efforts in Virginia, events soon heated up in the Old North State in early 1863. With the onset of winter, the opposing forces in Virginia suspended campaigning, thus presenting an opportunity for Lee to "put his idle forces to good use during the colder months." In February, as part of a general consolidation of subordinate departments following Lee's victory at Fredericksburg, the Confederate War Department assigned Lieutenant General James Longstreet to command of the Department of North Carolina and Southern Virginia. The recent transfer of the U.S. Army's Ninth Corps that same month from the Army of the Potomac to the Virginia Tidewater concerned Longstreet as it potentially threatened the area's rich agricultural resources, which included northeastern North Carolina. Longstreet responded by planning operations in both states designed to allow commissary officers to gather food and forage stocks before the enemy destroyed or confiscated the valuable supplies.[3]

To enable supply convoys to operate in North Carolina without fear of Federal attacks, Longstreet ordered demonstrations against Union-occupied New Bern and Washington. The veteran general sought to pin down the Federals behind their defensive perimeters at these two locations, thereby gaining freedom to operate unmolested. Longstreet chose Major General D. H. Hill to command the Carolina phase of the operation. Although deemed an outcast from Lee's Army of Northern Virginia, Hill remained widely popular in North

2. Chris Mackowski and Kristopher D. White, *Simply Murder: The Battle of Fredericksburg*, December 13, 1862 (El Dorado Hills, CA, 2012), 100; "Wounded North Carolinians in the Hospitals in Richmond," *Daily Progress* (Raleigh, NC), January 9, 1863; Warren, *A Doctor's Experience*, 309-10. Two of the surgeons employed by Warren were Eugene Grissom and David T. Tayloe. Early in the war, Tayloe played a significant part in hiding the valuable Hatteras Lighthouse Fresnel Lens from the U.S. government to prevent further use. See Kevin Duffus, "Historic Lighthouse Lens' Odyssey Continues," accessed on December 3, 2021, https://coastalreview.org/2021/04/historic-lighthouse-lens-odyssey-continues/.

3. Newsome, *The Fight for the Old North State*, 14; William R. Trotter, *Ironclads and Columbiads: The Civil War in North Carolina, The Coast* (Winston Salem, NC, 1989), 191. Longstreet also ordered operations against Union-held Suffolk, Virginia, thereby enabling Confederate authorities to collect commissary items in that region of the state.

Carolina. Beginning in mid-March, Hill executed a three-prong attack on the fortified port city of New Bern. Although one Confederate infantry brigade achieved minor success against a point on the city's outer defenses, Hill's remaining two brigades (one infantry and one cavalry) failed to achieve their objectives, forcing the general to withdraw his forces.[4]

After the failure at New Bern, Hill quickly turned his attention to Washington, 40 miles to the north, where he hoped to have better luck against the 1,200-man garrison stationed there. One step ahead of Hill, the Federal commander at New Bern, Maj. Gen. Foster, personally traveled to Washington upon receiving intelligence of Hill's planned move, and by the time Hill's forces had reached the town, the Federals had strengthened the town's existing fortifications and constructed a series of forts and blockhouses protecting the approaches to Washington, by both land and water. Hill's orders from Generals Lee and Longstreet favored a limited engagement, advising against a general attack because of the anticipated heavy losses normally associated with attacking a prepared defense. By March 30, Hill's Confederates, which now included an additional infantry brigade and field artillery, had Washington under siege. But by mid-April, the unimpeded ability of the U.S. Navy to resupply the besieged garrison with supplies and further reinforcements showed the futility of such an operation. More importantly, the spring campaign in Virginia had begun, and Lee's Army of North Virginia required every available rifle. Despite Hill's solid reputation as a fighter, the lack of a supporting naval element and an insufficient number of ground forces hampered any effort on his part to conduct the required offensive operations to retake either of the coastal towns. However, Hill's actions against both points did provide the necessary time and freedom for gathering critical war supplies.[5]

It was during Hill's brief siege against Federal-controlled Washington that Confederate authorities identified the need for a general hospital at the river town of Tarboro. Unlike Hill's demonstration against New Bern, where the Atlantic and North Carolina Railroad enabled the timely evacuation of any sick and wounded back toward Kinston and Goldsboro if required, Confederate medical personnel encountered greater challenges during the

4. *OR*, 8:950-51; Barrett, *The Civil War in North Carolina*, 151-55; White, *New Bern and the Civil War*, 77-88; Report of Maj. Gen. D. H. Hill, March 16, 1863, *OR*, 18:188-89. Longstreet and Hill were West Point classmates and old friends.
5. *OR*, 18:1,007; Barrett, *The Civil War in North Carolina*, 156-61; Newsome, *The Fight for the Old North State*, 15; During Hill's operation commissary officials successfully obtained approximately "35,000 pounds of bacon, and a great deal of corn, potatoes, and lard." Barrett, *The Civil War in North Carolina*, 157.

subsequent siege of Washington. The closest general hospital was at Wilson, an approximately 50-mile overland trip, and, unlike New Bern, there was no connecting railroad, only dirt roads. Tarboro's selection as a hospital site mitigated transportation issues by providing both water and rail accessibility. Although the road distance between Tarboro and Washington was about 45 miles, the Tar River allowed for an alternate transportation means to evacuate the sick and wounded from the latter. The Tarboro Branch Line, a short 14-mile length railroad, connected the town to Rocky Mount and the strategically important Wilmington and Weldon Railroad. These transportation advantages made Tarboro ideal as an alternate supply and medical base for aiding ongoing operations and as a post to support those Confederate units garrisoned permanently in the area. On the other hand, it was risky to maintain a hospital at Tarboro because of its proximity to Union-occupied New Bern, Plymouth, and Washington, and the likelihood of Federal raids.[6]

On April 6, Hill contracted Dr. Laurence A. Stith, a Wilson physician, to oversee the newly established Tarboro General Hospital (later designated General Hospital No. 11). Stith began the war as an assistant surgeon in the 2nd North Carolina, however, a terrible accident while assisting the wounded from a train to an ambulance resulted in the amputation of his arm. He subsequently resigned from the service in July 1862 and returned to North Carolina, where he resumed his private practice. On April 25, the *Tarboro Southerner* reported that authorities had recently established "a hospital for sick and disabled soldiers" in the town. Confederate authorities simply occupied the Tarboro Female Academy, which the army previously used for such purposes after the battle of New Bern. Hospital reports indicate the Tarboro General Hospital was small in comparison to the other general hospitals in North Carolina, fluctuating weekly between 40 and 50 beds, except during the week of May 14 when Stith reported 67 beds occupied.[7]

---

6. During the Confederate siege of Washington, river steamers and small schooners traveled down the Tar River from Greenville and Tarboro to Boyd's Ferry, approximately eight miles north of Washington. In addition to utilizing the river, supply wagons ran continually from Greenville, Tarboro, and Kinston. See "From the North Carolina Soldiers," *Fayetteville Semi-Weekly* (NC) April 16, 1863. The strategically important garrison at Fort Branch, along the Roanoke River, was located approximately 20 miles north of Tarboro.

7. L. A. Stith, CSR, M331, roll 237. Stith's service record suggests that he served at the hospital for only a brief period (April–July 1863) before Medical Director Covey reassigned him to Goldsboro; *Highland Recorder* (Monterey, VA), August 9, 1901; Manarin, et al., *North Carolina Troops*, 3:380; *Tarboro Southerner* (NC) April 25, 1863; Consolidated Weekly Reports, Week Ending May 14, 1863, NC Medical Director Reports, ch. 6, vol. 280, 2, RG109, NA.

War of Words

During the same time period of Hill's operations at New Bern and Washington, a debate took place in the Raleigh newspapers regarding the North Carolina Medical Department's wayside hospitals. Sources indicate that not all North Carolinians endorsed Governor Zebulon B. Vance and his surgeon general's initiative to establish wayside hospitals, especially because the Confederate government had recently assumed control of all the state-run general hospitals. One outspoken critic, John W. Syme, editor of the *Raleigh Register*, fervently questioned the state legislature's recent appropriations for such purposes: "Our new Surgeon General we are glad to hear, by dint of hard and unceasing efforts, makes a shift to find something to do, though not much, in an office which his distinguished predecessor thought useless, and therefore resigned, the State Hospitals having all been turned over to the Confederate Government, thus saving the expense of providing for them by the state."[8]

One aspect of the state-operated wayside facilities particularly rankled the editor. In addition to caring for transient soldiers, Warren allowed the wayside hospitals to feed and board family members of soldiers. Syme's reference to the Ladies Wayside Hospital in Raleigh as nothing more than a "Tavern Hospital" quickly resulted in a war of words with other Raleigh newspapers. In a piece titled, "Destructive Heartlessness," William W. Holden, editor of the *Standard*, defended Warren's actions, writing: "The pittance which is thus expended will never be felt by the State, and if it should, what of it? Let the soldiers be cared for. Let the wives and sisters of our soldiers . . . be given lodging."[9]

Despite Syme's criticism, Governor Vance directed his surgeon general to immediately establish a wayside hospital at Wilmington. On March 28, Warren ordered Assistant Surgeon John L. Neagle "to proceed to Wilmington without delay, and make arrangements for opening a 'Wayside Hospital' at that place." Neagle obtained use of a "large brick building" located near the depot, belonging to Wilmington merchant, Mr. W. B. Edmonson. Neagle successfully carried out Warren's order, and by March 31, the hospital was operational with a capacity of 50 beds. In addition to providing medical care at the hospital and lodging "in very comfortable beds," Neagle sent warm coffee to the depot with the arrival of every train, along "with a basket

---

8. "Profession and Practice," *Weekly Raleigh Register* (NC), March 4, 1863.
9. "Destructive Heartlessness," *Semi-Weekly Standard* (Raleigh, NC), March 20, 1863.

full of good things for their benefit." Neagle proudly announced, "The Wayside Hospital has been established by those noble patriots, Gov. Vance and Dr. Warren, Surgeon General for the State of N.C.," declaring it a permanent institution— "in for the war."[10]

Neagle's notice appeased Wilmington's citizens, who had been clamoring for the hospital to reopen for months. Delighted by the news, the *Wilmington Journal* reported the reestablishment of the wayside hospital "will relieve the anxiety of our lady readers." After the opening of the Wilmington Wayside Hospital, editor Syme predictably continued his negative attacks. The editor believed "it wasteful" when it came to matters concerning legislative appropriations for Surgeon General Warren's medical department, writing, "there is no necessity for a Surgeon General's department for North Carolina. The three hundred thousand dollars, if expended will be thrown away." However, Governor Vance did not waiver in his support for the well-being of the soldiers and in his confidence in Warren, who he steadfastly supported for the remainder of the war.[11]

North Carolina Soldiers' Home

In addition to establishing more wayside hospitals, Warren initiated efforts to establish a facility at Richmond solely for North Carolinians serving in Virginia. The forward-thinking surgeon general envisioned a facility where "the sick, wounded, and delayed soldiers and their friends, going to and from the army, will here find lodging and food." The Soldiers' Home contained 31 beds, but it could accommodate 50 soldiers. Warren supplied the home with "bacon, beans, apples, etc. from North Carolina." The *Fayetteville Observer* reported, "The table is good, and the soldier is better fed here for nothing than he is as the hotels for $6 and $8 a day." The Soldiers' Home proved an initial success, but it became increasingly difficult to sustain as supplies became scarce throughout the Confederacy due to the ongoing war. Despite its short-lived success, the Soldiers' Home

10. SO [no number], NC Surgeon General's Office, March 24, 1863, Civil War Collection, Medical Corps, NCOAH; *Wilmington Journal* (NC), May 14, 1863; See also Walker Meares, "The Wilmington Wayside Hospital," Eliza Parsley Papers, SHC/UNC. Neagle submitted a supply requisition on March 31, 1863, for 50 beds, 500 pounds of straw, and other necessary articles. See John L. Neagle, Unfiled Papers and Slips Belonging in Confederate Compiled Service Records, M347, roll 292, RG109, NA; The hospital was located at the corner of Front and Red Cross streets. Neagle previously served as a hospital steward in 49th North Carolina. On January 22, 1863, he received an appointment as an assistant surgeon in the state medical department. Manarin, et al., *North Carolina Troops*, 20:81.
11. *Raleigh Register* (NC), April 4, 1863, and May 2, 1863.

offered another example of the state government's commitment to the Confederate soldiers.[12]

Fire Destroys the Former First North Carolina Hospital

In April, a fire at the 1st North Carolina Hospital at Petersburg resulted in the total loss of the facility. Although no longer the responsibility of the North Carolina Medical Department, its destruction came as a shock to many due to its significance as the state's first general hospital established during the war. On April 11, at approximately 9:30 p.m., hospital attendants observed smoke and fire rising through the building's second floor. Despite efforts by staff to put out the fire, smoke compelled them to leave the building. At the time of the fire, the hospital contained no patients, as it had been undergoing repairs and thorough cleaning for several weeks. Fekarim M. Henderson, assistant surgeon-in-charge of the hospital, listed the loss to the Confederate government as "some 250 hospital shirts, 250 hospital drawers, 25 bed sacks, one cooking stove complete and some few other articles, all the other property belonged to the State of North Carolina."[13]

An investigation into the fire pointed to a nurse at the hospital, Morgan, an enslaved worker, who committed the act of arson after being "persuaded to do so by others, and another boy, also employed in that hospital." Morgan had hoped to prevent hospital administrators from discovering that he had stolen the "clothes of soldiers who died in the hospital." All in a matter of one day, Morgan pled guilty, the court sentenced him to death, and before sunset, officials carried out the hanging in the city's jail yard. The fate of his alleged accomplice is unclear. Accounts note that authorities held him "in jail pending investigation and trial."[14]

Confederate Negro Hospitals

Simultaneous with the opening of the Wilmington Wayside Hospital by the North Carolina Medical Department, the Confederate

---

12. *Semi-Weekly Standard* (Raleigh, NC), March 20, 1863; "The North Carolina Soldiers' Home," *Fayetteville Observer* (NC), September 21, 1863. The Soldiers' Home is comparable to the contemporary United Services Organization (USO) facilities that support traveling U.S. service members at select international airports.

13. "Fire in Petersburg—North Carolina Hospital Burnt," *Greensboro Patriot* (NC), April 16, 1863; Peter E. Hines to Wm. A. Carrington, April 13, 1863, and April 16, 1863, Peter E. Hines, CSR, M331, roll 128. See Appendix B for transcribed copies of the letters.

14. Ibid.; "Petersburg," *Richmond Dispatch* (VA), July 28, 1883.

government opened a hospital strictly reserved for impressed Blacks in the Lower Cape Fear region. At the beginning of the war, military authorities called upon enslavers to assist in the construction of North Carolina's coastal defenses. These loyal Confederates first volunteered the use of their enslaved workers out of a sense of patriotic duty or with the understanding they would receive compensation. As the war progressed, the Confederate government implemented an impressment program to meet the ever-increasing labor demands. In North Carolina, the army assigned enslaved, free Blacks, and Lumbee Indians to various strategic points, with the majority sent to Wilmington and the Lower Cape Fear River region.[15]

Enslaved individuals endured long hours of physically demanding work, laboring for a government that "routinely failed to provide adequate food, shelter, and medical care" for its own soldiers, much less its slaves. Although the enslaved had toiled on plantations as field hands, the construction of an earthen fortification, such as Fort Fisher, required, "if not greater effort, then at least more consistent and sustained effort." Because of these concerns, North Carolina slaveholders frequently complained of the neglect and abuse their slaves endured while laboring for the army. The government's perceived lack of concern regarding these workers led one Chatham County group of slaveholders to employ the services of a local physician to oversee the enslaved, thereby mitigating anxieties.[16]

The government recognized the need to guarantee the health and wellness of enslaved workers lest it incur the risk of financial liability and otherwise anger slaveowners. As early as 1862, the Confederate Engineer Bureau, the principal employer of most impressed laborers, established a hospital in Richmond specifically for the Black labor force. Strangely, the Richmond hospital did not fall under the management of Surgeon General Moore; the Engineer Bureau ran it with the assistance of contracted physicians. The earliest known such government-operated facility, commonly called "Negro Hospitals," in North Carolina was located at Wilmington. In early May 1863, Dr. Benjamin F. Fessenden, Maj. Gen. William H. C. Whiting's chief

---

15. A discussion of Confederate slave impressment goes beyond the scope of this study. For the best account see, Jaime A. Martinez, *Confederate Slave Impressment in the Upper South* (Chapel Hill, NC, 2013); During the Civil War, the North Carolina government considered Robeson County Indians (now known as Lumbee) as free people of color. And, as such, authorities often forced them to perform hard labor for the Confederacy. See NC Dept. of Natural and Cultural Resources, "Lumbee Legend," accessed October 10, 2021, https://www.ncdcr.gov/blog/2012/07/03/lumbee-legend. Other locations in North Carolina included: Fayetteville, Goldsboro, Kinston, Raleigh, and Weldon.

16. Martinez, *Confederate Slave Impressment*, 45-46, 48; ibid., 50, 65.

surgeon, reported, "There is a good deal of sickness amongst the Negroes, and no surgeon or asst. surgeon can be spared from this post to attend them." Strangely, despite the large number of Blacks working in the Wilmington area, the Confederate Engineer Bureau had not yet established a hospital there.[17]

Alarmed by Fessenden's report, Whiting ordered an African American hospital established immediately. Because of a shortage of medical officers within the command, Fessenden contracted a local physician, Dr. Alexander R. Medway, to superintend operations at the hospital, with the justification: "[F]or the Negroes employed by the government on the fortifications and defenses of Wilmington, N. C." Officially identified as the "Negro Hospital," the government leased the upper two stories of a building belonging to Henry von Glahn. Documents indicate the government maintained the building as a hospital through April 1864; however, the hospital's presence is undetermined beyond that date.[18]

To assist Dr. Medway, in October 1863, Whiting's headquarters detailed Private John Giles of the 10th Battalion North Carolina Heavy Artillery as a hospital steward for the Negro Hospital. Other than Giles, Medway probably utilized Blacks, nearly all enslaved persons, as nurses, cooks, and general laborers at the hospital. Not surprisingly, Medway's hospital was not a priority when resources were scarce, which required him to seek alternative sources beyond Wilmington. The commander of the Confederate arsenal at Fayetteville, Lieutenant Colonel Frederick L. Childs, reported to authorities in Wilmington that Medway had sent a "free Negro" to purchase articles for his hospital. Unfortunately, supply shortages were not Medway's only challenge. On December 29, Medway complained to Whiting's newly assigned medical director, Dr. Archibald M. Fauntleroy—Surgeon Fessenden had taken over the newly established general hospital at Fayetteville—regarding the removal of his nurses and cooks, who, likely, authorities in Wilmington reallocated to work on the local defenses. He also requested of Fauntleroy that "a more commodious building be secured" to accommodate the increased workload at the hospital. The few extant documents pertaining to the hospital indicate Medway's workload was anything but easy.

17. Prior to Medway's assignment at the Negro Hospital, the government had contracted him to serve at the Fort Fisher Post Hospital. Alexander R. Medway, CSR, M331, roll 175. Medway's service record contains the May 12, 1863 copy of his contract. For additional documents pertaining to Medway's service at the Negro Hospital, see Citizens or Business Papers, M346, roll 675, under the names, A. Medway, and A. R. Medway.
18. Alexander R. Medway, CSR, M331, roll 175; H. von Glahn, Citizens or Business Papers, M346, roll 1,058, RG109, NA.

*Surgeon Holt F. Butt served in the 3rd Virginia and 32nd North
Carolina before his assignment as the surgeon-in-charge of
Wilmington's General Hospital No. 5 in December 1863.*

(Courtesy of Marshall W. Butt Jr.)

According to one, at a cost to the government of 50 cents per individual, Medway examined a total of 1,079 enslaved patients who had been impressed to work on the Wilmington defenses. Medical Director Fauntleroy succeeded in retaining Medway's hospital attendants but failed at obtaining a larger building. This is likely because the government already had plans to put into operation a second Black hospital in the area, which would mitigate the stress on Medway's small facility.[19]

* * *

By July 1863, with Charleston besieged by Federal forces, Wilmington "assumed the mantle of the most important seaport in the Confederacy." In addition to the city's position strategically, the opening of the wayside and Black hospitals also signified the growing importance of Wilmington as a hospital center within the Old North State. The Lower Cape Fear region was now home to three general hospitals, a wayside, and a separate hospital for African Americans.[20]

The hospital expansion at Wilmington was not an isolated event, as other wayside hospitals were soon to emerge in the coming months. Coinciding with the expansion at Wilmington and elsewhere, the Confederate Medical Department was beginning to assert more control over the military hospitals throughout the Confederacy. In North Carolina, this change would bring further hospital growth throughout the remainder of the year, but it also caused closures, and along with it, controversy.

19. John Giles, CSR, M270, roll 83; F. L. Childs to A. M. Fauntleroy, February 14, 1864, Letters, Gen. W. H. C. Whiting's Command, 1863–1865, Randall Library, University of North Carolina Wilmington (UNCW). Hereafter cited as Whiting's Letters; Negro Hospital Report, December 14, 1863, Whiting Letters, UNCW; A. R. Medway, Citizens or Business Firms, M346, roll 675, RG109, NA; A. R. Medway to A. M. Fauntleroy, December 29, 1863, Whiting Letters, UNCW; The second Negro Hospital, which was located at Smithville, opened in early 1864.
20. Fonvielle, *The Wilmington Campaign*, 118.

Surgeon Edward N. Covey, who had served in the U.S. Army before the war, was the first medical director of North Carolina general hospitals. As a Marylander, some North Carolinians considered him an outsider.

(Confederate Veteran)

Chapter Eight

1863: Government Centralized Control

"If it is the Genl.'s wish I will have it reestablished."

Authority over North Carolina's General Hospitals

In March 1863, the Confederate War Department issued General Orders No. 28, creating the position of medical director of hospitals, thus relieving all responsibility and control of general hospitals from commanders in the field. Confederate Surgeon General Samuel P. Moore selected Surgeon Edward Napoleon Covey as the Medical Director of North Carolina General Hospitals. Covey would prove an able administrator and have a profound impact on the Confederate hospital system in the state. However, certain aspects of his personality and leadership style would ultimately limit his tenure. A Maryland native and former U.S. Army medical officer, he had served since the start of the war in the Trans-Mississippi Theater, primarily in New Mexico and Texas. In February 1863, the War Department reassigned Covey to Major General Earl Van Dorn's cavalry command in Spring Hill, Tennessee. At the time of Covey's appointment to North Carolina, the Confederate government operated 11 general hospitals in the state, administered by 26 medical officers and 256 attendants.[1]

Covey discovered, upon assuming the director's duties, that none of the government-operated general hospitals had been assigned a

---

1. SO No. 80, AIGO, dated April 2, 1863, see the file of Edward N. Covey, CSR, M331, roll 63; Covey attended the University of Maryland, followed by a two-year hospital internship in Paris. Upon his return to the United States, Covey served as a surgeon in the U.S. Army. While assigned at Salt Lake City, Utah, Covey aided the escape of several young Mormon girls, resulting in religious leader Brigham Young placing a $10,000 bounty out for him. Following the Civil War, Covey traveled to London, where he remained for almost a year before returning to Maryland. In 1869, a yellow fever epidemic spread throughout the South, and Covey, the dedicated physician, volunteered his services in Houston, Texas. Unfortunately, one day while treating the ill, he caught the fever and died the next day. Covey died at the age of 40, leaving no family. "Dr. Edward N. Covey, of Maryland," in *CV* (June 1926), 34:210; Consolidated Weekly Reports, April 1863, North Carolina Medical Director Reports, ch. 6, vol. 280, 1, RG109, NA.

numerical identification, as required under Confederate law. According to records, Covey corrected the noncompliance by the end of April (see table 8.1). While it is unclear what method Covey used to assign each hospital a number, it is certain, however, he did not base it on when authorities established an individual institution—a common contemporary misconception. For example, the Department of North Carolina established Wilson's General Hospital No. 2 almost a year after Smithville's General Hospital No. 6 began operation. It appears that Covey assigned individual numbers based on geographic location, beginning in the northeast at Weldon and working south along the railroad to Wilmington and Smithville, and then west along the railroad to Charlotte.[2]

Table 8.1: Numeric Designation of North Carolina General Hospitals[3]

Location	Designation Week Ending April 14, 1863	Designation Week Ending April 30, 1863
Weldon	Weldon General Hospital	General Hospital No. 1
Wilson	Wilson General Hospital	General Hospital No. 2
Goldsboro	Female College Gen. Hospital	General Hospital No. 3
Wilmington	Wilmington General Hospital	General Hospital No. 4
Wilmington	Marine General Hospital	General Hospital No. 5
Smithville (Southport)	Smithville General Hospital	General Hospital No. 6
Raleigh	Fair Grounds General Hospital	General Hospital No. 7
Raleigh	Peace Institute General Hospital	General Hospital No. 8
Salisbury	Military Prison Hospital	General Hospital No. 9
Charlotte	Charlotte General Hospital	General Hospital No. 10
Tarboro	Not Reported	General Hospital No. 11

Government Wayside Hospitals

Two weeks after Covey's arrival, a major shift in policy occurred regarding government-operated hospitals in North Carolina. On May 1, 1863, the Confederate Congress passed an amendment to the September 1862 act that directed Surgeon General Moore "to establish, in addition to pre-existing hospitals, a number of wayside hospitals."

2. See Consolidated Weekly Reports, NC Medical Director Reports, ch. 6, vol. 280, RG109, NA; Another aspect regarding the numeric identification of North Carolina hospitals is that several North Carolina hospitals changed locations or designation (wayside versus general) during the war. For example, General Hospital No. 1 in Weldon later became Way Hospital No. 1 in June 1863; however, the medical director did not use the No. 1 designation again until August 1864 to identify the newly established hospital at Kittrell.
3. Data from Consolidated Weekly Reports, April 1863, North Carolina Medical Director Reports, ch. 6, vol. 280, 1-3, RG109, NA.

Despite Moore's earlier hesitancy in accepting the concept, waysides proved beneficial in the care of soldiers and gained extreme popularity in those cities or towns where thousands of transient soldiers traveled along the railroad. Covey, as medical director, was responsible for implementing the Confederate Medical Department's wayside program within North Carolina. He immediately began executing by converting existing smaller general hospitals to waysides, assuming control of privately or state-operated hospitals, or, simply creating new waysides when necessary. Beginning in late June and continuing throughout July, Covey re-designated the smaller general hospitals at Tarboro and Weldon into waysides and assumed control of the once privately operated waysides at Charlotte, Wilmington, and Salisbury. In late July, Covey converted the camp hospital at Goldsboro's fairgrounds into a wayside. In less than 60 days, Covey had implemented the wayside concept by establishing six hospitals within North Carolina's network of government hospitals.[4]

Salem and Barbee Wayside Hospitals

In addition to the newly established government wayside hospitals, during the summer of 1863, local citizens established privately operated waysides at Salem and High Point. In early June, the Salem Soldiers' Relief Society established a wayside for the "accommodation of sick soldiers." According to Carrie L. Fries, whose mother volunteered at the hospital, the society first used the woefully inadequate former Salem post office for a short period before seeking a more accommodating building. Through the generosity of the Moravian Church, the society obtained permission to take over the town hall as a more suitable location. The June 23, 1863, entry from the Moravian Church congregational diary included the following: "The Soldiers' Relief Society having . . . taken possession of the Town Hall with the consent of the members of this body for the purpose of establishing a way-side hospital and lodging place for soldiers passing thro' town." The Church Board did charge the women rent "in consideration of the benevolent object of the society."[5]

---

4. Cunningham, *Doctors in Gray*, 38-39; See the Compiled Service Records of surgeons Marcellus Whitehead and Lawrence A. Stith, M331, RG109, NA; See Consolidated Weekly Reports, NC Medical Director Reports, ch. 6, vol. 280, RG109, NA.
5. C. Daniel Crews and Lisa D. Bailey, eds., *Records of the Moravians in North Carolina*, vol. 12: 1856–1866 (Raleigh, NC, 2000), 6,488; Carrie Fries' fiancé, Captain Charles F. Bahnson, a Confederate soldier and Salem native, wrote that the "ladies then cleaned up town hall for use as a hospital." Sarah Benson Chapman, ed., *Bright and Gloomy Days: The Civil War Correspondence of Captain Charles Frederic Bahnson, a Moravian Confederate* (Knoxville, TN, 2003), 52.

Barbee Hotel, High Point, N.C., ca. 1900. Later called Bellevue Hotel. In September 1863, locals established the privately operated Barbee Wayside Hospital. During the war's final two months, Confederate authorities redesignated it General Hospital No. 3.

(Courtesy of High Point Historical Society, High Point, N.C.)

The Salem Wayside Hospital, like its counterpart at Asheville, was different from the other waysides in the state due to the inaccessibility of the railroad. Despite the hospital's unconventional location, it operated successfully at least through the summer of 1864. A hospital report from July 1864 shows that many transient soldiers cared for at the hospital were from the Piedmont region; but some individuals from as far away as Kentucky, Tennessee, and Texas found comfort there as well.[6]

Later that summer, a second privately operated wayside, the Barbee Hotel Wayside Hospital, began operations at High Point on September 1, 1863. The former three-story Barbee Hotel across from the North

6. "Salem Wayside Listing of Meals Served," June–July [no year], Zebulon Vance Papers, NCOAH. After analyzing the individual service records of those soldiers listed as receiving meals at the hospital, the author has determined the correct date of the document is June 2 to July 15, 1864.

Carolina Railroad depot served as the site for the hospital. William G. Barbee and his wife acquired the hotel in 1858, and established "an outstanding institution" in the few years preceding the Civil War. One post-war account notes that two months after the hotel's conversion into a hospital, Governor Vance issued an order exempting Mr. Barbee "from duties in the home guard so long as he keeps an open house for wounded soldiers." The Barbees and Dr. Andrew J. Sapp, a local physician who served as the surgeon-in-charge, managed the day-to-day operations of the hospital with the assistance of a team of doctors and volunteers from the community. The Barbee Wayside continued to operate privately until the government seized it in March 1865. According to the hospital's patient registry, the wayside cared for approximately 5,000 sick and wounded soldiers during its 18 months of operation.[7]

Table 8.2 below displays that by September 1863 a total of 10 wayside hospitals existed in North Carolina: six managed by the Confederate government; two operated by the state surgeon general; and the remaining two were privately operated hospitals. It is unclear why Way Hospital No. 2 is absent from the medical director's consolidated weekly hospital reports during April 1863 and April 1864, as Medical Director Covey assigned the government numbering system through Way Hospital No. 7. Documents indicate the Confederate Medical Department did not use the Way No. 2 designation until May 1864, when the government assumed control of the newly opened state-operated wayside hospital at Greensboro. One possible reason for the absence of Way No. 2 is that when Covey began the takeover of private and state-run hospitals during the summer of 1863, he may have initially planned on incorporating the Ladies Wayside Hospital at Raleigh into the government system. But because North Carolina Surgeon General Edward Warren took a great interest in the wayside—it was the first state-run wayside established—based on the hospital's location in the capital city, Covey acquiesced, opting not to push the issue.[8]

---

7. "Old High Point Hotels Have Interesting History," *Greensboro Daily News* (NC), January 9, 1933; *High Point Enterprise* (NC), March 24, 1935; Mrs. J. S. Welborn, "A Wayside Hospital," *CV* (March 1930), 38:95-96; "Doctor Left His Mark on Early Community," Richard McCaslin, *News & Record* (Greensboro, NC), March 24, 1994; Bradly R. Foley and Adrian L. Whicker, comps., "The Wayside Hospital Registry, Part 13 Final Edition," *Guilford Genealogist* (Winter 2013), 40:36. The hospital registry contains entries for 5,795 patients; however, compilers Foley and Whicker have determined that although the registry contains listings for 5,795 patients, their analysis concludes that the number is actually less than 5,000.
8. See Consolidated Monthly Report, Month of May 1864, NC Medical Director Reports, ch. 6, vol. 280, RG109, NA.

Table 8.2: North Carolina Wayside Hospitals, September 1863[9]

Location	Designation	Authority
Weldon	Way Hospital No. 1	C.S. Med. Dept.
Not Used	Way Hospital No. 2	C.S. Med. Dept.
Salisbury	Way Hospital No. 3	C.S. Med. Dept.
Goldsboro	Way Hospital No. 4	C.S. Med. Dept.
Wilmington	Way Hospital No. 5	C.S. Med. Dept.
Charlotte	Way Hospital No. 6	C.S. Med. Dept.
Tarboro	Way Hospital No. 7	C.S. Med. Dept.
Asheville	Asheville Wayside Hospital	N.C. Med. Dept.
Raleigh	Ladies Wayside Hospital	N.C. Med. Dept.
High Point	Barbee Wayside Hospital	Privately Operated
Salem	Salem Wayside Hospital	Privately Operated

Plans for Further Construction

By the summer of 1863, the hospital system required larger, more efficient general hospitals to meet the ever-increasing numbers of sick and wounded soldiers arriving from Virginia, notably at Raleigh and at points farther west along the railroad toward Charlotte. Beginning in June, Covey initiated what would become his greatest contribution as the state's medical director—the construction of pavilion-style hospitals at Charlotte, Raleigh, and Salisbury. The design consisted of separate single-story buildings with multiple windows on each side, allowing for excellent lighting and cross ventilation. Although Covey was no longer serving in the state when the hospitals opened in 1864, breaking ground occurred during his time as medical director, and for that fact alone, he deserves credit.[10]

The June 17, 1863, edition of the *Raleigh Weekly Register* announced, "We learn that another Hospital is soon to be established in the grove to the North East of the Fair Grounds [Hospital]." A few

---

9. Data from Consolidated Weekly Reports, September 1863, North Carolina Medical Director Reports, ch. 6, vol. 280, 8-9, RG109, NA; *Asheville Citizen-Times*, February1, 1919; *Weekly Standard* (Raleigh), March 27, 1862; Welborn, "A Wayside Hospital," *CV*, 38:95-96; Crews and Bailey, eds., *Records of the Moravians in North Carolina*, 12:6,488.

10. Cunningham is incorrect in stating that the pavilion-style hospital constructed in Raleigh "was the only one especially built for hospital purposes." See Cunningham, *Doctors in Gray*, 54.

weeks later, Medical Director Covey detailed Surgeon James F. McRee, who helped establish Wilmington's hospitals earlier in the war, to superintend the construction of the new hospitals at Raleigh and Salisbury. Two local business partners, Thomas Briggs, and James Dodd, began initial work in August 1863 on the Raleigh hospital. It is unclear what construction firm the government contracted to build the Salisbury hospital, but the Quartermaster Department paid Briggs and Dodd for use of the blueprint plans in its construction. Unfortunately, McRee encountered significant challenges in obtaining building materials for the Salisbury project, which pushed its start date into the following year.[11]

Covey next turned his attention toward Charlotte, where in July he assigned Assistant Surgeon Ignatius D. Thomson to superintend the construction of a new 500-bed hospital. Thomson had recently arrived from Lynchburg, Virginia, where, by 1863, the city was home to one of the largest hospital complexes in Virginia, apart from Richmond. The government acquired the fairgrounds, located approximately one mile south of Charlotte's public square, for the site of the new hospital. At that time, the Mecklenburg Agricultural Society owned the property, which consisted of approximately 12 acres of land, along with several wooden structures. The location was ideally suited for the construction of multiple one-story, open-bay wooden structures. As with the hospital project at Salisbury, it is unclear whom the government paid for constructing the hospital.[12]

Because of the lengthy project time required to complete the pavilion hospitals, in the interim, Covey identified Fayetteville as a suitable site for establishing a general hospital. Covey's choice of Fayetteville as the building site was somewhat unorthodox, considering a major railroad serviced each of North Carolina's general hospitals. Although the Western Railroad connected Fayetteville with the coal mines located approximately 25-miles away in Chatham County (present-day Lee County), it did not connect to other railroads. Fayetteville's primary transportation modes consisted of roads and the Cape Fear River.

Despite the lack of a major railroad, the establishment of a hospital in Fayetteville offered several advantages from a military perspective.

11. *Weekly Raleigh Register* (NC), June 17, 1863; McRee's service record notes that he performed the duty through the end of the year. James F. McRee, CSR, M331, roll 174; Briggs and Dodd, Citizens or Business Papers, M346, roll 97, RG109, NA.
12. Upon completion of No. 11's construction, Surgeon Thomson relocated to Charlotte's Way Hospital No. 6 in September 1863, serving there as surgeon-in-charge until his parole in April 1865. Ignatius D. Thomson, CSR, M331, roll 247.

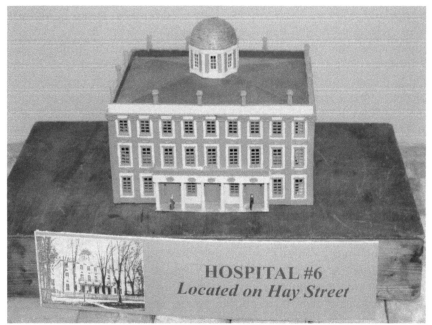

HOSPITAL #6
Located on Hay Street

A model of the Fayetteville Female Seminary displayed in the Fayetteville Area Transportation and Local History Museum, Fayetteville, N.C. The school served as General Hospital No. 6 (second wartime location) from September 1863–April 1865.

(Image courtesy of Frank Hall)

First, the town itself was mostly isolated from Union attacks, although mounted raids were not entirely out of the question. Second, because steamboats routinely used the Cape Fear River for transporting goods and people, medical officers could easily evacuate patients between Fayetteville and Wilmington's general hospitals. Lastly, Fayetteville had a growing military population relative to personnel assigned to the Confederate Arsenal and Armory located there, as well as other government agencies. Before Covey decided to establish a general hospital at Fayetteville, Dr. Benjamin W. Robinson, a contracted local physician, treated military personnel at the small post hospital located within the arsenal. However, by the summer of 1863, Fayetteville's growing military presence necessitated the need for a general hospital.[13]

In August, Covey detailed Surgeon Thomas R. Micks from Wilmington to identify a suitable site for the hospital and begin making necessary arrangements. Micks selected the Fayetteville Female Seminary, located on the south side of Hay Street, as the site. The

13. See file of Benjamin W. Robinson, CSR, M331, roll 215; In July 1863, the Federal raid at Warsaw and Kenansville demonstrated the possible vulnerabilities to a similar operation against Fayetteville.

three-story building, with a large front balcony, provided sufficient space for patient rooms and supporting staff. The following month, with his temporary duties completed in Fayetteville, Micks returned to Wilmington, and Surgeon Benjamin F. Fessenden arrived as the surgeon-in-charge of the newly designated General Hospital No. 6. Lucy Anderson, a Fayetteville resident, recalled that "each ward or floor was presided over by four ladies, who attended to their wants, giving medicine, nourishments, etc., also reading to them, writing to their absent loved ones, and making them as comfortable as was possible."[14]

The Closing of Hospitals

Early on in his tenure as medical director, Covey sought to economize where he could, which, if needed, included closing existing government general hospitals deemed unnecessary or inefficient. Covey's superior, Surgeon General Moore, "favored" the larger institutions more than the smaller ones, and he had instituted a similar policy in Richmond resulting in the closure of 12 hospitals between September 1862 and April 1863. Essentially, Moore frowned upon any hospital with a capacity of fewer than 100 patients. Table 8.3 indicates that more than half of the 11 general hospitals operating in May 1863 were clear candidates for closure, according to the surgeon general's guidance.[15]

Table 8.3: Total Bed Capacity of North Carolina General Hospitals, week ending May 14, 1863[16]

Location	Designation	Bed Capacity	Subsequent Medical Director's Action
Weldon	General Hospital No. 1	54	Converted to Wayside
Wilson	General Hospital No. 2	175	No Change
Goldsboro	General Hospital No. 3	226	No Change
Wilmington	General Hospital No. 4	196	No Change
Wilmington	General Hospital No. 5	51	Possible Expansion
Smithville	General Hospital No. 6	42	Closed
Raleigh	General Hospital No. 7	150	No Change
Raleigh	General Hospital No. 8	300	No Change
Salisbury	General Hospital No. 9	14	Future Pavilion
Charlotte	General Hospital No. 10	40	Future Pavilion
Tarboro	General Hospital No. 11	57	Converted to Wayside

14. Thomas R. Micks, CSR, M331, roll 177 and file of Benjamin F. Fessenden, CSR, M331, roll 92; The October 10, 1863, edition of the *Fayetteville Semi-Weekly* (NC) reported, "The High School Seminary Building having been

Beginning in May, Covey carried out Moore's wishes by closing General Hospital No. 6 at Smithville. An analysis of the hospital's consolidated weekly reports from the period of April 14 to May 7 indicates that the hospital consistently maintained a capacity of 42 beds, but its occupancy rate never exceeded 11 patients. Covey's decision to close the hospital appears justified based on the number of staff members assigned to the hospital: one assistant surgeon, one hospital steward, two detailed nurses, and a cook.[17]

Covey later re-designated General Hospital No. 11 at Tarboro as a wayside by the end of July. Although the Charlotte and Salisbury hospitals qualified for closure based on limited capacity, both remained in operation pending the completion of the new pavilion-style hospitals at each location. Likewise, Wilmington's General Hospital No. 5, which throughout the war consistently maintained a mere 51-bed capacity, met the surgeon general's criteria for closure; however, the property upon which the former U.S. Marine Hospital stood proved ideal for a potential pavilion hospital.

A Summer of Federal Raids

Throughout July 1863, the commander of the U.S. Army's Department of North Carolina, Maj. Gen. John G. Foster carried out a series of raids targeting key points along the strategically important Wilmington and Weldon Railroad designed to sever the line of communication between North Carolina and Richmond. On July 4, a 650-man mounted force, led by Lieutenant Colonel George W. Lewis of the 3rd New York Cavalry, struck the town of Kenansville, destroying the Confederate armory before continuing west toward the town of Warsaw, a key stop along the railroad. The following day, Lewis' force raided Warsaw and successfully destroyed several miles of track and rolling stock, along with valuable quartermaster and commissary stores. Alerted to possible Confederate forces in the area, Lewis withdrew toward New Bern, bringing along 150 head of livestock and 30 prisoners, as well as several hundred Blacks.[18]

taken by the government for a hospital."; Lucy Anderson, "Work by the Women of Fayetteville during the War Between the States," 3.

15. Cunningham, *Doctors in Gray*, 50.

16. Data from Consolidated Weekly Report, May 14, 1863, North Carolina Medical Director Reports, ch. 6, vol. 280, 3, RG109, NA.

17. Consolidated Weekly Reports, Week Ending May 14, 1863, NC Medical Director Reports, ch. 6, vol. 280, 2-3, RG109, NA; Edwin S. Ray, CSR, M331, roll 207. With the closing of the hospital, Covey reassigned Edwin S. Ray to General Hospital No. 8 in Raleigh.

18. Foster to Halleck, June 21, 1863, *OR*, 27, pt. 3, 242; Halleck to Foster, July 5, 1863, ibid., 553; Report of Maj. Gen. John G. Foster, ibid., pt. 2, 859-60. General-in-Chief of the Armies of the U.S., Maj. Gen. Henry W. Halleck,

Encouraged by Lewis' success, Foster ordered a second raid on a much grander scale. Brigadier General Edward E. Potter led a Federal expedition of 800 soldiers from New Bern targeting Greenville, Rocky Mount, and Tarboro. On July 19, Potter's raiders entered Greenville uncontested and proceeded to burn the Tar River Bridge. Potter later noted in his official report the presence of a hospital at Greenville, where his forces discovered "a few convalescents and sick" soldiers. Sources describe Greenville's military hospital as "a small post," which suggests it primarily supported the local military units in the area. According to one Confederate officer's account published in the *Raleigh Register*, the "Ladies of Greenville" established the hospital in September 1862 to care for the wounded following a failed attempt to recapture Union-occupied Washington. Ann K. Pearce, whose husband was a member of the 35th North Carolina, volunteered as a nurse at the hospital.[19]

That same afternoon, Potter's force continued north into Edgecombe County, where the raiders established camp at Sparta for the night. In the predawn hours of July 20, Potter divided his force, sending one element toward Rocky Mount and the other in the direction of Tarboro. The Rocky Mount contingent successfully destroyed both private and government property—notably, the cotton mills and important infrastructure and equipment belonging to the Wilmington and Weldon Railroad. Nearly simultaneous with the attack on Rocky Mount, Potter's second force reached Tarboro and destroyed a partially-built ironclad gunboat, two large government warehouses, the jail, the market house, and other military goods. At the rail depot, the raiders destroyed "a large quantity of cotton, several railroad cars, and some medical stores found in the depot."[20]

ordered raids carried out in North Carolina and Virginia in response to Confederate general Robert E. Lee's invasion of Pennsylvania; Although the author discovered no extant documents, according to local history, the Confederates utilized the Pierce-Bowden House at Warsaw as a hospital throughout the war. If the Confederates did establish a hospital there, the paucity of information suggests it served only in a temporary basis, or at the most, a post hospital; Following the raid, Confederate authorities assigned additional forces at Kenansville. Records indicate Assistant Surgeon W. S. Dubose of the 7th Confederate Cavalry established a post hospital at Kenansville in July 1863. See, W. S. Dubose, CSR, M258, roll 13; Assistant Surgeon James F. Davis later replaced Dubose as surgeon-in-charge. In December 1863, Davis requisitioned ten pounds of nails "in order to make bunks for the use of the hospital." See, James F. Davis, CSR, M331, roll 72.

19. Report of Brig. Gen. Edward E. Potter, *OR*, 27, pt. 2, 965; David A. Norris, *Potter's Raid: The Union Cavalry's Boldest Expedition in Eastern North Carolina* (Wilmington, NC, 2007), 1, 61. Potter's Raid is by far the best written account about the Union expedition; *Raleigh Register* (NC), October 4, 1862; "Pitt's Past," *Greenville Times* (NC), April 28, 2004, 8.

20. Report of Maj. George W. Cole, *OR*, 27, pt. 2, 969.

Other than the destruction of the medical supplies found at the depot, it is difficult to assess what consequences, if any, Potter's raid had on the Tarboro hospital, as such details are absent from Federal and Confederate accounts. However, one must assume that the damage to the Tarboro Branch Line Railroad immediately impacted the hospital's timely access to the Wilmington and Weldon Railroad at Rocky Mount. Additionally, the raid surely awakened Covey to the potential threats that existed in maintaining a hospital there, a reality that rang truer two weeks later when Potter conducted a third raid in the region.

In response to the Potter's raid, the surgeons in charge of the general hospitals at Goldsboro and Wilson organized *ad hoc* military formations consisting of staff members and convalescing soldiers. At Wilson's General Hospital No. 2, Surgeon Samuel S. Satchwell formed the "Hospital Defenders," and his counterpart at General Hospital No. 3 in Goldsboro, Surgeon George W. Graves, led a group identified as the "Hospital Invincibles." In a July 22, 1863, letter to Graves, Satchwell provided an interesting account of how his "Hospital Defenders" aided in the defense of Wilson. According to Satchwell, upon receipt of intelligence that an "immense armament of negroes and negro-stealers were advancing upon this point, the citizens flew ...to their trunks and wardrobes, the militia flew to the woods," which left only the volunteers from General Hospital No. 2 to counter the approaching threat. The surgeon's reference to armed Blacks suggests that Potter's marauding force may have enticed both enslaved individuals as well as Union sympathizers to raise up in arms against the Confederacy.[21]

Based on Satchwell's account, the militia rallied upon observing the deployment of the "Hospital Defenders." Commodore William F. Lynch, who commanded the local forces assigned to defend Wilson, organized a defense at a nearby bridge on an unidentified road leading into Wilson. The local forces destroyed the bridge, felled timber across the road, and constructed two lines of entrenchments "at least sixty yards in length," which the enemy upon observing, retired. With Wilson no longer under immediate danger, the "Hospital Defenders" returned to the general hospital.[22]

In late July, the Federals carried out a third raid targeting the strategically important Wilmington and Weldon Railroad Bridge

21. S. S. Satchwell to George W. Graves, July 24, 1863, William A. Holt Papers, SHC/UNC. Satchwell's reference to "armed African Americans" should not be confused with the 1st North Carolina Colored Volunteers (35th U.S. Colored Troops) formed in North Carolina during summer 1863. See Appendix C for a transcribed copy of Satchwell's letter.
22. S. S. Satchwell to George W. Graves, July 24, 1863, William A. Holt Papers, SHC/UNC.

spanning the Roanoke River at Weldon. As part of a diversion, a predominantly infantry force advanced from Union-occupied Plymouth to compel Confederate units stationed along the Roanoke River at Fort Branch and Hamilton to remain in position, thus preventing them from responding to the Federals. The departure of the force from Plymouth caused "great alarm" amongst Confederate authorities in the area, especially for Dr. A. Howard Scott, surgeon-in-charge of Way Hospital No. 7 at Tarboro. Because of Tarboro's proximity to Hamilton, Scott inquired of Covey, "Shall I remove the Hospital Stores, &c. The enemy are advancing in force from Plymouth and Washington?" It is unclear what actions Covey or Scott may have taken toward protecting the medical supplies. Luckily for them though, the enemy bypassed Tarboro entirely. However, the fact that for a second time in less than a month Federal raiders had spared the government hospital did not go unnoticed by Covey.[23]

In the aftermath of the final raid toward Weldon, Covey directed the closure of the Tarboro hospital, a decision that caught Brigadier General James G. Martin, commander of Confederate forces in the region, completely off guard. Because Martin was unsure as to whom ordered its closure, the general inquired of Captain G. H. Brown, the post quartermaster at Tarboro, for possible answers. Captain Brown knew it was Covey who had directed the hospital closed, so he referred the general's inquiry to the medical director, writing, "I do not know by what authority the Hospital was discontinued as Genl. Martin recommends it reestablishment." Covey responded, "The hospital was discontinued by an order from this office on the ground that it was not necessary." Covey based his decision on the fact that the wayside's weekly reports revealed that the hospital admitted and treated few patients. But to avoid further confrontation, Covey responded stating, "If it is the Genl.'s wish I will have it reestablished." To which the captain replied, "As Genl. Martin recommends the reestablishment of the hospital, it had better be done." Covey complied with the general's wish and reopened the hospital.[24]

Covey's decision to close the hospital seemed acceptable from a business perspective, principally because of the hospital's low occupancy rate—one that had been steadily declining since the recall of

23. Report of Maj. Gen. John G. Foster, *OR*, 27, pt. 2, 981; David Norris, "The Yankees Have Been Here!: The Story of Brig. Gen. Edward E. Potter's Raid on Greenville, Tarboro, and Rocky Mount, July 19–23, 1863," *NCHR* (1996), vol. 73, no. 1, 301-03; Report of Col. Theodore F. Lehman, *OR*, 27, pt. 2, 986-89; A. Howard Scott, CSR, M331, roll 220; *Fayetteville Semi-Weekly Observer* (NC), July 30, 1863.
24. G. H. Brown to E. N. Covey, August 25, September 7, 1863, Whiting Letters, UNCW.

Maj. Gen. William H. C. Whiting

(Histories of the Several Regiments and Battalions from North Carolina)

Confederate forces to Virginia. The end-of-week report for June 21 noted patients occupied only 14 of 40 available beds. Covey's decision was also justifiable considering the two close calls with Federal raiders. Without a sizeable Confederate troop presence in the Tarboro area, the hospital would have risked more raids if it had continued operating. Regardless, Covey had learned a valuable lesson as medical director in the pitfalls of acting autonomously. Despite the fact Surgeon General

Moore served as his superior, the controversy that erupted surrounding the hospital's closure revealed the complications Covey had to negotiate to execute the surgeon general's policy regarding discontinuing those institutions deemed inefficient.[25]

Troubles in Wilmington

Covey's unpleasant encounter with Martin in August 1863 was not an isolated event. Maj. Gen. Whiting, commander of forces in the Wilmington area, questioned Covey's decision to replace the general's brother-in-law, Dr. Joshua C. Walker, assistant surgeon-in-charge at General Hospital No. 5, with Dr. Thomas R. Micks, a recent transfer who was senior in rank to Walker. By the time Micks reported for duty, Wilmington's government hospitals were no longer the responsibility of Whiting or his command's medical director. That authority now rested with Covey, as the Medical Director of North Carolina General Hospitals. The Walker-Micks controversy that ultimately transpired included acts of favoritism, nepotism, and undo command influence, all of which Medical Director Covey had to carefully navigate.

In addition to Walker's personal connections with the commanding general, he was also a local from New Hanover County and had served faithfully as an assistant surgeon in the 3rd North Carolina since the spring of 1861. In January 1863, authorities granted Walker a furlough to return home to Wilmington to wed Elizabeth C. Bradley. Upon his return to Virginia in February, Walker actively sought a replacement in the regiment so that he might return to Wilmington and take charge of General Hospital No. 5 (Marine Hospital). Walker specifically seeking the head position at the hospital in February leads one to assume that during his wedding furlough Whiting discussed the possible position with him. Importantly, as of January 1863, general hospitals still fell under the purview of the medical director and senior commander of the department or district. Thus, Whiting was able to influence the assignment of medical officers in his command. Coincidentally, the surgeon-in-charge of the General Hospital No. 5, Dr. Peter B. Custis, had not yet fully recovered from complications resulting from his service at the hospital during Wilmington's yellow fever epidemic—a fact of which Whiting was probably aware. Custis passed away on March 27, and two days later,

25. NC Medical Director Reports, ch. 6, vol. 280, 3, RG109, NA.
26. *Wilmington Journal*, January 21, 1863; Wood, *Doctor to the Front*, 52; Peter B. Custis, CSR, M331, roll 69. Surgeon Custis died of Phthisis Pulmonalis (tuberculosis or consumption) while on duty at the hospital; W. H. C. Whiting to E. N. Covey, July 31, 1863, Whiting Letters, UNCW.

authorities in Virginia reassigned Walker to Wilmington. According to Whiting, Walker was "ordered to report to me by Genl. Lee and at my request assigned by the Med. Dir. of the Dept. of N.C. [and] Va. to this Hospital."[26]

In late July, Surgeon Thomas R. Micks arrived in Wilmington from the Confederate Army of Tennessee, where he had served in various Confederate hospitals in Georgia. Although a native of Sampson County and the son of a prominent Clinton physician, at the start of the war, Micks was practicing medicine in New Orleans, so he enlisted as an assistant surgeon in the 1st Louisiana. It was during his early months of service that he became acquainted with another North Carolinian—Confederate General Braxton Bragg.[27]

Covey informed Maj. Gen. Whiting that Micks, as the senior officer, had requested the position, and his seniority justified the placement. Whiting, who until this point had remained professional and courteous in their correspondence, was displeased with Covey's justification and immediately referred the matter to the Confederate Medical Department. Whiting expressed to Surgeon General Moore, "I cannot regard the reasons given for the action of Dr. Covey as at all satisfactory or sound." Although Surgeon General Moore's response is unknown, Walker remained in charge of General Hospital No. 5 through the end of the year, suggesting that he possibly agreed with Whiting. Ironically, when Covey's successor, Surgeon Peter E. Hines, later reassigned Walker to Wilmington's larger General Hospital No. 4 in December 1863, the surgeon-in-charge was none other than Surgeon Micks.[28]

Concurrent with the Walker-Micks issue, Whiting had the surgeon-in-charge of Wilmington's General Hospital No. 4, Dr. Milton W. Ritenour, arrested on multiple charges, notably for disobedience of general orders and violation of quarantine regulations. Whiting eventually dismissed all charges against Ritenour, calling it a misunderstanding; however, Whiting, seemingly at his wits' end regarding General Orders No. 28, wrote Confederate Adjutant General Samuel Cooper requesting clarification as to "the limits assigned to Department Commanders in the matter of General Hospitals." Unclear regarding the order, Whiting wrote, "I cannot understand from that order that Medical Officers assigned to General Hospitals are entirely independent of the Military Commander." Whiting stated to

27. S. M. Bemiss, M.D. and W. S. Mitchell, M.D., eds. *Index to Vol. XXII: The New Orleans Journal of Medicine* (New Orleans, 1869), 858; Thomas R. Micks, CSR, M331, roll 177.
28. Thomas R. Micks, CSR, M331, roll 177; W. H. C. Whiting to Surgeon General Moore, August 7, 1863. Whiting Letters, UNCW; Joshua C. Walker, CSR, M270, roll 133.

the Adjutant General that he did not interfere with the day-to-day operations of the hospitals at Wilmington. However, pointedly, Whiting wrote, "I know but one commanding officer here and that is myself . . . but I cannot tolerate anything like insubordination or that Medical Officers . . . violate standing orders–or to violate any regulations within their limits of their hospitals."[29]

Although Ritenour returned to his duties at General Hospital No. 4, his time at the hospital proved brief, as he became part of a tumultuous period of personnel turnover. On September 17, Whiting's senior command surgeon, Benjamin F. Fessenden, who had requested to return to hospital duty, replaced Ritenour. Strangely, Fessenden lasted only 10 days before Covey reassigned him to the recently established general hospital at Fayetteville to create a position for Surgeon Micks. Medical Director Covey's initiative to find positions for senior medical officers while simultaneously appeasing Whiting by retaining his brother-in-law at General Hospital No. 5, led to three head surgeons at one hospital in a brief 18-day period. Unlike the Tarboro hospital controversy that Covey remedied by simply reopening the hospital, matters in Wilmington did not resolve as easily.[30]

Covey continued to generate problems. Along with frustrating Confederate generals Martin and Whiting, Covey was equally successful in losing favor with the state's chief executive officer, Governor Vance, who by August, had grown weary of this obstinate outsider. The governor even made Covey a topic of discussion with President Davis during a trip to Richmond that summer. In a follow-up letter to the Confederate secretary of war, James Seddon, Vance reiterated his meeting with the president regarding Covey and stressed the need for quick change: "[M]y complaint to President Davis was the presence of such a number of Virginians and Marylanders in our State filling the offices which were local and permanent in their character." Vance described Covey and the other officers as "a brood of his own countrymen avoiding conscription and making themselves generally very obnoxious to our people." The governor reminded Seddon that President Davis promised to have them replaced, but had yet to honor the agreement. Vance further stated that he provided the president a half dozen names "who were most obnoxious, among them that of a Dr. Covey."[31]

29. W. H. C. Whiting to Samuel Cooper, August 17, 1863, Whiting Letters, UNCW.

30. Milton W. Ritenour, CSR, M331, roll 213; Benjamin F. Fessenden, CSR, M331, roll 92.

31. Governor Vance to Hon. J. Seddon, September 3, 1863, *OR*, ser. 4, 2:787-88.

A New Hospital Czar

By the first week of September, Covey, as medical director, was equally wary of serving in the Old North State and had seemingly had enough; he requested of the surgeon general that he relieve him from his current duty and reassign him elsewhere. Although Covey's motivation for such a drastic change is unknown, one could deduce that the two separate incidents involving generals Martin and Whiting, neither of whom was in his chain of command, along with the caustic work environment in Raleigh stemming from the governor's personal feelings toward him, all of this weighed heavily in his decision. From the beginning of his service in North Carolina, authorities in Raleigh considered Covey an outsider. It may seem trivial, but in the Confederate army, a Marylander responsible for North Carolina hospitals staffed mostly with Tar Heels did not bode well.

Upon learning of Covey's resignation, Surgeon Edmund B. Haywood, who at the time superintended Raleigh's General Hospital No. 7, immediately wrote Surgeon General Moore expressing his desire for the position. "I am informed by my friend Dr. Covey that he desires to be relieved as Medical Director . . . I have the honor to apply for this position." Many of Haywood's contemporaries, particularly Dr. Samuel S. Satchwell, surgeon-in-charge at Wilson's General Hospital No. 2, also lobbied for Haywood to get the position. Satchwell went so far as to collect signatures from the other surgeons to demonstrate support for Haywood. Satchwell shared with Haywood a copy of the letter he had drafted in which he and the other surgeons intended to send to the surgeon general. One key aspect of Satchwell's letter is that it presented an opposite opinion of Medical Director Covey than the rhetoric echoed by Governor Vance and others toward the Marylander. Satchwell wrote, "We take occasion to say that he has made in our opinion an efficient and faithful Medical Director—that he is in every aspect acceptable to us . . . We believe also that the Medical Profession and the public generally of North Carolina, have no objection to him, and are satisfied that he should remain in his present position." In addition to his fellow medical officers, Haywood found support from local civilians. One individual, D. W. Barringer, wrote a letter to the Secretary of War Seddon, with the heading: "citizens of North Carolina," touting Haywood's qualifications.[32]

But things did not work out for Haywood. Despite the extensive lobbying, in the end, Surgeon General Moore selected another North

---

32. E. Burke Haywood to Surgeon General Moore, September 12, 1863, Haywood Papers, SHC/UNC; S. S. Satchwell to Haywood, September 1863, ibid; D. W. Barringer to James A. Seddon, September 18, 1863, ibid.

Carolinian and a close friend of Haywood, Surgeon Peter E. Hines, as Covey's replacement. Although some may have disapproved of Hines' selection, few North Carolina medical officers were as qualified. He began the war as a regimental surgeon, and later perfected the craft of hospital management at the hospitals in Yorktown, and at Petersburg, where he served as the surgeon-in-charge of the 1st North Carolina Hospital. Before his assignment as North Carolina's medical director, Hines served as the Chief of Hospitals for all of Petersburg's general hospitals. Undoubtedly, Hines was equally as qualified as Haywood was. It is worth noting that Hines initially declined the job, perhaps upon learning of the tremendous support for Haywood's assignment.[33]

Hines recalled years later that he began his duties as the medical director "without even a list of where or how many hospitals the state had operating at the time," which suggests Covey departed Raleigh before Hines' arrival and without taking the time to prepare, at a minimum, a transition paper for his incoming replacement. Although Hines' jab at Covey may seem like condemnation, he did not begin the medical director position fumbling in the dark. A simple glance at Covey's medical director book would have revealed the weekly reports from all the hospitals dating back to April 1863. Nonetheless, it does reveal a somewhat unprofessional attitude on the part of his predecessor.[34]

Hines was a doctor of extraordinary talent, possessing great leadership and administrative skill, and within weeks of becoming North Carolina's new medical director, he immediately instituted initiatives to improve the state's hospital system. In October, Hines ordered Surgeon Haywood to "proceed to Richmond, Va. and examine . . . the arrangements for heating, ventilating, bathing, cooking, and washing," at Camp Jackson Hospital and other hospitals. The Camp Jackson Hospital was a large institution established in the summer of 1863. The hospital's wooden barracks accommodated 2,500 patients. Dispatching Haywood to Richmond was a wise decision considering the planned construction of pavilion-style hospitals at several locations in the state.[35]

---

33. Cunningham, "Edmund Burke Haywood and Raleigh's Confederate Hospitals," *NCHR*, 159; Samuel Moore to Samuel Cooper, September 12, 1863, Letters Received, AIGO, M474, roll 83; Hasegawa, *Matchless Organization*, 35. Hasegawa contends that it is unclear as to who ultimately ordered Covey's dismissal. Based on the extant letters written by both Haywood and Satchwell, it is the author's belief that Surgeon General Moore accepted Covey's resignation to avoid further conflict with Governor Vance.
34. Hines, "The Medical Corps," Clark, *Histories*, 4:625.
35. SO No. 3, Office Medical Director, General Hospitals, North Carolina, October 19, 1863, John and Edmund Burke Haywood Papers, Sec. A Box 63 items 1-26, c.1, Rubenstein Library, Duke University, Durham, NC (DU);

As Haywood visited the Richmond hospitals, Hines explored options to mitigate the issues associated with General Hospital No. 4 in Wilmington. Surgeon Micks, the hospital's newly assigned surgeon-in-charge, reported to Hines that the "locality of this Hospital is bad." Micks explained that the hospital's location near the Wilmington riverfront exposed it to the rowdiness of the port city. Micks stressed to Hines, "[I]t is difficult to keep convalescents from straggling and the noise . . . is certainly prejudicial to the very sick." The hospital's duty log for October 16, 1863, validated Micks' concerns. The duty officer wrote, "[t]wo intoxicated sailors were placed in the guard house last night."[36]

When Micks arrived at General Hospital No. 4 in September 1863, the facility consisted of four separate structures. The former Seaman's Home constituted the main part of the hospital, which officials later expanded by leasing three nearby residential properties. Although leasing the additional properties increased the hospital's capacity, it made administrative control difficult. With no other suitable structures available in Wilmington, Micks recommended to Hines that expanding the current General Hospital No. 5 (Marine Hospital) was the best option. The hospital was ideally located away from the bustle of the Wilmington riverfront, and the property upon which the building stood provided sufficient acreage for the "erection of shed buildings" as additional hospital wards. On November 14, Micks informed Wilmington's assistant quartermaster, Captain C. W. Styron, of the plan to enlarge the general hospital with buildings "sufficient to accommodate two hundred patients." Unfortunately for Micks, Capt. Styron responded that the severe lumber shortage and the limited number of sawmills in the Wilmington area prevented the Quartermaster Department from providing the necessary material to complete the project. For the remainder of the war, Micks, along with his accompanying staff, would continue to operate General Hospital No. 4 from its original location.[37]

Cunningham, "E. Burke Haywood and Confederate Hospitals, *NCHR*, 159; Cunningham, "Confederate General Hospitals: Establishment and Organization," *The Journal of Southern History* (1954), 20:376-79.

36. Entry, October 16, 1863, Reports of the Officer of the Day, General Hospital No. 4, Oct. 16, 1863–May 10, 1864, vol. 402, 7, RG109, NA.

37. Thomas R. Micks to C. W. Styron, November 14, 1863, Letters Received, General Hospital No. 4 Papers, ch. 6, vol. 399, 22, RG109, NA; Thomas R. Micks to Peter E. Hines, November 18, 1863, ibid., 23. In October 1863, Micks requisitioned materials for "erection of a shed" for the use of General Hospital No. 4. See, Thomas R. Micks, CSR, M331, roll 177.

Conclusion

On December 24, 1863, Senator A. G. Brown from Mississippi stood on the Senate floor and delivered a speech titled "State of the Country." Speaking directly to President Davis, Brown asked: "Shall the Confederacy stand or shall it fail? This is the question which today, more potentially than at any former period of our brief history, urges itself upon our attention, and in thunder tones demands our consideration." Brown urged President Davis of the necessity "to strengthen the army and improve the currency." History shows that the year 1863 witnessed a high point of the Confederacy in battle. Union victories at Gettysburg, Vicksburg, and Chattanooga placed the Confederate army on the strategic defensive for the remainder of the war. Moving forward the Confederacy faced a rapidly deteriorating situation, both economically and militarily.[38]

In North Carolina, tangible threats to Governor Vance and Confederate control began to occur. Peace advocates such as editor William W. Holden of the *Standard* became more vocal and clamored "for a negotiated end to the war." The mothers and wives of Confederate soldiers rioted in the streets at Salisbury in protest of shortages and soaring food costs. And the recent string of military defeats only worsened the situation by sapping the morale of soldiers, resulting in the problem of "frequent desertions from" the Tar Heel regiments serving in Virginia and the Army of Tennessee.[39]

Despite such issues at the national and state levels, by year's end, a significant maturation regarding the Confederate hospital system in North Carolina had occurred. Centered around the increasing importance of North Carolina's various railroads, wayside hospitals emerged from Wilmington on the coast to Salisbury in the Piedmont, thus providing an important service to the army's transient soldiers. Although private and state-operated wayside hospitals continued to function at a lesser scale through 1863 (two each private and two each N.C. Med. Dept.), by the end of the year, the Confederate Medical Department controlled most hospitals functioning within the Tar Heel State (see table 8.4).

---

38. *State of the Country: Speech of Hon. A. G. Brown of Mississippi, in the Confederate Senate, December 24, 1863* (Richmond, VA, 1863), 2697 Confederate, Rare Book Collection, Wilson Library, the University of North Carolina at Chapel Hill.

39. Newsome, *The Fight for the Old North State*, 35; Barrett, *The Civil War in North Carolina*, 190; In Wilkes County, "a band of 1,100 draft evaders and deserters" marched through the streets of Wilkesboro. Hardy, *Last Capital of the Confederacy*, 43.

Table 8.4: North Carolina Hospital System, December 1863[40]

Location	Designation	Authority
n/a	General Hospital No. 1	Not Used
Wilson	General Hospital No. 2	C.S. Med. Dept.
Goldsboro	General Hospital No. 3	C.S. Med. Dept.
Wilmington	General Hospital No. 4	C.S. Med. Dept.
Wilmington	General Hospital No. 5	C.S. Med. Dept.
Fayetteville	General Hospital No. 6	C.S. Med. Dept.
Raleigh	General Hospital No. 7	C.S. Med. Dept.
Raleigh	General Hospital No. 8	C.S. Med. Dept.
Salisbury	General Hospital No. 9	C.S. Med. Dept.
Charlotte	General Hospital No. 10	C.S. Med. Dept.
Weldon	Way Hospital No. 1	C.S. Med. Dept.
n/a	Way Hospital No. 2	Not Used
Salisbury	Way Hospital No. 3	C.S. Med. Dept.
Goldsboro	Way Hospital No. 4	C.S. Med. Dept.
Wilmington	Way Hospital No. 5	C.S. Med. Dept.
Charlotte	Way Hospital No. 6	C.S. Med. Dept.
Tarboro	Way Hospital No. 7	C.S. Med. Dept.
Asheville	Asheville Wayside Hospital	N.C. Med. Dept.
Raleigh	Ladies Wayside Hospital	N.C. Med. Dept.
High Point	Barbee Wayside Hospital	Privately Operated
Salem	Salem Wayside Hospital	Privately Operated

Led by the capable Medical Director of North Carolina Hospitals, Surgeon Covey, the government hospital system in North Carolina totaled nine general hospitals and six wayside hospitals. Despite Federal raids and troublesome confrontations with senior officers and the leadership in Raleigh, Medical Director Covey accomplished a great deal during his brief six-month tenure in the Old North State. He instituted the numerical identification system for North Carolina

40. Data from Consolidated Weekly Reports, December 1863, North Carolina Medical Director Reports, ch. 6, vol. 280, RG109, NA; *Asheville Citizen-Times*, February 1, 1919; *Weekly Standard* (Raleigh), March 27, 1862; Welborn, "A Wayside Hospital," *CV*, 38:95-96; Crews and Bailey, eds., *Records of the Moravians in North Carolina*, 12:6,488.

hospitals. Covey implemented the use of wayside hospitals as mandated by the Confederate Congress. And probably his greatest contribution, although he never witnessed the final products, was the implementation of the pavilion-style hospitals in North Carolina. Though these hospitals never approached the sheer size of Richmond's Chimborazo or Winder hospitals, Covey's ordering of their construction demonstrated forward-thinking as medical director as he attempted to incorporate best practices known at the time into the state's hospital system. Fortunately for the Confederates, his successor, Surgeon Hines, moved forward with completing the construction of the pavilion hospitals at Charlotte, Raleigh, and Salisbury. As history shows, the availability of the pavilion hospitals proved invaluable in the war's final two years.

* * *

The story of North Carolina Confederate hospitals during the war's final two years, 1864 to 1865, continues in Volume II. By 1864 the Confederacy was clearly on the defensive, as its armies could no longer wage war on their own terms. After three years of fighting, the Confederate soldiers were unpaid, undernourished, and poorly clad. The citizens on the home front shared in the soldiers' sufferings. A protracted war had wrecked the Southern economy. Shortages of essentials coupled with inflationary prices made life extremely difficult for Southerners. The scarcity of food and medical supplies also affected the ability of surgeons overseeing various military hospitals to provide a proper diet and care for patients.

Despite such challenges, it was during these last years when the Medical Department would expand the hospital network along the state's vital railroads further into the Piedmont region to meet an ever-increasing flow of sick and wounded. North Carolinians would also witness several titanic events beginning with the fall of both Fort Fisher and Wilmington and Major General William T. Sherman's 1865 Carolinas campaign. These events brought the Confederate hospital system in the state to the brink of failure. Lastly, Major General George Stoneman's devastating cavalry raid through much of western North Carolina exacerbated an already desperate situation.

Archibald M. Fauntleroy, Served as General Whiting's medical director from August 1863-July 1864. During his service at Wilmington, the Confederates opened a second Negro Hospital at Smithville (Southport).

(American Civil War Museum, under the management of
Virginia Museum of History & Culture [FIC2013.00125])

Appendix A

Letters Pertaining to
the Waring Controversy

For several weeks after the battle of New Bern, Surgeon James J. Waring engaged in a letter-writing campaign with Confederate authorities refuting his sudden dismissal as Medical Director of the Department of North Carolina. Transcribed below are letters submitted by Waring, as well as other principal participants in the controversy. Although the letters focus primarily on the alleged misconduct of Surgeon Waring, several of the letters provide insightful information regarding the New Bern hospitals in the hours leading up to, during, and immediately following, the battle of New Bern. The author transcribed the letters verbatim, with minimal corrections to spelling or grammatical. The letters are currently in Letters Received, Adjutant & Inspector General's Office, microfilm (M474), roll 52, Records Group 109, National Archives and Records Administration, Washington, D.C.

Letters written by Surgeon James J. Waring, former Medical Director of the Department of North Carolina

Letter One: James J. Waring to Brig. Gen. Joseph R. Anderson, commander of the Department of North Carolina, March 21, 1862, Goldsboro, N.C.

Sir,

Your order suspending me has so overwhelmed me that it is only since my arrival here [Goldsboro] that I have been able to determine upon the course to be pursued. It must be seen by you, sir, that a <u>suspension</u> under such an order not only injures my fair name but irrevocably for the future. I respectfully suggest that I am prejudged and ruined in the estimation of the people without a hearing, <u>me</u> who have labored night and day in our cause.

I respectfully ask a Court of Inquiry without <u>delay</u>. A communication has been received from the Surgeon General throwing light upon this subject. The business of my office is <u>extremely</u> pressing at this juncture, it is natural to suppose that no one can understand its particulars as well as myself. I am making considerable purchases for the Purveyor at Richmond. My papers and my property are at this most critical juncture <u>the end of the fiscal quarter</u>, and shall I turn them over to an officer who is not in your Department and assigned to a special duty by the Surgeon General viz: "the Army Medical board"?

I appeal to you to suspend your "order" until a Court of Inquiry can decide on the merits of this very serious case to me.

Letter Two: James J. Waring to Surgeon General Samuel P. Moore, March 21, 1862, Goldsboro, N.C.

Sir,

I indignantly deny the accusation made through some unknown party to Senator William T Dortch. I respectfully ask for a Court of Inquiry upon my whole conduct in the recent attack upon NewBern and do not fear the result. It is very important in view of the large increase of troops in this vicinity that I be not hampered in my efforts to serve the country and therefore urge upon you that this Court of Inquiry sit without delay. In the meantime I submit to you an order issued by Gen. Anderson suspending me for the present from my duties and calling upon me to turn over all the property and stores in my possession. I have just received a letter from Surgeon Johns in relation to whiskey which I am purchasing for him from various parties. The Scuppernong [wine] 3000 gallons has been at Tarboro for three weeks, the rest of it is also arriving as also sheeting.

How can I turn over all this business to a gentleman who is not in this Department and who is serving on an Army Medical Board convened for a specific purpose by you? Surgeon Warren is not subject to the orders of Gen. Anderson. This blow has fallen upon me so suddenly and unexpectedly that I hardly can find language to express the injustice of it and its cruel mockery of a man who in spirit at least is more than willing to work in this our cause.

Letter Three: James J. Waring to Surgeon General Samuel P. Moore, April 1, 1862, Richmond, Va.

Sir,

I have this evening for the first time seen anything tangible as to the nature of the information found prejudicial to my usefulness. The witnesses are named one of whom, W. W. Gaither was seen by me only late in the evening at Kinston on the day of the attack on Newbern. He walked with me to the railroad where I got upon the train to go to Goldsboro in order to superintend the arrangements for the sick that had been forwarded.

The evidence against me, therefore, upon which has been based my suspension and the forestalling of public opinion is derived from one individual and [who had] been the acting substitute in my office. I regret extremely if I do injustice to another. I care for nothing now but my personal character and for that I must and shall stake everything.

Letter Four: James J. Waring to Surgeon General Samuel P. Moore, April 1, 1862, Richmond, Va.

Sir,

If it be necessary to my personal defense that the <u>source</u> of this attack upon me be understood, thus, the following facts which have come to my knowledge are submitted. They implicate another and therefore I reluctantly do this, <u>only</u>, in my personal vindication. Surgeon Warren was not under my control in the Dept. of N.C. His opposition, therefore, to the course proposed by me tended to <u>embarrass</u> me. He <u>asserted</u> his determination to stay and take care of the wounded of that day; and, yet, Dr. Pitman, a militia surgeon and a citizen of Newberne, who did <u>stay</u> and is now paroled, complains that Dr. Warren left after the promise above was made to him. Dr. Pitman made this statement to Surgeon Wm. H. Moore before he left Newberne. Surgeon I. G. Thomas openly asserts that Dr. Warren has been striving to get my place. I refer you to Asst. Surg. Holt. Surgeon Warren remarked to Asst. Surg. Martin, that Dr. Crowell had been his friend and was now mine (Dr. Waring's). Why was not friendship for me compatible with friendship for Dr. Warren? Again, to Dr. Martin, Surgeon Warren remarked later after hearing that I had been reinstated that perhaps he had been talking too freely on the 19th of March, <u>before</u> the order for my suspension had been issued by Gen. Anderson. I was told by Surgeon Shields and Asst. Surgeon Moore that a paper was submitted to them for signature which they had flung aside as if it had been a serpent and that learning I had or would resign they, three, consented to the signature of a paper expressing a preference for Surgeon Warren. As it was impossible to know that I had expressed a wish to resign and as the above order had not been issued, for Gen. Anderson had not taken command on the 18th. The above action I submit was un officer like as well as premature. Enough has been said to me to lead me to the conclusion that Surgeons Wyatt M. Brown and W. J. Blow were the parties who submitted the first paper. The first has been introduced to me as the future Medical Purveyor of N.C. and the latter has been placed in a Hospital at Kinston though refusing openly to appear before the Army Medical Board. Surgeons Shields and Asst. Surg. Moore can throw light upon their point. I by no means desire that this paper should be submitted to you, sir, without the knowledge of Surgeon Warren.

I have submitted my authority on all these points. I may finally state that the majority of those who signed that paper have personally stated to me that they by no means desired to express any wish for my removal.

Letter Five: James J. Waring to the Hon., Secretary of War, April 2, 1862, Richmond, Va.

Sir,

By order of Gen. Anderson, Genl. Commanding Dept. of N.C. I was suspended from my duties in his Dept. I confess, sir, that the <u>suddenness</u> and as I have thought <u>un-deservedness</u> of the charges and insinuations which persons said had been made against me both mortified me and conduced largely to my unhappiness. Yesterday evening I, for the first time, saw these charges. I <u>deny</u> them <u>absolutely</u> and <u>in every sense</u>.

Briefly, to Charge I - I was <u>not</u> on duty at the hospital in Newberne. My office and duties were in Goldsboro and I left them permitted to do so <u>reluctantly</u> by Gen. Gatlin, ([see] Gen. G's letter) <u>volunteering</u> my supervision of the removal of the sick in my anxiety. Does a night of sleepless effort go for naught? And does the removal of over 200 sick under my instructions go for naught? <u>Four</u> wounded men or <u>five</u> at most with a few desperate cases of Typhoid from which could not and ought not to have been removed were all that was left. These few wounded men had been assigned by me to two or three volunteer aides and this was done by me in the absence of both responsible officers of the Hospital. The surgeon was in the field and the assistant surgeon was removing the sick under my instructions. These aides had it explained to them that I ought not to be taken prisoner, and yet they persisted in remaining to operate on and dress wounded men that might have been put up on the train with the sick. Does Gen. Branch forget the sleepless night of effort I made to get an order from him for a train?

To Charge II - My official duties in instructing the officers under me were performed and successful. ([see] written testimony of Hosp. Surgeons Martin and Holt.) No fear, therefore, prevented their performance and no need to deny the fear. Such an insinuation becomes only a <u>scandal</u>. I am or was a <u>staff officer</u> of Gen. Gatlin, at his side was my post; or rather my bureau at his headquarters was my post, <u>that</u> I abandoned by permission of Gen. G.: upon consideration that Surgeon Brown be left in my place. ([see] Gen. G's letter). But how many men on that day who had posts awaited orders from Gen. B. [Branch] to leave them? Have <u>they</u> been Court Martialed? I fear in no respect, nor challenge the scrutiny of all just and impartial men.

* * *

Letters Written by Surgeon Edward Warren, member, Medical Examination Board, Department of North Carolina

Letter One: Edward Warren to Surgeon General Samuel P. Moore, March 22, 1862, Goldsboro, N.C.

Sir,

In ordering me to report on the circumstances referred to in the Communication of the Hon. W. T. Dortch, you have imposed a most painful duty. I regret that I am compelled to say the charge thus brought against Surgeon J. J. Waring, is in the main correct. A number of wounded men had been brought from the battlefield to the General Hospital, where these injuries were being attended to by the attending surgeons. Before this work was completed, a bomb shell was thrown over the town, which exploded in the vicinity of the hospital. Surgeon Waring, without giving direction as to the disposition of the wounded, immediately left the hospital, and escaped from the Town. When it was [ ] ascertained that the town had been fired at several points, the wounded were brought off, by the surgeons who remained behind, and cared to a place of safety. Permit me to add that Surgeon N. S. Crowell, President of the Examining Board, displayed great coolness and courage in bringing off the sick and wounded. I had the honor to submit.

Letter Two: Edward Warren to Surgeon General Samuel P. Moore, March 22, 1862, Goldsboro, N.C.

Sir,

In response to your order to report on the circumstances referred to you in a communication from the Hon. W. T. Dortch, in regard to the conduct of Surgeon J. J. Warring at New Bern, I beg leave to make the following statement. In company with Surgeon N. S. Crowell, I repaired to New Bern on the night of Thursday the 13 [March] inst. for the purpose of volunteering my services in the engagement which was anticipated on the succeeding day. The Medical Director, failing to assign me to any particular duty on the morning of Friday, as he had promised, I repaired to the Depot for the purpose of procuring transportation to the "Battle Field," 3 miles distance from the town. While waiting for this mode of conveyance, the announcement was suddenly made, that our Army had been defeated and was in full retreat. About the same moment I was informed that the wounded were being transported to the General Hospital in Newberne, and that they were in want of surgical assistance. I immediately repaired there, and on my arrival met Dr. Waring, who had just fled from the field among the earliest fugitives. The scene of confusion in around the Hospital surpassed anything that I had ever conceived of or witnessed. The sick not having been previously removed from the hospital, we're running about all directions, in the greatest state of terror, eagerly asking permission to escape, without succeeding in obtaining any definite order from the Director. The wounded were arriving momentarily in every possible conveyance, bleeding and begging for assistance. The employees of the Hospital were clamorous for "Commands" which they would obtain from no one, and not knowing whether to fly or to remain at their post, overwhelmed the Director with questions as to the course they should pursue. The Surgeons did not know what to do, and could get no orders. And the Medical Director was in such a condition of excitement and nervous agitation as to be entirely incapable of performing the duties of his office. In this condition of things, I procured a train of cars from the President of the Road

[Atlantic and North Carolina Railroad], and with the assistance of N. S. Crowell sit off the sick, and slightly wounded, retaining only the more desperately wounded, whose injuries required medical attention. The latter were carried into the hospital, and the proper attention given to their cases, by the surgeons in attendance. Dr. Waring insisted that Dr. Crowell and myself should leave, as he could do so in that event without rendering himself obnoxious to public odium. We peremptorily refused to leave, declaring that it was the duty of surgeons to remain with the wounded at all hazards, and insisting that there should be no desertions from the hospital at that time. After these things had transpired, and while we were all engaged in performing an amputation, a Bomb was suddenly thrown over the hospital, where the medical director, exclaimed "My God, they are shelling the town," and without giving a single direction as to the disposition of the sick fled precipitately from the town, leaving all the wounded behind him, to the utter surprise of all the medical officers present.

It seems that he [Waring] had detailed the Hospital Steward to keep his Horse in readiness, and leaving upon his "Pony," led the retreat to Kinston getting there among the earliest, and arriving even in Goldsboro before the "Calvary Regiment" had reached the former place.

Finding that the town had been fired in several places, and that the place was being thoroughly shelled, we determined to remove the wounded, and then to retreat ourselves. Acting upon this resolution the patients were immediately hurried off, some being sent upon the "last train" of Cars, and others being placed in Wagons and in that way transported from the town. When the last man had been removed from the Hospital Surgeon Crowell, and myself retired, and without difficulty or danger made our escape.

These Sir, are the facts of the Case, as I witnessed them myself, and as will he[,] testified to by a number of responsible persons who were present on the occasion. I must add, that many miles from Newberne, I saw a number of ambulances, which should have been used on the field, in the possession of Citizens and Soldiers escaping for their lives from the enemy.

It is a source of infinite pain to be constrained to make these statements, but being called upon by yourself and prompted by an earnest desire to advance the public interest, I had given you a faithful, honest and impartial account of what occurred in New Bern at the time designated in the Communication of the Hon. M. [Mr.] Dortch. Permit me to add that a number of medical officers were present, who will testify to the above mentioned facts. Among these, I can recall Surgeons Crowell, and Pittman, Asst. Surgeons W. A. Blunt, and Gaither, Acting Asst. Surgeon Martin and Hospital Steward Rhodes.

Letter Three: Edward Warren to Surgeon General Samuel P. Moore, April 2, 1862, Richmond Va.

Sir,

I have been ordered to this place [Richmond] by General Holmes on special duty, and shall proceed to report to you in person at 2:00 p.m., if it meets with your approval. Before doing this however, I deem it one to myself to make some explanations in order that you understand in advance my connection with what has recently occurred in the Department of N.C. In the first place, I will state, and the assertion can be readily established, that tho: applied to presently by my medical friends in that Department, to permit my name to be used in order to deprive Dr. Waring of his position, I invariably and peremptorily refused to do so, upon the ground that such a course was contrary to my ideas of propriety. Secondly, I would remark, that my friends did not recommend me to the Commanding General until Dr. Waring had announced that he had applied to you to be relieved from duty. In this connection, permit me to say, that there is a Communication to this effort on the letter book of the Medical Directors office dated march 19th, and that the application of my friends, which was drawn up without my knowledge, began, as I am informed, with these words "understanding that the Office of Medical Director is to be vacated, we recommend Dr. Warren, MD." Thirdly, I beg leave to state in the most emphatic manner, that all I have done in this connection was under the most positive and peremptory orders from Generals Anderson and Holmes, both of whom are cognizant of all the facts of this case, and are prepared to justify me to the <u>fullest extent</u>. Indeed, the latter who is an officer of the Old Army, and a most rigid disciplinarian has been my friend and adviser in this whole matter, and requested me to refer you to him for a thorough vindication of my character and conduct if any misinformation had been attempted against me. If there has been any mistake made in this regard, I am sure therefore you will acquit me of all connection with it, in as much, as I have simply obliged the positive orders of my superiors—orders which I could not have disobeyed without subjecting myself to an immediate arrest. <u>Fourthly</u>, I most respectfully and emphatically urge, that my appointment to this place by the Commanding General, not only took me by surprise but was not agreeable to me in the least, and that my only reason for accepting it under the circumstances was, that I conceived it my duty to make any personal sacrifice to serve the Cause in a great emergency. In conclusion I must say that the appointment of Acting Purveyor was conferred upon personally by General Holmes, and that I have no desire to retain the position.

In this whole matter, I have in endeavored to do my whole duty, faithfully, honestly and fearfully, and it is a source of satisfaction to know that I have secured the good will and hearty approval of the Commanding Officers, men who were on the spot and had an opportunity of judging of all the facts of the case. With Dr. Waring I have had no quarrel at any time, and no one would rejoice me at his through vindication. Trusting that your <u>judgment</u> has not been biased by ex parte statements in this matter, and that you will give it an impartial consideration.

* * *

Letter Written by Dr. Nathaniel S. Crowell, president, Medical Examination Board, Department of North Carolina, to Surgeon General S. P. Moore, March 22, 1862, Goldsboro, N.C.

Sir,

I have the honor to acknowledge the receipt of a communication of Senator Dortch of North Carolina in reference to the conduct of Surgeon J. J. Waring at the attack on New Bern referred to me from your office.

In accordance with your wishes, I have to state that Surgeon Waring did not leave the hospital at New Bern until some time after the issue of the action was known. Previous to leaving and before the shelling of the town commenced, he explained that holding as he did, the important position of Medical Director and Purveyor of the Department, he deemed it his duty to avoid capture. While he remained in the hospital he was actively engaged at tending the wounded.

* * *

Letter Written by Dr. William H. Moore, former surgeon-in-charge, Neuse General Hospital (New Bern), to Surgeon General S. P. Moore, March 21, 1862, Goldsboro, N.C.

Sir,

Having heard that charges are preferred against Surgeon Waring I deem it my duty to throw what light I can upon the subject. Surg. Waring came to my hospital Thursday evening after dark. He immediately procured an engine. And went over to General Branch's headquarters, five or six miles beyond town to get transportation for the sick to Goldsboro. He returned about four o'clock in the morning. At eight o'clock I assisted him in an amputation. After which we immediately started for the field. Dr. Waring riding Dr. Worrell and myself walking. After we had gone some distance beyond the river the firing being rapid at our left. Dr. W. urged us to go immediately with him to the that point, which we refused to do until we could get our horses which were at Col. S[inclair]'s Camp a few hundred yards to the right. We hurried on to the Camp, and found everything in great confusion. Striking tents and running in every direction in the panic. I lost sight of Dr. Waring and did not see him again. On reaching New Bern I found that Drs. Waring, Warren, Crowell and M[artin] had all left the town there being in possession of the enemy. I also deem it but justice to say that Dr. Waring has labored faithfully in this cause.

Letter Written by Dr. William A. Holt, former assistant surgeon-in-charge, Branch General Hospital (New Bern), to Surgeon General S. P. Moore, March 21, 1862, Goldsboro, N.C.

Sir,

At the request of Dr. Waring, I take pleasure in stating the following facts. I was the assistant surgeon in charge of the Branch Hospital NewBerne. Seeing the sick under my charge safely placed upon the train, in pursuance of instructions received from Surg. Waring on the morning of the attack on NewBerne, and one now safely housed in [the] hospital prepared by Dr. Waring in this place [Goldsboro].

On that morning about 10:00 o'clock, I met Dr. Waring on the NewBerne side of the County Bridge, and said to him that all the excitement and confusion he saw was due to the fact that the army was retreating. I went with Dr. Waring to the [Neuse] Genl. Hospital and then went to look after my sick in [Branch] Hospital. I afterwards met Dr. W. at the RR depot, when the enemy were shelling the town. He seemed to be looking for someone, when the shelling became more violent and the trains moved off. We then rode away from the RR Track which being shelled by a Gun Boat being near the RR Depot. We had not gone far from the town when the last Locomotive left without any trains.

* * *

Letter Written by Dr. Thomas D. Martin, former assistant at Neuse General Hospital (New Bern), to Surgeon General S. P. Moore, March 21, 1862, Goldsboro, N.C.

Sir,

I have communication from you in relation to the conduct of the Medical Director of this Department at the attack on New Berne. I was the asst. Surgeon of the General Hospital New Berne. On the morning of the attack on New Berne Dr. Waring was engaged with Surgeon Moore of the [Neuse] General Hospital in the amputation of a leg. This amputation was completed about half past eight or nine o'clock a.m. Dr. Waring & Dr. Moore with Dr. [Cyrus E.] Worrell of 2nd Cavalry Regt. then left for the battlefield. Dr. Waring returned about half past ten o'clock a.m. with Dr. Holt of Branch Hospital. Previous to this the Militia and the 35th Regt. N.C.T. had passed the hospital in full treat. During the early part of the day I had been engaged in making preparations to remove the sick in pursuance to orders received from Dr. Waring, who had been engaged during the night previous until 5 o'clock a.m. trying to get a train from Genl. Branch and the president of the R. Road.

A few moments after Dr. Waring returned to the hospital from the battlefield, several wounded were brought to the hospital. Dr. Waring ordered them dressed and put on the train. Dr. Waring requested me to invite Drs. Warren and Crowell, who were in the hospital then, to come in to the hospital and assist in dressing the wounded. This they did. Such as men only slightly wounded after their wounds had been dressed were told to get on board the train. After this, the wounded were not removed to the train. Dr. Waring seemed undecided and worried, and said he wanted the wounded all sent to Goldsboro. In a conversation with Drs. Warren, Waring and Crowell, I heard Dr. Waring say that he thought that proper preparation should be made to leave. That as Medical Director and Purveyor of this Department his responsibilities and duties required that he should not be taken prisoner.

The sick were all removed except such as were too ill to bear the journey to Goldsboro. After his Dr. Warren began giving chloroform to a patient upon whom Dr. Crowell was about to operate. About this time the enemy began to shell the town. One shell passed very nearly over the Hospital. The railroad bridge and lower part of the city were on fire. Dr. Waring and my self then left the Hospital. This is the last time I saw Dr. Waring in New Berne. Dr. Waring overtook me some 4 or 5 miles out of town on his way to Kinston.

* * *

Letter Written by Brig. Gen. Richard C. Gatlin, former commander of the Department of North Carolina, to Surgeon General S. P. Moore, March 19, 1862, Goldsboro, N.C.

Sir,

Understanding from Surgeon Waring, that for certain reasons, he is about to apply to be relieved from the duties of Medical Director of this Department, I avail myself of the occasion to express to you, my entire satisfaction of the manner in which he has performed the very arduous duties incident to the organization of his department. He has worked with untiring energy and with a zeal which cannot be too highly Commended. I recommend him to your favorable notion.

\# \# \#

Appendix B

Destruction of the 1st North Carolina Hospital (Petersburg, Va.)

Letter One:

Petersburg, Va., April 13, 1862

Sir,

I'm very sorry to have to inform you of the total destruction of the 1st North Carolina Hospital, by fire, last night between the hours of 9 and 12 o'clock.

The fire was first discovered about 9 ½ o'clock, the alarm given and every effort made to put out the fire, but all in vain. Everything in the hospital was destroyed except the books and the greater [portion] of the medicines which were saved. It was either the act of an incendiary or of spontaneous combustion, for the room in which the fire was first discovered was that in which the effects of men who had died in the hospital was deposited. The ward master had the key in his pocket and had not had occasion to enter the room in weeks.

Assistant Surgeon F. M. Henderson who was in charge, informed me that he had visited that portion of the hospital about 8 o'clock and found everything in good order. As you are aware there has been no patients in this hospital for several weeks, and it was being repaired and thoroughly cleaned and would have been in readiness for the reception of patients on Wednesday.

There were seven white men, six of them attendants, in the hospital when the fire was first discovered. Three of them in the office, one on the second floor and three on the third. They continued to try to put out the fire, until they were compelled to leave the building by the smoke. I have examined all of them who saw the fire at first and they all give it the same location viz. in the closet adjoining the dining room. One of the men went through the kitchen and dining room to the closet and looked into the pantry adjoining the closet and did not see fire or signs of any, except in the closet, and when first discovered the smoke and fire was coming through the floor of the 2nd story over the closet. There are some reasons for suspecting that it was fired, by a negro boy who had been and was employed there, and I will endeavor to have it thoroughly investigated.

The government lost some 250 hospital shirts, 250 hospital drawers, 25 bed sacks, one cooking stove complete and some few other articles, all the other property belonged to the State of North Carolina. Enclosed I send you a plot of the ground on the 1st floor of the hospital, where the fire originated with remarks.

I will distribute the medical officers and attendance to the other hospitals, where they may be needed until I hear from you. They will be required if we receive any wounded from below. I also enclose the remarks of Assistant Surgeon Henderson on the morning report for this day.

I Am Sir, Very Respectfully

Your Obt. Servant

P. E. Hines, Surgeon
In Charge of Hospitals

Surgeon Wm. A. Carrington
Medical Director, Richmond, Va.

[Assistant Surgeon Henderson log entry]

April 13, 1863

Remarks. At 9 o'clock last night the first North Carolina hospital building was discovered to be on fire. The entire building, with beds, furniture, etc. was concerned. Medical and commissary stores and records saved. Minute examinations with the probable cause of the fire, as well as the secluded location of its origin all tend strongly towards incrimination. Morgan a slave nurse has not reported for duty today.[1]

Letter Two:

Petersburg, Va., April 16, 1863

Sir,

I have the honor to acknowledge the receipt of your letter of the 15th instant; and to report that the boy Morgan, an employee of the 1st N.C. Hospital had been arrested, tried for burning that hospital, pleaded guilty and was sentenced to be hanged, by the court today. He acknowledged that he set the house on fire and said that he was persuaded to do so by others, and another boy, also employed in that hospital is held in jail, for investigation and trial, as an accessory. It seems that the fire was caused to prevent the discovery of some thefts of clothes of soldiers who died in the hospital, of which he and others had been guilty and which would have been certainly discovered on Monday or Tuesday, if the hospital had not been burned up.

I beg leave to respectfully recommend that some person be appointed to receive and store and take care of the effects of all blank, who die, in all the hospitals in this place, outside and apart from any of the hospital buildings.[2]

I Am Sir, Very Respectfully

Your Obt. Servant

P. E. Hines, Surgeon
In Charge of Hospitals

Surgeon Wm. A. Carrington
Medical Director, Richmond, Va.

---

1. P. E. Hines to Wm. A. Carrington, April 13, 1863, Peter E. Hines, M331, roll 128, RG109, NA. See Hines' compiled service record for the enclosed sketch of the hospital's first floor.
2. P. E. Hines to Wm. A. Carrington, April 16, 1863, ibid. The author did not transcribe the final two pages of Hines' April 16 letter, as the contents did not pertain to the destruction of the hospital.

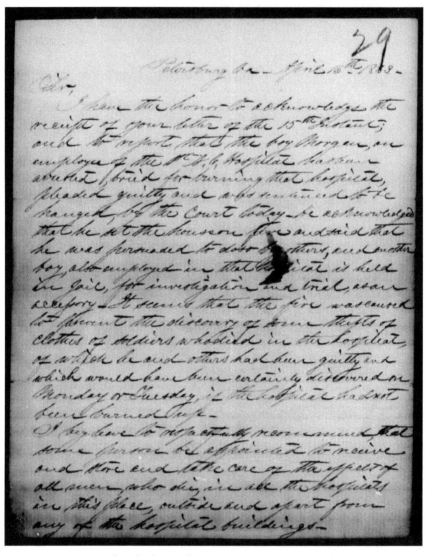

Example of a letter from Surgeon Peter E. Hines.

(National Archives)

Appendix C

Satchwell's "Hospital Defenders"

General Hospital No. 2, Wilson, N.C.
July 24, 1863
Surgeon Graves,

My Dear Sir,

I have the honor to acknowledge your communication of July 22nd, offering for the defense of this late beleaguered garrison your gallant corps. Allow me to congratulate you upon the brilliant successes, achieved in behalf of Goldsboro and Southern Independence by the "Hospital Invincibles" under your command. Let me also call your attention to the activity displayed and the valor shown in defense of Wilson.

Immediately upon the reception of the intelligence that and immense armament of negroes and negro-stealers were advancing upon this point, the citizens flew ...to their trunks and wardrobes, the militia flew to the woods, and the "Hospital Defenders" flew to arms, to rally in defense of their bunks, their rations, their homes, and all they hold dear (and what is there not dear now?) This glorious band, composed of the half and the maimed, and the blind, of those who have [ ] miseries in the bowels, in the back, and especially in the breast, were stationed where the mighty toss not rolls its languid tide, to guard the bridge there placed, which was the key to this situation. Soon, too, the militia rallied handsomely and reinforced the "Defenders," and the whole army was put under command of Commodore [William F.] Lynch (that never flinches) who promptly offered to lead our troops to victory and glory. By his skill and energy, and with incredible alacrity and diligence, the bridge was destroyed, timber felled abreast the road, and two lines of entrenchments at least sixty yards in length were thrown up. The enemy hearing the defiant sound of axe and spade, and the ring of arms, wisely concluded to retire without attack.

Col. [Stephen D.] Pool with his command of one hundred and eighty men, was sent with discretionary powers to protect Wilson, Rocky Mount or Tarboro, wherever he might be more efficient. He arrived here between the hours of six and seven, and was urged by many to proceed immediately to the defense of Rocky Mount, which place the enemy did not reach till nine o'clock. Commodore Lynch having assumed the responsibility of defending this point, and Col. Pool assembling thereto. He was urged, and it was expected that he would go with all possible dispatch to the defense of Rocky Mount. For some cause or other, Col. Pool delayed and hesitated until late in the forenoon, and then rode to within eight miles of the place, saw the smoke of its burning property, and retired. By the conduct, he has gained no glory, in the popular esteem, as a strategist or fighter, but is rather considered like the war horse of old, to delight in snuffing the battle afar off. And thus, has Rocky Mount been desolated, and immense destruction of property ensued, which might have been prevented, as is currently believed, had Col. Pool gallantly rushed forward to protect the point. But I am no military man. The enemy has retired. His spies informed him doubtless of the impracticability of taking this citadel. The "Defenders" wearied of the inactivity of this post have been transferred to the regular army.

Yet the post is safe. The militia now used to scenes of daring and danger, will rush to protect Wilson from attack, and add to the laurels they have earned.

A great achievement for your gallant "Invincibles" and my "Defenders" would be to return the compliment of such visits, by taking possession of the fair towns that now suffer so much from the iron bondage under which they groan. Any feasible plan you may suggest for accomplishing so important an enterprise, I will readily entertain, and most heartily cooperate with you in effecting it.[1]

I have the honor to be
Very Respectfully
Your ob't. servt and friend

S. S. Satchwell
Surgeon P.A.C.S. in charge

---

1. S. S. Satchwell to Graves, July 24, 1863, William A. Holt Papers, SHC/UNC.

BIBLIOGRAPHY

Newspapers

Carolina Watchman (Salisbury, NC)
Daily Bulletin (Charlotte, NC)
Charlotte Observer (NC)
Daily Progress (Raleigh, NC)
Daily Standard (Raleigh, NC)
Fayetteville Observer (NC)
Fayetteville Semi-Weekly Observer (NC)
Goldsboro Tribune (NC)
Greensboro Daily News (NC)
Greensboro Patriot (NC)
Greenville Times (NC)
High Point Enterprise (NC)
Highland Recorder (Monterey, VA)
Kinston Free Press (NC)
News and Observer (Raleigh, NC)
News and Record (Greensboro, NC)
Newbern Daily Progress (New Bern, NC)
Newbern Weekly Progress (New Bern, NC)
North Carolina Standard (Raleigh, NC)
North Carolina Weekly Standard (Raleigh, NC)
North Carolina Whig (Charlotte, NC)
Our Living Dead (New Bern, NC)
Raleigh Register (NC)
Richmond Dispatch (VA)
Semi-Weekly State Journal (Raleigh, NC)
Semi-Weekly Standard (Raleigh, NC)
Siler City Grit (NC)
Spirit of the Age (Raleigh, NC)
State Journal (Raleigh, NC)
Tarboro Southerner (NC)
Weekly Progress (Raleigh, NC)
Weekly Raleigh Register (NC)
Weekly State Journal (Raleigh, NC)
Wilmington Daily Journal (NC)
Wilmington Journal (NC)

Manuscripts and Collections

Charlotte-Mecklenburg Public Library, Carolina Room, Charlotte, NC
Wilkes-Smedberg Family Papers

Duke University, Perkins Library, Durham, NC
Gertrude Jenkins Papers, 1859-1908
John and Edmund Haywood Papers
Thomas Hill "Sketch of General Hospital No. 8, Peace Institute, Raleigh"
Tillinghast Family Papers
Miss Sarah Ann Tillinghast, "Sherman's Army in Fayetteville"

East Carolina University, Joyner Library, Greenville, NC
Thomas Sparrow Papers

Greensboro History Museum, Greensboro, NC
Thomas Lee Doster Papers

High Point Public Library, North Carolina Collection, High Point, NC
Barbee Hotel Confederate Hospital Registry (1863–1865)

Lower Cape Fear Historical Society, Wilmington, NC
Confederate Veteran Talks

National Archives and Records Administration, Washington, D.C.
Record Group (RG) 94: Records of the Adjutant General's Office, 1780s–1917

Letters Received by the Adjutant General, 1861-1870
RG 109: War Department Collection of Confederate Records
Chap. I: Adjutant and Inspector's Generals Office (AIGO)
Vol 474: Letters Received by the Confederate AIGO, 1861–1865
Chap. II: Department of North Carolina (NC) and the Department of North
Carolina and Southern Virginia
Vol. 259 1/ 2: Orders and Circulars Issued, 1861–1865
Vol. 262 1/2: Letters and Telegrams Sent, Aug. 25, 1861–March 7, 1862
Vol. 331: Letters Sent and Orders Issued by the Wilmington Command,
Apr.–May 1861
Chap. VI: Medical Department
Vol. 35: Letters, Orders, and Circulars Issued and Received, Military
Prison Hospital, Salisbury, N.C., May 1, 1864–Mar. 22, 1865
Vol. 151: Statistical Reports of Hospitals in Virginia, 1862–64

Vol. 280: Statistical Reports of Patients and Attendants, Office of the Medical Director of Hospitals in North Carolina, 1863–65

Vol. 399: Letters Sent, General Hospital No. 4, Sept. 12, 1863–Feb. 19, 1865

Vol. 401: Letters, Telegrams and Orders Received, General Hospital No. 4, Sept. 5, 1863–Feb. 19, 1865

Vol. 402: Reports of the Officer of the Day, General Hospital No. 4, Oct. 16, 1863–May 10, 1864

Vol. 415, Letters, Orders, and Circulars Received General Hospital No. 2, Jan. 13, 1864–March 1, 1865

Vol. 644: Record of Reports Received, Inspector of Hospitals, Richmond, 1863–64

Vol. 739–741: Letters, Orders, and Circulars Sent, Surgeon General's Office, 1861–65

Microfilm M251: Compiled Service Records of Confederate Soldiers Who Served in Organizations from the State of Florida

Microfilm M266: Compiled Service Records of Confederate Soldiers Who Served in Organizations from the State of Georgia

Microfilm M267: Compiled Service Records of Confederate Soldiers Who Served in Organizations from the State of South Carolina

Microfilm M270: Compiled Service Records of Confederate Soldiers Who Served in Organizations from the State of North Carolina

Microfilm M324: Compiled Service Records of Confederate Soldiers Who Served in Organizations from the State of Virginia

Microfilm M331: Compiled Service Records of Confederate Generals and Staff Officers, and Nonregimental Enlisted Men

Microfilm M346: Confederate Papers Relating to Citizens or Business Firms, 1861–1865

Microfilm M347: Unfiled Papers and Slips Belonging in Confederate Compiled Service Records

Microfilm M474: Letters Received by the Confederate Adjutant and Inspector General, 1861–65

Microfilm M901: General Orders and Circulars of the Confederate War Department, 1861–65

Microfilm M1761: Muster Rolls and Lists of Confederate Troops Paroled in North Carolina

U. S. Federal Census (1860)

New Hanover Public Library, Wilmington, NC
Bill Reaves Collection, Seaman's Bethel File

North Carolina Office of Archives and History, Raleigh, NC
Governor's Papers: Henry T. Clark
Governor's Papers: John W. Ellis

Governor's Papers: Zebulon B. Vance
Ira Heath Papers
Military Collection-Civil War
    Joseph B. Cheshire, Jr. Memoirs "Some Account of My Life for My Children"
    North Carolina Surgeon General Edward Warren Report, 1864
    Special Orders, Surgeon General Edward Warren
Thomas Merritt Pittman Collection
Shaffner Diary and Papers
Lowry Shuford Collection
"Record of a Soldier in the Late War"
"The Confederate Hospital of Charlotte, N.C."

Rowan County Public Library, Edith Clark History Room, Salisbury, NC
    Louis A. Brown File

University of North Carolina at Asheville, Ramsey Library
    "Medicine in Buncombe County Down to 1885"

University of North Carolina at Chapel Hill, Wilson Library, Southern Historical Collection
    DeRosset Family Papers
    Earnest Haywood Collection of Haywood Family Papers
    William A. Holt Papers
    Drury Lacy Papers
    McKay-Stiles Papers
    Eliza Hall Parsley Papers
    James Ryder Randall Papers
    Jonathan Worth Papers

University of North Carolina at Wilmington, Randall Library, Special Collections
    Letters Sent Gen. W. H. C. Whiting's command, July 1863–August 1864

Virginia Museum of History & Culture, Richmond, VA
    New Bern Relief Society
    Kate S. Sperry Diary

Wilson County Public Library, History and Genealogy Room, Wilson, NC
    Records of the Wilson Confederate Hospital

Private Collections

Marshall W. Butt, Jr., Surgeon Holt F. Butt Personal Papers
Robert J. Cooke, Wilmington's Civil War Hospitals
Frank Hall, J. A. Warner Civil War Letters

Government Publications

Surgeon General's Office, United States Army, *The Medical and Surgical History of the*
Civil War, 6 volumes. Wilmington, NC: Broadfoot Publishing Company, 1990-1992.
Supplement to the Official Records of the Union and Confederate Armies. 100 volumes.
United States Navy Department. *Official Records of the Union and Confederate Navies in the War of the Rebellion.* 30 volumes. Washington, D.C.: Government Printing Office, 1900-1901.
United States War Department. *The War of the Rebellion: A Compilation of the Official Records of the Union and Confederate Armies.* 128 volumes. Washington, D.C.: Government Printing Office, 1880-1891.

Articles and Books

Adams, George Worthington. *Doctors in Blue: The Medical History of the Union Army in the Civil War.* Baton Rouge, LA: Louisiana State University Press, 1996.
_____. "Confederate Medicine." *Journal of Southern History* 6, no. 2 (May 1940): 151-66.
Ainsley, W. Frank. *The Historic Architecture of Warsaw, North Carolina.* Timberlake, NC: Righter Publishing Co., 2008.
Amis, Moses N. *Historical Raleigh: With Sketches of Wake County (from 1771) and Its Important Towns.* Raleigh, NC: Commercial Printing Co., 1913.
Anderson, Lucy London. *North Carolina Women of the Confederacy.* (1906), Updated and compiled by the Cape Fear No. 3 United Daughters of the Confederacy Wilmington, NC: Winoca Press, 2006.
Archbell, L. V. "Whitfield House." *Carolina and the Southern Cross* 1, no. 1 (November 1912): 2.
Barnett, D. Christopher. "Hospital Life within the Confederate Medical Department." *The Museum of the Confederacy Journal* 75 (1997).
Barrett, John G. *The Civil War in North Carolina.* Chapel Hill, NC: University of North Carolina Press, 1963.
Baxley, Haughton, M.D. "Surgeons of the Confederacy." *Confederate Veteran* 34, no. 5 (May 1926): 172-173.

Bemiss, S. D., M.D. and W. S. Mitchell, M.D., eds. Index to Vol. XXII: *The New Orleans Journal of Medicine*. New Orleans: n.p., 1869.

Bishir, Catherine W. The "Unpainted Aristocracy." Raleigh, NC: Division of Archives and History, Third Printing, 1983.

Black, Mary Gardner. "Confederate Surgeons and Hospitals." *Confederate Veteran* 36, no. 5 (May 1928): 183-185.

Black, III, Robert C. *The Railroads of the Confederacy*. Chapel Hill, NC: University North Carolina Press, 1952.

Branch, Paul. *Fort Macon a History*. Charleston, SC: Nautical & Aviation Publishing Company of America, 1999.

Brewer, James H. *The Confederate Negro: Virginia's Craftsmen and Military Laborers, 1861–1865*. Durham, NC: Duke University Press, 1969.

Brown, Louis A. *The Salisbury Prison: A Case Study of Confederate Military Prisons 1861–1865*. Wendell, NC: Avera Press, 1980.

Bryan, Mary Norcott. *A Grandmother's Recollection of Dixie*. New Bern, NC: O. G. Dunn, printer, 1912.

Caknipe, John, Jr. *Randolph Macon College in the Early Years*. Jefferson, NC: McFarland Publishing, 2014.

Calcutt, Rebecca Barbour, *Richmond's Wartime Hospitals*. Gretna, LA: Pelican Publishing Company, 2005.

_____. *South Carolina's Confederate Hospitals*. Self-published, CreateSpace, 2015.

Cashman, Diane, et. al., ed. *The Lonely Road: A History of the Physics and Physicians of the Lower Cape Fear, 1735–1976*. n.p.: privately published, 1978.

Chamberlain, Hope S. *History of Wake County North Carolina: With Sketches of Those Who Have Most Influenced Its Development*. Raleigh, NC: Edwards & Broughton Printing Co., 1922.

Chapman, Sarah Benson, ed. *Bright and Gloomy Days: The Civil War Correspondence of Captain Charles Frederic Bahnson, a Moravian Confederate*. Knoxville, TN: University of Tennessee Press, 2003.

Cheshire, Joseph B. *The Church in the Confederate States: A History of the Protestant Episcopal Church in the Confederate States*. New York, NY: Longmans, Green, and Co. 1912.

Churchill, Winston. *My Early Life: A Roving Commission*. London, London: Thornton Butterworth, Ltd., 1930.

Clark, Walter, ed. *Histories of the Several Regiments and Battalions from North Carolina in the Great War 1861-'65. Written by members of the Respective Commands*. 5 vols. Goldsboro, NC: Nash Brothers, 1901.

Clinard, Karen L. and Richard Russell, comps. and eds. *Fear in North Carolina: The Civil War Journals and Letters of the Henry Family*. Asheville, NC: Reminiscing Books, 2008.

Crenshaw, Doug. *Richmond Shall Not Be Given Up: The Seven Days' Battles, June 25–July 1, 1862*. El Dorado Hills, CA: Savas Beatie, 2017.

Crews, C. Daniel and Lisa D. Bailey, eds. *Records of the Moravians in North Carolina, vol. 12: 1856–1866*. Raleigh, NC: Division of Archives and History, 2000.

Cunningham, H. H. *Doctors in Gray: The Confederate Medical Service.* Baton Rouge, LA: Louisiana State University Press, 1958, 2nd edition, 1986.

_____. "The Confederate Medical Officer in the Field." *Bulletin of the New York Academy of Medicine* 34, no. 7 (July 1958): 461-88.

_____. "Edmund Burke Haywood and Raleigh's Confederate Hospitals." *North Carolina Historical Review* 35, no. 2 (April 1958): 153-66.

_____. "Confederate General Hospitals: Establishment and Organization." *Journal of Southern History* 75, no. 3 (July 1954): 376-94.

Crute, Joseph H. Jr. *Confederate Staff Officers: 1861 – 1865.* Powhatan, VA: Derwent Books, 1982.

Curtis, Dr. Walter G. *Reminiscences of Wilmington and Smithville.* Southport, NC: Herald Job Office, 1905.

Cushman, Diane, et. al., ed. *Lonely Road: A History of the Physics and Physicians of the Lower Cape Fear, 1735–1976.* Privately Published, 1978.

Dammann, Gordon, D.D.S., and Bollet, Alfred Jay, M.D. *Images of Civil War Medicine: A Photographic History.* New York, NY: Demos Medical Publishing, 2008.

Dargan, C. P. "A Wayside Hospital." *Confederate Veteran* 24, no. 8 (August 1916): 1.

"Patriotic Mrs. Armand J. DeRosset." *Confederate Veteran* 3, no. 7 (July 1895): 218-19.

Edwards, James D. *Memories: A Pictorial History of Vance County, North Carolina.* Henderson, NC: D-Books Publishing, Inc. 2006.

Edwards, Tom J. and William H. Rowland. *Through the Eyes of Soldiers: That Battle of Wyse Fork: Kinston, North Carolina, March 7-10, 1865.* Kinston, NC: Lenoir County Historical Association, 2006.

Faust, Drew Filpin. *Mothers of Invention: Women of the Slaveholding South in the American Civil War.* Chapel Hill, NC: University of North Carolina Press, 1996.

First Baptist Church, High Point, N.C. History Committee. *History of the First Baptist Church, 1825 – 1968.* High Point, NC: The Church, 1969.

Fisher, R. H. *Biographical Sketches of Wilmington's Citizens.* Wilmington, NC: Wilmington Stamp and Printing, 1929.

Fleming, Monika. *Edgecombe County: Along the Tar River.* Charleston, SC: Arcadia Publishing, 2003.

Foley, Bradley R., and Adrian L. Whicker, comp. "The Wayside Hospital Registry in High Point, Part 13, Final Edition." *The Guilford Genealogist* 40, no. 4 (Winter 2013): 36-57.

Foley, Bradley R., ed., with Adrian L. Whicker. *The Civil War Ends: Greensboro, April 1865. A Historical Study of the Civil War in Guilford County.* Greensboro, NC: Guilford County Genealogical Society, 2008.

Fonvielle, Chris E., Jr. *The Wilmington Campaign: Last Rays of Departing Hope.* Campbell, CA: Savas Publishing, 1997.

_____. "Welcome Brothers! The 1865 Union Prisoners of War Exchange in North Carolina." *North Carolina Historical Review* 92, no. 3 (July 2015): 278-311.

Gaddis, James L., Jr. *Richard Gatlin and the Confederate Defense of Eastern North Carolina*. Charleston, SC: The History Press, 2015.

Gadski, Mary Ellen. *The History of the New Bern Academy*. New Bern, NC: Tyron Palace Commission, 1986.

Gallagher, Sallie. "Dr. John A. Gallagher." *Carolina and the Southern Cross*, no. 8 (October 1913): 21.

Greene, A. Wilson. *The Second Battle of Manassas*. Fort Washington, PA: Eastern National Park and Monument Association, 2006.

Green, Carol C. Chimborazo: *The Confederacy's Largest Hospital*. Knoxville, TN: University of Tennessee Press, 2004.

Hall, Lewis P. *Land of the Golden River: Historical Events and Stories of Southeastern North Carolina and the Lower Cape Fear*, 3 vols., Wilmington, NC: Wilmington Printing, 1975.

Hairr, John. *Bizarre Tales of the Cape Fear Country*. Fuquay-Varina, NC: Triangle Books, 1995.

Hardy, Michael. *Civil War Charlotte: Last Capital of the Confederacy*. Charleston, SC: Arcadia Publishing, 2012.

Hasegawa, Guy R. *Matchless organization: The Confederate Army Medical Department*. Carbondale, IL: Southern Illinois University Press, 2021.

Herring, Ethel, and Carol Williams. *Fort Caswell: In War and Peace*. Wendell, NC: Broadfoot Bookmark, 1983.

Hilde, Libra R. *Worth a Dozen Men: Women and Nursing in the Civil War South*. Charlottesville, VA: University of Virginia Press, 2012.

Houck, Peter W. *A Prototype of a Confederate Hospital Center in Lynchburg, Virginia*. Lynchburg, VA: Warwick House Publishing, 1986.

Howell, E. Vernon. *"Medical and Pharmaceutical Conditions in the Confederacy," Proceedings of the Eighteen Annual Session of the State Literary and Historical Association of North Carolina*. Raleigh, NC: Edwards & Broughton Printing Co., 1918.

Hufham, J. D., Rev. *Memoir of Rev. John L. Prichard: Late Pastor of the First Baptist Church, Wilmington, N. C.* Raleigh, NC: Hufham and Hughes, Publishers, 1867.

James, Mrs. W. C. *Fannie E. S. Heck: A Study of the Hidden Springs in a Rarely Useful and Victorious Life*. Nashville, TN: Broadman Press, 1939.

Johnson, K. Todd. *Historic Wake County: The Story of Raleigh and Wake County*. San Antonio, TX: Historic Publication Network, 2009.

Johnston, Hugh Buckner, Jr. *Records of the Wilson Confederate Hospital, 1862–1865*. Wilson, NC: Johnston, 1954.

_____. "The Wilson Confederate Hospital 1862-1865." *United Daughters of Confederacy Magazine* 52, no. 10 (October 1989): 35-41.

Jones, Harry A., Jr. *Tarborough and Its Academies*. Greenville, NC: Ira Press, 1975.

Kearns, Randy D., M.D. *Sanatoriums and Asylums of Eastern North Carolina*. Charleston, SC: Arcadia Publishing, 2018.

Kenny, Stephen C. "A Dictate of Both Interest and Mercy: Slave Hospitals in the

Antebellum South." *Journal of the History of Medicine and Allied Sciences* 65, no. 1 (January 2010): 1-47.

Koonce, Donald B., ed. *Doctor to the Front: The Recollections of Confederate Surgeon Thomas Fanning Wood 1861-1865.* Knoxville, TN: University of Tennessee Press, 2000.

Kratt, Mary N. *Charlotte: Spirit of the New South.* Winston Salem, NC: J. F. Blair Publishing, 1992.

Kulikowski, Jennifer A., and Kenneth E. Peters. *Historic Raleigh.* Charleston, SC: Arcadia Publishing, 2002.

Kyle, James, Mrs. *"No. 25—Fayetteville and Wytheville," Our Women in the War: The Lives they Lived; The Deaths They Died, from the Weekly News and Courier, Charleston, S.C.* Charleston, SC: News and Courier Book Press, 1885, 144-48.

Lawrence, R. C. "Dr. E. Burke Haywood." State 10, no. 4 (June 1942): 3, 22.

Loehr, Walter J., M.D. "Civil War Medicine in North Carolina." *North Carolina Medical Journal* 43, no. 2 (February 1982): 121-22.

Long, Dorothy, ed. *Medicine in North Carolina: Essays in the History of Medical Science and Medical Service, 1524–1960,* 2 vols. Raleigh, NC: the North Carolina Medical Society, 1972.

Lounsbury, Carl, *The Architecture of Southport.* Southport, NC: Southport Historical Society, 1979.

Mallison, Fred M. *The Civil War on the Outer Banks: A History of the Late Rebellion along the Coast of North Carolina from Carteret to Currituck.* Jefferson, NC: McFarland & Co., Inc. 1998.

Manarin, Louis H., Weymouth T. Jordan, Jr., Matthew M. Brown, and Michael W. Coffey, comps. *North Carolina Troops 1861-1865 A Roster,* 20 vols. to date. Raleigh, NC: Division of Archives and History, Department of Cultural Resources,1966-.

Marshall, Mary Louise. "Nurse Heroines of the Confederacy." *Bulletin of the Medical Library Association* 45, no. 3 (July 1957): 319-36.

Martinez, Jaime Amanda. *Confederate Slave Impressment in the Upper South.* Chapel Hill, NC: University of North Carolina Press, 2013.

Mast, Greg. *State Troops and Volunteers: A Photographic Record of North Carolina's Civil War Soldiers.* Raleigh, NC: North Carolina Division of Archives and History, Department of Cultural Resources, 1995.

Mathews, James M. "Public Laws of the Confederate States of America, passed at the First Session of the First Congress; 1862," The statutes at large of the Confederate States of America. Richmond, VA: R. M. Smith, printer to Congress, 1862),

Matthews, Mary G., and M. Jewell Sink. *Wheels of Faith and Courage: A History of Thomasville, North Carolina.* High Point, NC: Hall Printing Co., 1952.

McEachern, Leora H. and Williams, Isabel M. "The Prevailing Epidemic—1862." *Lower Cape Fear Historical Society, Inc. Bulletin* 11, no. 1 (November 1967): 1, 3-20.

_____. "Miss Buie, The Soldier's Friend." *Lower Cape Fear Historical Society, Inc. Bulletin* 18, no. 1 (October 1974): 1-4.

McKean, Brenda C. *Blood and War at My Doorstep: North Carolina Civilians in the War Between the States*, vol. 2. Xlibris Corporation, 2011.

McMahan, Margaret T. *John A. Oates and the Campbellton Children: Including a Story of Campbellton on the Cape Fear*. Clinton, NC: Bass Publishing Co., 1957.

Merrill, James M. *The Rebel Shore: The Story of Union Sea Power in the Civil War*. Boston: Little, Brown & Co., 1957.

Miller, Brian Craig. *Empty Sleeves: Amputation in the Civil War*. Athens, GA: University of Georgia Press, 2015.

Moore, Carol. *Guilford County and the Civil War*. Charleston, SC: The History Press, 2015.

Murray, Elizabeth Reid. *Wake: Capital County of North Carolina, Vol. I: Prehistory through Centennial*. Raleigh, NC: Capital County Publishing, 1983.

Moore, James, M.D., *Kilpatrick and Our Cavalry: Comprising a Sketch of the Life of General Kilpatrick*. New York, NY: W. J. Widdleton, Publisher, 1865.

Morrill, Dan L. *Historic Charlotte: An Illustrated History of Charlotte and Mecklenburg County*. San Antonio, TX: Historical Publishing Network, 2001.

Munson, E. B., ed. *Confederate Incognito: The Civil War Reports of "Long Grabs," a.k.a. Murdoch John McSween, 26th and 35th North Carolina Infantry*. Jefferson, NC. McFarland & Company, Inc. Publishers, 2013.

Newsome, Hampton. *The Fight for the Old North State: The Civil War in North Carolina, January – May 1864*. Lawrence, KS: University Press of Kansas, 2018.

Nifong, Dorothy R. *Brethren with Stethoscopes*. Winston-Salem, NC: Hunter Pub. Co., 1965.

Nightingale, Florence. *Notes on Hospitals*. London: John W. Parker and Sons, 1859.

Norris, David A. *Potter's Raid: The Union Cavalry's Boldest Expedition in Eastern North Carolina*. Wilmington, NC: Dram Tree Books, 2007.

_____. "For the Benefit of Our Gallant Volunteers." *The North Carolina Historical Review* 75, no. 3 (July 1998): 297-326.

_____. "The Yankees Have Been Here!: The Story of Brig. Gen. Edward E. Potter's Raid on Greenville, Tarboro, and Rocky Mount, July 19-23, 1863." *The North Carolina Historical Review* 73, no. 1 (January 1996): 297-326.

Oliver, F. E. and S. L. Abbot, eds. *The Boston Medical and Surgical Journal* 66 (1862): 279-80.

Paschal, George W. *History of Wake Forest College*, 2 vols. Raleigh, NC: Edwards & Broughton Co. 1943.

Pearce, T. H. "Kittrell Remembers." *State* 41, no. 1 (June 1973): 18-20.

Perry, Octavian Jordan and Whipple, Mildred. *History of the First Presbyterian Church, High Point, North Carolina, 1859 – 1959*. High Point, NC: Hall Printing Co., 1959.

Pezzoni, J. Daniel. *The History of Architecture of Lee County, N.C.* Sanford, NC: Railroad House Historical Association, Inc., 1995.

Pollitt, Phoebe A. *The History of Professional Nursing in North Carolina, 1902–2002*. Durham, NC: Carolina Academic Press, 2014.

Pollitt, Phoebe A. and Camille Reese. "When One Goes Nursing, All Things Must Be Expected." *Confederate Veteran* 2 (2002): 23-31.

Phillips, Robert L. *History of the Hospitals in Greensboro*. Greensboro, NC: Printworks, 1996.

Powell, William S. *Higher Education in North Carolina*, 2nd edition. Raleigh, NC: Department of Archives and History, 1964.

_____, ed. *Dictionary of North Carolina Biography*, 6 vols. Chapel Hill, NC: University of North Carolina Press, 1979.

Raper, Charles Lee, *The Church and Private Schools of North Carolina: A Historical Study*. Greensboro, NC: Jos. J. Stone, Book and Job Printer, 1898.

Rodman, Lida T. "William Blount Rodman." *Carolina and the Southern Cross* 1, no. 8 (October 1913): 3-7.

Sandbeck, Peter B. *The Historic Architecture of New Bern and Craven County, North Carolina*. New Bern, NC: Tyron Palace Commission, 1988.

Salsi, Lynn and Burke. *Guilford County: Heart of the Piedmont*. Charleston, SC: Arcadia Pub., 2002.

Sauers, Richard A. *A Succession of Honorable Victories: The Burnside Expedition in North Carolina*. Dayton, OH: Morningside, 1996.

Schroeder-Lein, Glenna R. *Confederate Hospitals on the Move: Samuel H. Stout and the Army of Tennessee*. Columbia, SC: University of South Carolina Press, 1994.

Schurr, Nance. "Inside the Confederate Hospital: Community and Conflict during the Civil War." PhD diss., University of Tennessee, 2004.

Seth, Joseph B. "Dr. Edward N. Covey, of Maryland." *Confederate Veteran* 34, no. 6 (June 1926): 210.

Shafer, Steve. *The Order Book of Brigadier General Lawrence O'Bryan Branch, Confederate Army*. Independently Published, 2021.

Silkenat, David. *Driven from Home: North Carolina's Civil War Refugee Crisis*. Athens, GA: University of Georgia Press, 2016.

Sloan, John A. *Reminiscences of the Guilford Grays, Co. B, 27th N. C. Regiment*. Washington, D.C.: R. O. Polkinhorn, Printer, 1883.

Smith, Gustavus W. *Confederate Papers*. New York: Atlantic Publishing & Engraving Co., 1884.

Smith, Robert K. and Earl O'Neal, Jr., ed. *The History of Fort Ocracoke in Pamlico Sound*. Charleston, SC: The History Press, 2015.

Sokolosky, Wade and Mark A. Smith. *To Prepare for Sherman's Coming: The Battle of Wise's Forks, March 1865*. El Dorado Hills, CA: Savas Beatie, 2015.

Sondley, F. A. *Asheville and Buncombe County*. Asheville, NC: The Inland Press, 1922.

Sparrow, Joy W., ed. *Sparrow's Nest of Letters*. Wake Forest, NC: Scuppernong Press, 2011.

Sprunt, James. *Chronicles of the Cape Fear River, 1660–1916*. Wilmington, NC: Broadfoot Publishing Co., 1992.

Stancil, Jerry. "Confederate Deaths at the Wilson Hospital." *Trees of Wilson: the Newsletter of the Wilson County Genealogical Society* 9, no. 5 (May 2000): 8-9.

Stockard, Sallie W. *History of Guilford County, North Carolina*. Knoxville, TN: Gaut-Ogden, Co., Printers & Book Binding, 1902.

Straubing, Harold Elk, comp. *In Hospital and Camp: The Civil War through the Eyes of Its Doctors and Nurses*. Harrisburg, PA: Stackpole Books, 1993.

Strong, Charles M., M.D. *History of Mecklenburg County Medicine*. Columbia, NY: New Printing House, 1929.

Tompkins, Daniel A. *History of Mecklenburg County and the City of Charlotte: From 1740 to 1903, Vol. I*. Charlotte, NC: Observer Print House, 1903.

Trotter, William R. *Ironclads and Columbiads: The Civil War in North Carolina, The Coast*. Winston Salem, NC: John F. Blair, Publisher, 1989.

Tyndall, Cliff. *Threshold of Freedom: Lenoir County, NC During the Civil War*. Kinston, NC: Lenoir County Historical Association, 2003.

Valentine, Patrick M. *The Rise of a Southern Town: Wilson, North Carolina 1849–1920*. Baltimore, MD: Gateway Press, Inc., 2002.

Waitt, Robert W., Jr. *Confederate Military Hospitals in Richmond*. Richmond, VA: Richmond Civil War Centennial Committee, 1964.

Wall, Bennett H. "Medical Care of Ebenezer Pettigrew's Slaves." *The Mississippi Valley Historical Review* 37, no. 3 (1950): 451-70.

War Department (Confederate). *Regulations for the Army of the Confederate States, 1863*. Richmond, VA: J. W. Randolph, 1863.

Ward, Patricia S. *Simon Baruch: Rebel in the Ranks of Medicine, 1840–1921*. Tuscaloosa, AL: University of Alabama Press, 1994.

Waring, Joseph I. *A History of Medicine in South Carolina: 1825–1900*. Charleston, SC: South Carolina Medical Society, 1968.

Warner, Ezra J. *Generals in Blue*. Baton Rouge, LA: Louisiana State University Press, 1964.

Warren, Edward, M.D. *A Doctor's Experiences in Three Continents*. Baltimore, MD: Cushing & Bailey, Publishers, 1885.

Watford, Christopher M. ed. *The Civil War in North Carolina: Soldiers' and Civilians' Letters and Diaries, 1861-1865, Vol. I: The Piedmont*. Jefferson, NC: McFarland & Company, Inc., 2003.

_____. *The Civil War in North Carolina: Soldiers' and Civilians' Letters and Diaries, 1861-1865, Vol. II: The Mountains*. Jefferson, NC: McFarland & Company, Inc., 2003.

Weatherly, Andrew E. *The First Hundred Years of Historic Guilford County, 1771–1871*, Greensboro, NC: Greensboro Print Co., 1972.

W., G. B. and Mrs. F. H. "Kinston in the Sixties." *Carolina and the Southern Cross* 1, no. 9 (November 1913): 1-3.

Welborn, J. S. Mrs. "A Wayside Hospital." *Confederate Veteran* 38, no. 3 (1930): 95-96.

White, James E., III. *Portsmouth Divided: Portsmouth Island and the Civil War*, Trent Woods, NC: Mount Truxton Publishing Co., 2013.

_____. *New Bern and the Civil War*, Charleston, SC: The History Press, 2018.

Wilbur, C. Keith, M.D. *Civil War Medicine 1861-1865*. Guilford, CT: The Globe Pequot Press, 1998.

Zartaga, Michael P. *Battle of Roanoke Island: Burnside and the Fight for North Carolina*. Charleston, SC: The History Press, 2016.

Internet Sources

Angley, Wilson. "A History of Fort Johnston on the Lower Cape Fear, vol. 1, March 1983." Accessed on October 1, 2020. https://digital.ncdcr.gov/digital/collection/p16062coll6/id/12460/rec/1.

Brawley, James S. "Josephus Wells Hall." Accessed on December 10, 2018. https://www.ncpedia.org/biography/hall-josephus-wells.

Brisson, Jim D. "City of the Dead: The 1862 Yellow Fever Epidemic in Wilmington, North Carolina." Accessed on November 1, 2019. http://commons.lib.jmu.edu/cgi/viewcontent.cgi?article=1022&context=mhr.

"Casualties of Battle." Antietam. Accessed on February 25, 2021. https://www.nps.gov/anti/learn/historyculture/casualties.htm.

Clifton, Angie. "Thomas Henry Briggs Sr. (1821–1886)." Accessed on February 6, 1861. https://ncarchitects.lib.ncsu.edu/people/P000037.

Curtis, Walter G., M.D. "Reminiscences of Wilmington and Smithville—Southport, 1848-1900." Accessed on October 1, 2020. http://digital.lib.ecu.edu/17079.

Gerad, Phillip. "During the Civil War, Sisters of Mercy Provide Medical Attention." Accessed on December 1, 2020. https://www.ourstate.com/sisters-mercy/.

Haywood, Marshall De Lancey. "Edmund Burke Haywood." Accessed on September 8, 2021. https://www.ncpedia.org/biography/haywood-edmund-burke.

Long, R. B. "7th Regiment North Carolina Volunteers." 7th Regt. North Carolina Volunteers. Accessed on December 12, 2020. http://7thncvols.wordpress.com.

Lewis, Marie. "Wayne's Early History Swirls about Old House." Accessed on December 21, 2000. https://files.usgenarchives.net/wayne/history/overet30.tx.

"Main Building, Peace College Raleigh, NC." *The Journal of Presbyterian History* (1997-) vol. 89, no. 2 (2011), 98–98, Accessed January 1, 2021. http://www.jstor.org/stable/23338049.

Medical Society of the State of N.C., *Provisional Record of Confederate Medical Officers: Offered by the Confederate Veterans Committee, Medical Society, N.C., for corrections and additions*. Accessed on August 21, 2020. http://digital.lib.ecu.edu/16951.

NC Historic State Sites. "The Road to Secession." Accessed on November 24, 2020. https://historicsites.nc.gov/resources/north-carolina-civil-war/road-secession.

Whitford, J. D. Whitford to Gov. Clark, letter, Accessed on January 17, 1862. https://digital.ncdcr.gov/digital/collection/p15012coll8/id/10553/rec/11.

P. A. Cox to Dear Brother, September 17, 1863, "1862-64: Peyton Alexander Cox to His Siblings," Spared and Shared, Accessed on November 11, 2021. https://sparedshared22.wordpress.com/2021/10/22/1862-64-peyton-alexander-cox-to-john-henderson-cox/.

Pollitt, Phoebe, "Information about North Carolina Women in the Civil War." North Carolina Nursing History. Accessed on October 17, 2020. http://nursinghistory.appstate.edu.

Heritage Sunday Committee, "Our Christian Heritage: Faith through the Ages." Queen Street United Methodist Church, November 19, 2006, 3, Accessed on September 8, 2018. https://nccumc.org/history/files/Queen-street-UMC-history.

Rowland, Thomas, and Kate Mason Rowland. "Letters of Major Thomas Rowland, C.S.A. from North Carolina, 1861 and 1862." *The William and Mary Quarterly*, vol. 25, no. 2, 1916, pp. 73–82, www.jstor.org/stable/1915189, Accessed on June 29, 2020.

Salisbury Way-Side Hospital Committee. "An Appeal for the Sick and Wounded Soldiers." Accessed on July 25, 2015. https://docsouth.unc.edu/imls/salisbury/image.html.

Schroeder-Lein, Glenna R. "The Wounded," Essential Civil War Curriculum." Accessed on November 9, 2020. https://www.essentialcivilwarcurriculum.com/the-wounded.html.

Smith, Jr., Claiborne T. "Pete Evans Hines." Accessed on January 9, 2021. https://www.ncpedia.org/biography/hines-peter-evans.

Wilkins, Ida. "History of the Weldon Methodist Church." 4, Accessed on October 4, 2019. https://nccumc.org/history/files/Weldon-UMC-History.

Wyche, Mary Lewis. "The History of Nursing in North Carolina." Accessed on July 13, 2017. https://www.scribd.com/document/63816424/The-History-of-Nursing-in-North-Carolina.

Unpublished

Hambrecht, F. T., and J. L. Koste, "Biographical Register of Physicians who Served the Confederacy in a Medical Capacity." Unpublished database.

Index

About the Author

Colonel Wade Sokolosky (Ret.), a native of Beaufort, North Carolina, is a graduate of East Carolina University and a 25-year veteran of the U.S. Army. He is one of North Carolina's leading experts of the 1865 Carolinas Campaign. Wade has lectured throughout the country speaking to roundtables, various societies and organizations, and at historical sites. He is the recipient of the Raleigh Civil War Round Table's 2017 T. Harry Gatton Award for his important efforts to study, preserve, and share the Civil War heritage of his native North Carolina.

Wade is co-author (with Mark A. Smith) of "No Such Army Since the Days of Julius Caesar": Sherman's Carolinas Campaign from Fayetteville to Averasboro (revised edition 2016) and To Prepare for Sherman's Coming: The Battle of Wise's Forks, March 1865 (2015), and the compiler of Final Roll Call: Confederate Losses during the Carolinas Campaign (2013).

Lightning Source UK Ltd.
Milton Keynes UK
UKHW022255080223
416650UK00006B/975/J